Notes on the
Botany of the Bible

David Gordon Rose

RoseTintedSpecs Imprint

Copyright Matters

Notes on the Botany of the Bible is Number One in the publisher's Reference series. It includes facsimile reproduction of a manuscript of the same name with additional comment and supplementary illustrations. My thanks for permission to publish the manuscript and illustrations go to Mike Beech and John Taylor.

Front cover image "The Dominion restored (Isaiah 11:6)" courtesy of Rose Photo Archive (RPA). Back cover image of a double page of the original manuscript courtesy of RPA. "Temple at Jerusalem from the Mount of Olives" on page eight courtesy of RPA. All manuscript pages and original drawings (identified as framed) reproduced courtesy of RPA. All other images are from J. H. Balfour's **The Plants of the Bible** published by T. Nelson & Sons, 1885 and provided courtesy of RPA. **The Plants of the Bible** is out of copyright and in the public domain.

ISBN 978-1-912152-03-2 (paperback)
Also available in e-book as a facsimile of the paperback ISBN 978-1-912152-04-9 (.ebook).

RoseTintedSpecs Imprint
Publisher: David G. Rose
Butchers Farm, Molash, Kent, United Kingdom
www.rosetintedspecs.com
e-mail: publisher@rosetintedspecs.com

British-English spelling is used in this book. Font licensing correct at time of publication.

To John and Mike

With many thanks for allowing access
to the manuscript in your care

Introduction

It is not every day that one discovers an old school exercise book in which is written a meticulously researched account of plants and trees mentioned in the Bible. I was staying with friends in Poitou-Charente in Central France and was looking through the old books and manuscripts in their extensive library. I saw immediately the possibility of preparing this gem and accompanying botanical drawings for publication and was delighted with the positive and generous response from my hosts.

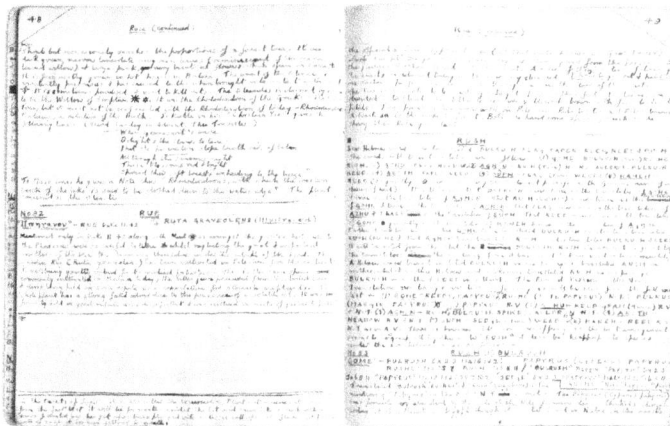

There are no clues in the manuscript to its author and few to when the material was compiled. From the style of the exercise book, its utility binding, degradation of the paper and the type of green ink postcards used for the illustrations I believe the book was written in the 1920s. The sometimes untidy handwriting and forthright style are those of an adult. Supporting the notion the author was not a senior school or seminary student is the lack of guidance during the work's progress. There are errors in entry and page numbering and in spelling. There is no indication of source material apart from reference to an unknown **All the Plants of the Bible** to which the author directs the reader, or writes that a particular subject is not illustrated in this book.

It seems the author, who I shall refer to as the MS author, first drew 34 botanical specimens on the back of post cards and wrote accompanying text on the address side. He or she then copied the text to the exercise book adding more entries to bring the total to 115. About 137 plants, trees and shrubs in total are described. The drawings accompany the manuscript in a hand-made envelope marked SUPPLEMENTARY SKETCHES.

A further pointer to the austerity of the Interwar years is that blank post cards were probably a cheap form of card on which to draw. These appeared in Britain in the early years of the 20th. Century. On page 134 (MS page 57) the MS author writes incidentally in the Spikenard entry that the Roman Denarius is worth 8½d (eight pence halfpenny). It should be possible to work out a manuscript date from this, though I haven't attempted to do this. However, the spikenard entry in **Easton's Bible Dictionary** (1897) is very close to the MS author's entry but giving the contemporary value of the Denarius as 7½d. This dictionary would still have been a major source of information on biblical matters in the 1920s. I note too, the MS author's first entry Algum-Tree is very close in content to that in the eleventh edition of the **Encyclopædia Britannica** (1911, or the 12th. edition of 1923 whose main text was the same). This reference work would also have been current during the 1920s.

Nothing of what I suggest in the preceding paragraphs is negative criticism. **Notes on the Botany of the Bible** is a remarkable endeavour. It is full of factual material and interesting sidelights and surprisingly current considering how long ago it was written. If the labours of a seminary student it would have been awarded a prize and commendation. If the effort of a keen amateur botanist it would have been considered worthy of publication. There is a grasp of the classical languages and a deep interest in the Scriptures. The MS author is well-read, or had good reference material on the geography and botany of the British Isles as well as the Near East. Sources are diverse. Material and comment might be dated but much is still relevant.

Regarding the place of origin of the manuscript the only information is that it was bought in auction about thirty years ago in Doncaster near Sheffield in the North of England. Inside the exercise book is a sticker of E. Weston & Sons, Change Alley, Sheffield and the price of 2/- (two shillings). Westons was a bookshop and stationers before the Second World War and after this a newsagents until about 1962 when this area of the city was cleared for redevelopment.

I considered making corrections to and expanding the original work but decided this was presumptuous. There is expert work on the subject of the botany of the Bible and Holy Land that people interested in this book will know of. That of Michael Zohary, Harold and Alma Moldenke and F. Nigel Hepper, for example. There are also interesting recent publications on this subject and that of the associated planting of Bible gardens.

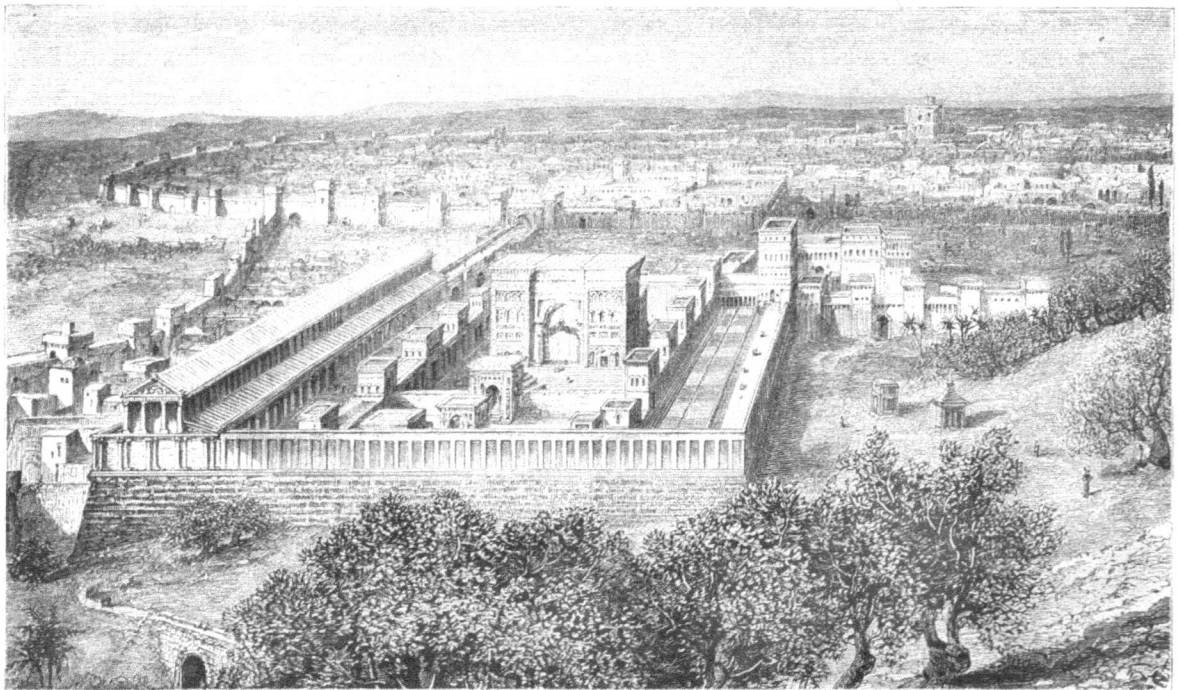

Temple at Jerusalem from the Mount of Olives

ASPEN, OR TREMBLING POPLAR.—(*Mulberry-tree of Scripture.*)

Because of the missing illustrations from the unknown **All The Plants of the Bible** I have supplemented the MS author's line drawings with several from J. H. Balfour's **The Plants of the Bible**[1] published in London in 1885 (sample left). This is also because the drawings listed in the MS author's index and referred to throughout the manuscript do not match those 34 that accompany the manuscript. This might be because the text was to be read in conjunction with the unknown **All the Plants of the Bible**. The illustrations are inserted in the text of my general notes.

The reproduction of the manuscript pages is at 100 per cent of the original size of 6¾ by 8¾ inches. That of the MS author's original illustrations (sample below) of 3½ by 5½ inches is at 50 per cent. A margin has been added on all sides because the MS author wrote to the edges of the exercise book pages. The text and illustrations can be enlarged in the e-book (ISBN 978-1-912152-04-9) which is a facsimile of the paperback.

In deciding what plants are actually referred to in biblical texts the difficulties are slowly being overcome. These are the fragmentary form of manuscripts, species being closely related, synonyms, local names, context, the technical knowledge needed for accurate identification and ultimately, inadequate translation.

Taxonomical reclassification and the improving of botanical nomenclature is ongoing around the world. This is not easy with, for example, near-identical thorn bushes across an arid sandy region that need to be studied in field trips. The scientific name of almost every plant in the manuscript needed updating and reflects how long ago it was compiled. I give the scientific name in full since the point of this book and others on the subject is ever more accuracy in the determination of biblical plants. Identifying plants by shared common names is unsatisfactory, especially those on which accurate field work has been done.

Along with these difficulties come those of translating common, or local names. With some Bible verses you only get a sense you are reading the same passage across different publications. A random example is part of Ezekiel chapter 27 verse 19 (the Book of Ezekiel was compiled *c*. 590-560 BCE). It shows "bright iron, cassia, and calamus, were among thy merchandise" (American Standard Bible); "wrought iron, cassia and sweet cane were among your merchandise" (New American Standard Bible); "They exchanged wrought iron, cinnamon, and spices for your wares" (Common English Bible); "bright iron, cassia, and calamus, were in thy market" (King James Version); "wrought iron: stacte, and calamus were in thy market" (Douay-Rheims Catholic Bible); "wrought iron, and gum of myrrh, and calamus, that is, a sweet smelling spice, for thy merchandise"

(Wycliffe); "wrought iron, cassia, and sugar cane in payment for your good things" (New Century Version).

With regard to my notes on the MS author's work, of hundreds of plants studied by eminent researchers in recent decades there is concensus agreement so far on 95 mentioned in the Bible. These were put forward by Zophia Włodarczyk of the Agricultural University of Krakow in 2007[2]. In addition to the 95 species are a further 111 Dr. Włodarczyk suggests are a basis for continuing discussion on the subject. The botanists who have worked on the plant species are named in full in the General subject index under botanists (pages 73 and 74).

Fundamental to my **Notes on the Botany of the Bible** is this 'master' list of 206 species. The Index of plants by scientific name (pages 65-70) is, in effect, this list. Entries total 150 and include the MS author's 115. Forty-seven plants do not have entries of their own but are mentioned or described under other entries throughout the book. Nine plants listed are missing, that is, they that are not mentioned anywhere else in the text. I will attend to this in the next edition of the book.

My notes should be enough for readers coming fresh to the subject to get an overall picture of plants of the Bible. With the briefest description and usage, clarification of plant species, cross-referencing, updating of the botanical nomenclature, plant indexes by common and scientific name, expanded biblical references and a general subject index covering the facsimile pages and notes, my addition to the original material ends since it is not the purpose of this publication to write a new work.

I have enjoyed researching this material and bringing a forgotten manuscript to light. The Old and New Testament era spans *c.* 700 BCE to 200 CE, making the subject of the botany of the Bible one of the earliest *flora* while also alluding to climate, geography, farming, social conditions, environmental changes and medicine. The greatest botanical treatise of the Ancient World is the ***Historia Plantarum*** by Theophrastus (*c.* 371-287 BCE). However, biblical botanical references date from three centuries earlier and it is commendable the subject continues to be refined. DGR.

---

[1] There is a .pdf file of Balfour's book here: https://archive.org/details/plantsofbible00balfrich and that of several other Nineteenth-century books on the natural history of the Bible courtesy of the University of California Libraries.

[2] Zophia Włodarczyk, Agricultural University of Krakow, Poland 2007. You can see pp. 67-85 of Dr. Włodarczyk's paper with plant listing here:
http://www.ptno.ogr.ar.krakow.pl/Wydawn/FoliaHorticulturae/Spisy/FH2007/PDF19012007/fh1901p07.pdf

Contents

NB. Page numbers refer to the numbers at the foot of the page, not those showing on the facsimile Index and pages.

Abbreviations

Ar. Arabic
archit. architectural
b. born
BCE before the common era
c. circa 'about'
CE common era
cont. continued
d. died
etc. et cetera 'and so forth'
ff. following
fig. figurative

Gk. Greek
ie. id est 'that is'
illust. illustration
intro. Introduction
MS manuscript
Mt. Mount
NB. nota bene 'note well'
N° number
p. page
.pdf portable document format
pl. plural

pp. pages
[*qv.*] *quod vide* 'which see'
ref. reference
refs. references
sp. spelling
St. Saint
subsp. subspecies
var. variant
viz. videlicet 'namely'

Bible versions referred to in the notes

BBE The Bible in Basic English, **CEBA** Common English Bible with Apocrypha, **CJB** The Complete Jewish Bible, **DBY** The Darby Translation, **GNTA** Good News Translation with Apocrypha, **GW** God's Word translation, **KJV** King James Version, **KJVA** King James Version with Apocrypha, **KJV 2000** King James 2000 Bible, **LEB** Lexham English Bible, **LXX** Septuagint with Apocrypha, **MSG** The Message Bible, **NAS** New American Standard Bible, **NIRV** New International Reader's Version, **NIV** New International Version, **NLT** New Living Translation, **NRS** New Revised Standard, **OJB** Orthodox Jewish Bible, **RHE** Douay-Rheims Catholic Bible, **RSVA** Revised Standard Version with Apocrypha, **TYN** Tyndale, **WYC** Wycliffe, **YLT** Young's Literal Translation.

There are well-organised Internet sites that access these bibles and provide biblical comment here:

http://www.biblestudytools.com/

and here:

http://biblehub.com/

Botanical nomenclature

The botanists cited in this book are listed in the General subject index under botanists: (pp. 145-146). Their full name and dates and recognized abbreviation is shown. It is a convention that the abbreviated name and initials have no spaces between them. Wikipedia has a list of botanists by abbreviation here:

https://en.wikipedia.org/wiki/List_of_botanists_by_author_abbreviation_(A)

The list is kept up-to-date by the International Plant Names Index located here:

http://www.ipni.org/index.html

Utah State University has a comprehensive article titled **Nomenclature, names and taxonomy** here:

http://herbarium.usu.edu/teaching/4420/botnom.htm

Notes on the Botany of the Bible

Entries Nos. 1 - 18

NB. The numbering of the plant species in this book follows that of the MS author's entries which are generally in alphabetical order. The entries without a number are those suggested subjects for research. They are taken from Dr. Włodarczyk's 2007 paper (see endnote [2] page 10). Taxonomy and nomenclature are updated to 2017.

Looking up the biblical references across several Bible translations will give a broader view of the reference.

The list of abbreviations is on page 13 and general subject index pp. 73-77. The botanists by abbreviations are listed on pp. 73 and 74 in the General subject index.

Nº 1 algum, almug tree

The identity of this tree or trees remains unknown. The MS author suggests Lebanese cedar [*qv.*], red sandalwood (*Pterocarpus santalinus* L.f.) and juniper. Red sandalwood is most likely if the city of Ophir mentioned in 1 Kings is in India. See **Nº 51 juniper**; **Nº red sandalwood**.

Biblical references: 2 Chronicles 2:8 (sandalwood and algum), 9:10-11. 1 Kings 10:11-12 (almug).

Nº acacia

Vachellia tortilis var. *raddiana* (Savi) Kyal. & Boatwr., commonly known as the umbrella thorn acacia, umbrella thorn or Israeli babool is a fine-grained durable timber. Acacia references in the Bible include it being the wood of the Ark of the Tabernacle (Deuteronomy 10:3). Its pods and leaves provided fodder for animals. It is probably the biblical *shittah* (pl. *shittim*) tree. *Plicosepalus acaciae* (Zucc.) D.Wiens & Polhill is acacia mistletoe. See also **Nº 44 grove** and the MS author's entry **Nº 91 shittah tree** (page 130).

Specific to acacia: Exodus 25:5, 10, 13, 23, 28, 26:15, 26, 32, 37, 27:1, 6, 30:1, 5, 35:7, 24, 36:20, 31, 36, 37:1, 4, 10, 15, 25, 28, 38:1, 6. Deuteronomy 10:3. Isaiah 41:19. Joel 3:18.

Specific to *shittim*: Isaiah 41:19. Joshua 2:1, 3:1. Judges 7:27. Micah 6:5. Numbers 25:1, 33:49.

Nº agarwood, aloeswood

Aquilaria agallocha (Lour.) Roxb. *Aquilaria*, is a genus of trees known as lign-aloes. The resin-infused parts of the tree, its natural defence against a fungal attack, are used in perfumery and medicine. No biblical references are found under agar, agarwood or its Arabic name *oudh*. See headings **Nº 7 balm of Gilead** and **Nº 8 balsam** for general balm, resin and gum references.

Nº Aleppo oak

Quercus infectoria G.Olivier, see **Nº 69 oak** (page 38).

ALMOND-TREE.—(*Amygdalus communis.*)

N° Aleppo pine

Pinus halepensis Mill., see **N° 74 pine** (page 40).

N° 2 almond

Prunus dulcis D.A.Webb, sweet almond, is the first tree to blossom across the Near East and is revered for the quality of its seeds. These produce a high-grade oil that is used in complementary medicine and skin care. The symbolic status of blossom, fruit and tree in biblical times was maintained mostly though art to the Middle Ages. See also **N° 68 nuts**.

Ecclesiastes 12:5. Exodus 25:33-36, 37:17, 19-22. Genesis 30:37, 37:20, 43:11. Jeremiah 1:11. Numbers 17:8.

N° 3 aloes, lign-aloes

Aloe succotrina Lam., also *Aloe vera* (L.) Burm.f. The healing ability of aloe plant extract was recorded in Sumeria in 2,200 BCE. and in Egypt in 1,150 BCE. Biblical reference to aloes is probably to agar resin that was prized for use in incense and embalming. See **N° agarwood**.

John 19:39. Numbers 24:6 (lign-aloes). Proverbs 7:17. Psalm 45:8. Song of Solomon 4:14.

N° 4 anise

The MS author writes the herb dill (*Anethum graveolens* L.), rather than anise referred to in the Bible, is the correct plant. It grows wild around the Mediterranean. See **N° dill; N° 48 herbs**.

Matthew 23:23 (anise).

N° 5 apple

The MS author believes the apple *Malus pumila* Mill. (and crab apple *Malus sylvestris* Mill.) is not that referred to in the Bible. He suggests apricot (*Prunus armeniaca* L.). "Apples" ornamentation is better translated as "pomegranates" in 2 Chronicles 3:16, 4:13. Jeremiah 52:22-23. 1 Kings 7:18, 20, 42. 2 Kings 25:17. Similarly **mandrake** [*qv.*] for love-apple. There remain however, several references to apple, *viz. :*

Deuteronomy 20:20 (WYC), 32:10. Genesis 1:11 (WYC). Jeremiah 52:23. Joel 1:12. Lamentations 2:18. Leviticus 19:23 (WYC). Proverbs 7:2, 25:11. Psalm 17:8. Song of Solomon 2:3, 5, 5:1, 7:8, 8:5. Zechariah 2:8.

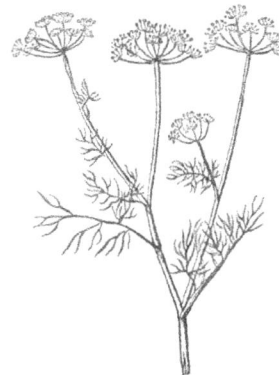

ANISE —(*Peucedanum graveolens.*)

N° 6 ash

The MS author writes this is not the European ash (*Fraxinus excelsior* L.) and refers the reader to Aleppo **pine** [*qv.*] and Scotch pine. The King James and American King James Bible translate the tree in the verse below as ash, though the KJV 2000 edition re-translates it as pine. Włodarczyk suggests the Syrian ash (*Fraxinus angustifolia* subsp. *syriaca* [Boiss.] Yalt.) for further research.

Isaiah 44:14.

Nº 7 balm of Gilead

This balm is a metaphor in the Bible for something healing and soothing. Its composition is unknown but the source of its gum or resin is likely to be that of the balsam tree *Commiphora gileadensis* (L.) C.Chr. The hills of Gilead today form the north-western part of Jordan. The words gum and resin are interchangeable in the Bible. Other plants from which gum or resin is extracted are **Nº 3 aloes, lign-aloes**; **Nº 10a bdellium**; **Nº 37 frankincense**; **Nº 40 galbanum**; **Nº Gum Tragacanth Milkvetch**; **Nº 52 ladanum**; **Nº** Mecca **myrrh**; **Nº** *Nardostachys jatamansi* (spikenard); **Nº** hairy **rockrose**; **Nº** drug **snowbell** (storax); **Nº 95 stacte**. See the following entry for gum and resin references.

General references to balm: 2 Chronicles 28:15. Ezekiel 27:17. Genesis 37:25, 43:11. Jeremiah 8:22, 46:11, 51:8.

Nº 8 balsam

Balsam is the aromatic resin (known as balm) of several species of tree when cut and is a valuable resource. The mastic tree (*Pistacia lentiscus* L.) is one such mentioned in Susanna and the Elders. Another is *Balanites aegyptiaca* (L.) Delile, Egyptian balsam. *Tetraclinis articulata* (Vahl) Mast., is the arar tree or Berber thuya, also thyine wood. See **Nº terebinth** and preceding entry.

General references to gum and resin: 1 Chronicles 14:14-15 (tree). Exodus 25:6, 30:23, 34, 35:8, 28, 37:25 (altar). Genesis 2:12, 37:25, 43:11. Isaiah 39:2. Jezekiel 27:17 (LXX). 2 Kings 20:13. Numbers 11:7. Psalm 45:8, 84:6. 2 Samuel 5:23-24. Song of Solomon 4:10, 5:1, 6:2.

BARLEY.
(*Hordeum distichon.*)

Nº 9 barley

Hordeum vulgare L., common barley, is a cereal staple and valuable in biblical times for food and in the brewing of beer and wine, as today. It is heat tolerant and ripens before wheat. It supplemented wheat flour (as did ground beans) in the making of poor people's bread. *H. distichon* L. is two-row barley and *H. hexastichon* L. six-row barley. See also **Nº 25 corn and wheat**.

1 Chronicles 2:15, 11:13. 2 Chronicles 2:10, 15, 27:5. Deuteronomy 8:8. Exodus 9:31. Ezekiel 4:12. Hosea 3:2. Isaiah 28:25. Job 31:40. Joel 1:11. John 6:9. Judges 7:13. 1 Kings 4:28. 2 Kings 4:42, 7:1, 16, 18. Leviticus 27:16. Numbers 5:15. Ruth 1:22, 2:17, 23, 3:2, 15, 17. 2 Samuel 14:30, 17:28, 21:9.

BAY-TREE.—(*Laurus nobilis.*)

Nº 10 bay tree

Laurus nobilis L., laurel or sweet bay, also known as true laurel, has culinary and alternative medicine uses. Some versions of the Bible translate bay as cedar. See also **Nº 48 herbs**.

1 Corinthians 9:25. Isaiah 44:14. Psalm 37:35.

Nº 10a bdellium

This is an aromatic gum resin from several trees of the *Commiphora* (Gk. 'gum bearing') genus used in incense, perfumery and traditional medicine. In Genesis 2:12 bdellium is placed with semi-precious stones implying costliness. Presumably more cheaply available it was used to adulterate myrrh [*qv.*]. See headings **Nº 7 balm of Gilead** and **Nº 8 balsam** for general balm, resin and gum references.

Nº 11 bean

Vicia faba L., the broad bean, is a legume that has been cultivated in the Middle East since 6,000 BCE and most likely that referred to. Shell and beans are edible when young. Dried and ground it could be added to bread. When dried after harvest it was fed to cattle. Other beans are the runner bean, haricot bean and kidney bean. Also of the family *Leguminosae* is *Cercis siliquastrum* L., the Judas Tree. This once-widespread deciduous tree has edible flowers and seed pods and was valued for its fine timber. See also **Nº 54 lentil**; **Nº 77 pulse**.

Ezekiel 4:9. Genesis 1:29, 9:3. 2 Samuel 17:28, 23:11-12.

BEANS.—(*Vicia faba.*)

BOX-TREE.—(*Buxus sempervirens.*)

Nº 12 bitter herbs

Reichardia tingitana (L.) Roth, also known as bitter herbs and false sow-thistle, is the poppy-leaved Reichardia. Apart from this plant, the bitter herbs referred to in the Bible include chicory (*Cichorium intybus* L.), wild chicory (*Cichorium pumilum* Jacq.), field eryngo (*Eryngium creticum* Lam.), wild lettuces, bitter cresses and hawkweeds. The leaves of *Sonchus oleraceus* L., common sow-thistle, are eaten in salads or cooked like spinach. See also **Nº 48 herbs**; **Nº 117** white **wormwood**.

Exodus 12:8. Lamentations 3:15. Numbers 9:11.

Nº 13 box, boxwood

Buxus sempervirens L. is the common box or European box. Its wood was highly regarded for its hardness and fine grain in carving and inlay work. It is not related to the box-thorn [*qv.*] shrub.

Ezekiel 27:6. Isaiah 41:19, 60:13.

Nº 14 burning bush

Translated as burning bush in Acts 7:30 but 'burning thorn bush' in the New American Standard Bible. It refers possibly to the box-thorn bush or wolfberry (*Lycium* genus). See **Nº 100-109 thorns.**

Acts 7:30. Exodus 3:2-4. Judges 9:15 (thornbush or bramble).

SWEET CANE.—(*Andropogon calamus-aromaticus*)

Nº Persian buttercup

Ranunculus asiaticus L. is probably a biblical 'flower of the field' as referred to in Isaiah 40:6; James 1:10; Job 14:2; Luke 12:27; Matthew 6:28; 1 Peter 1:24; Psalm 37:20, 103:15; Song of Solomon 2:1. It is a protected wild flower in Israel. See **Nº 56 lily of the field; Nº 79-81 roses.**

Nº 15 calamus

Acorus calamus L., calamus, sweet flag, sweet sedge, is a reed-like perennial herb with a fragrance that suggests ginger. Its habitat is close to, or in water. In the Bible it is also known as fragrant cane and fragrant reeds. Its root is used in medicine and its essential oil in perfumery and Temple incense. The genus *Andropogon* (now classed as *Cymbopogon)* is lemon grass and is not related to calamus. There is no biblical reference to lemon grass. See also **Nº lemon grass; Nº common reed.**

Exodus 30:23 (anointing oil). Ezekiel 27:19. Isaiah 43:24. Jeremiah 6:20. Song of Solomon 4:14.

Nº 16 camphire

Camphire is a transliteration of the Hebrew word *kopher* that has nothing to do with the camphor tree (*Cinnamomum camphora* [L.] J.Presl). Henna, from the Arabic *hinna* is the plant referred to. See **Nº henna.**

Song of Solomon 1:14, 4:13.

CAROB TREE (CERATONIA SILIQUA)
FLOWERS

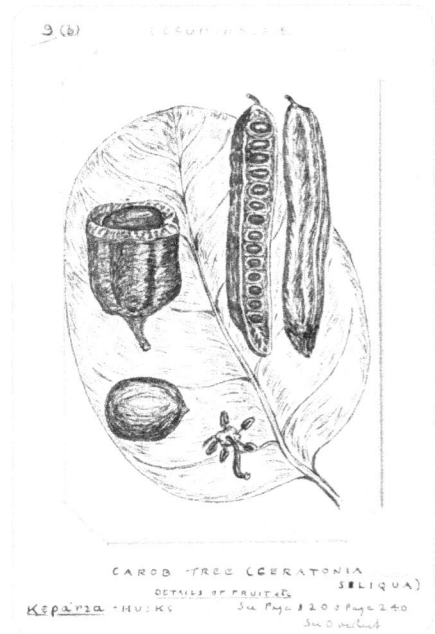

CAROB TREE (CERATONIA SILIQUA)
DETAILS OF FRUIT

N° capers

Capparis spinosa L., caper bush, is a hardy widespread shrubby plant whose flower buds (capers) and fruit (caper berries) are common, usually pickled, in Mediterranean cuisine. The flower buds of *Tetraena dumosa* (Boiss.) Beier & Thulin (bushy bean-caper) have been similarly used. See also **N° 48 herbs**.

Ecclesiastes 12:5.

N° carob

Ceratonia siliqua L., the carob tree, known also as St. John's Bread with reference to the story of John the Baptist surviving in the desert. The interior pulp of the pods (locust beans) is sweet. The wild tree was widespread in biblical times, is drought-tolerant and would have been a valuable food resource. A single seed was a unit of measurement known as a *gerah*, with 60 seeds (or three carob pods) equal in value to one *shekel*. Locust bean gum, or carob bean gum is derived from the seeds and is now used extensively in the food industry. This gum has no relationship to the African tree known as the locust bean or African locust-bean tree (*Parkia biglobosa* [Jacq.] G.Don). See also **N° Gum Tragacanth Milkvetch**; **N°** oriental **sweetgum**.

Exodus 30:13 (*gerahs*). Ezekiel 45:12 (*gerahs*). Luke 15:16. Mark 1:6 (translated as locusts). Numbers 3:47 (*gerahs*).

CASSIA-TREE.—(*Cinnamomum Cassia.*)

N° 17 cassia

Cinnamomum cassia (L.) J.Presl is commonly known as cassia or Chinese cassia. In biblical times it was an important ingredient of anointing oil and perfume. Its bark and buds are used (as a spice) for flavouring, partly for its stronger flavour but mostly because it is more readily available from *C. cassia* and other species. Cassia oil has a long tradition of medicinal use and is an ingredient of pharmaceutical products today including dental and cosmetic. It is that specified in the United States Pharmacopoeia as 'oil of Cinnamon.' *Cinnamomum verum* J.Presl is the true cinnamon with a less pungent and more subtle aroma. See **N° 21 cinnamon**; **N° 94 spicery**.

Ben Sira 24:15 (NRSA). Exodus 30:24 (anointing oil). Ezekiel 27:19. Jezekiel 27:17 (LXX). Proverbs 7:17 (perfume). Psalm 45:8. Song of Solomon 4:14.

FLORENTINE IRIS . IRIS FLORENTINA

KETZIOTH . CASSIA . in Psa 48

N° 18 *Iris florentina*

Iris florentina L, now *Iris germanica nothovar* is the white flower variant of *Iris germanica* L. (bearded iris). It was known to the ancient Egyptians for its fragrant properties. It has long been harvested for its root (known as orris root) for cosmetics, perfumery and traditional medicine. Orris is probably a corruption of iris. *Iris pseudacorus* L. is yellow iris.

Notes on the Botany of the Bible

Entries Nos. 19 - 39

CASTOR-OIL PLANT.—(*Ricinus communis*)

N° castor bean

Ricinus communis L. is the castor bean or castor-oil plant. The leaves and particularly the oil have medicinal and insecticidal uses. It was used in anointing but has an unpleasant smell when burnt as lamp oil.

Jonah 4:6-7, 9-10.

N° southern cattail

Typha domingensis (Pers.) Poir. ex Steud., see **N° 83-88 rushes**.

N° 19 cedar of Lebanon

Cedrus libani A.Rich., is valued for its fine grain, aroma, oil and durability. The destruction of cedar forests in Lebanon was first recorded in the 3rd. Millennium BCE. This was due to the demand for ships' timber, construction and agricultural land. References below include several to cedar generally.

Amos 2:9. Ben Sira 24:13, 50:8 (GNTA). Chronicles II 1:15, 2:3, 9:27 (LXX). 1 Chronicles 14:1, 17:1, 6, 22:4. 2 Chronicles 1:15, 2:3, 8, 16, 9:27, 25:18. Divrey Hayamim Bais 2:32 (OJB). Ezekiel 17:3, 27:5, 31:8, 13. Ezra 3:7. Hosea 14:5-6. Isaiah 2:13, 9:10, 14:8, 37:24, 41:19, 44:14, 23. Jeremiah 22:7, 15, 23. Job 40:17. John 18:1. Judges 9:15. Kings III 5:10, 6:9, 10:27 (LXX). 1 Kings 4:33, 5:6, 8, 10, 6:9-10, 16, 18, 36, 7:2-3, 7, 11-12, 9:11, 10:27. 2 Kings 14:9, 19:23. Leviticus 14:4, 6, 49, 51-52. Numbers 19:6, 24:6. Psalm 29:5, 37:35, 72:16, 80:10, 92:12, 104:16, 148:9. 2 Samuel 5:11, 7:2, 7. Song of Solomon 1:17, 4:11, 5:15. Zechariah 11:1-2.

N° chamomile

Cota palaestina Reut. ex Unger & Kotschy, Palestinian chamomile or Israel's chamomile, is a 'flower of the field' a biblical metaphor for something fleeting or transient. The plant has many medicinal uses. See also **N° Persian buttercup** (for flower of the field references); **N° 56 Lily of the field**.

N° 20 chestnut

The sweet chestnut *Castanea sativa* Mill. was a food staple across Western Europe for two millennia. The tree is valued for its

CEDARS OF LEBANON.

durable timber in the making of furniture, fencing and joists. Biblical chestnut is thought to be the plane tree *Platanus orientalis* L. See Nº Oriental **plane**. See also Nº **68 nuts**.

Ezekiel 31:8. Genesis 30:37. Isaiah 2:13.

Nº 21 cinnamon

Cinnamomum verum J.Presl. This is true cinnamon and native to Sri Lanka. There are several other *Cinnamomum* species from which the spice (the ground or powdered bark) is obtained. It is considered to have a more delicate flavour for culinary use than the cheaper cassia (*Cinnamomum cassia* [L.] J.Presl). It was used in anointing oil and, as today, in perfumery. Cinnamon and cassia are interchanged in many of the biblical translations. See Nº **17 cassia**; Nº **58 malabathron**; Nº **94 spicery**.

Ben Sira 24:15 (KJVA). Exodus 30:23. Ezekiel 27:19. Jeremias 6:20 (LXX). Proverbs 7:17. Psalm 45:8. Revelation 18:13. Song of Solomon 4:13-14.

CINNAMON-TREE.—(*Cinnamomum zeylanicum.*)

Nº Chinese cinnamon

Cinnamomum cassia (L.) J.Presl, see Nº **17 cassia**.

Nº 22 citron

Citrus medica L. is the citron or citron melon (*etrog*). There is pollen grain evidence of its existence in Israel in the 6th. Century BCE but the *etrog* and other citrus fruits are rarely mentioned in the Bible.

Leviticus 23:40 (goodly trees). Revelation 18:12 (wood). Song of Solomon 2:3 (wood), 5, 7:8, 8:5 (citron-tree). Vayikra 23:40 (OJB) (fruit).

Nº 23 cockle

Lolium temulentum L., known also as darnel. It is a toxic weed that resembles wheat and grows amongst it. See Nº **darnel**.

Nº 24 coriander

Coriandrum sativum L. When crushed all parts of the plant give off a pungent aroma. It is used in curries, meat dishes, bread, sweets and alcoholic drinks. See also Nº **48 herbs**.

Exodus 16:14, 31. Numbers 11:7.

Nº 25 corn and wheat

Triticum aestivum L. is the bread wheat or common wheat widely grown today. Two of the earliest subspecies are *Triticum turgidum* L. subsp. *dicoccum* (Schrank) Thell. (emmer, a hulled wheat of the

CORIANDER.—(*Coriandrum sativum.*)

WHEAT.—(*Triticum sativum.*)

COTTON.—(*Gossypium herbaceum.*)

Middle East since the 6th. Millennium BCE) and *Triticum turgidum* L. subsp. *durum* (Desf.) Husn. (durum or macaroni wheat, a naked wheat also from the 6th. Millennium BCE that has become the main Mediterranean subspecies.) Corn in the UK refers to the seeds of a cereal plant that can be ground into flour and is therefore, a generic term for many cereals. Grain refers to seeds not necessarily ground into flour. See also **N° 9 barley**; N° 36 flax; N° 61 millet; N° 89 rye; N° sorghum; N° cultivated emmer **wheat**.

Amos 8:5. 1 Corinthians 9:9. Deuteronomy 23:25. Exodus 22:6. Job 24:24. Joel 1:10, 17. Joshua 5:11-12. Judges 15:5. 2 Kings 4:42. Leviticus 2:14. Luke 6:1. Mark 2:23. Matthew 12:1.

Specific to wheat: 1 Corinthians 15:37. Isaiah 23:3, 28:25, 28. Joel 1:11. John 12:24. Revelation 18:13. Ruth 2:23. Shmuel Bais 17:28 (OJB). Song of Solomon 7:2.

Specific to grain: Acts 7:24. 2 Chronicles 31:5. Deuteronomy 25:4, 32:14. Ezekiel 45:17, 46:5, 14. Ezra 7:22. Genesis 2:5, 3:18, 42:2. Isaiah 17:5, 23:3, 28:28. Jeremiah 17:26. John 12:24. Leviticus 2:13-14, 16 (LXX), 19:10, 23:14. Mark 4:8, 28. Matthew 13:4, 8. Nehemiah 13:5. Numbers 6:4, 28:12. 2 Samuel 17:28.

Specific to seed: Ben Sira 7:3 (fig.). 1 Corinthians 15:38-39, 40 (fig.). 2 Corinthians 9:6, 10. Daniel 11:31 (LXX). Deuteronomy 11:10, 22:9, 28:38. Ecclesiastes 11:4, 6. 2 Esdras 4:36 (fig.), 8:41, 44 (fig.), 15:13. Ezekiel 4:9, 36:9, 30. Genesis 1:11-12, 29, 47:19, 23-24. Haggai 1:6, 2:19. Hosea 8:7, 10:12-13 (all fig.). Isaiah 5:10, 19:7, 28:25, 30:23, 32:20, 40:24, 55:10, 61:11. James 3:18 (fig.). Jeremiah 4:3, 31:27, 35:7, 50:16. Job 31:40. John 12:24. Judges 6:3. Kings I 8:15 (LXX). 1 Kings 18:32. Leviticus 11:37-38, 19:19, 25:5, 11, 20, 26:16, 27:16. Luke 3:17, 6:1, 8:5, 8, 11-15, 12:24, 16:17, 22:31. Mark 4:4-5, 7-8, 15, 16-27 (fig.). Matthew 3:12, 6:26, 13:3-5, 7-8, 18-20, 22-25, 27, 29, 32, 37-38 (fig.), 25:24. Micah 6:15. Numbers 24:7. 1 Peter 1:23. Proverbs 8:19, 11:30, 16:28, 18:20, 22:8 (fig.). Psalms 107:37, 126:6. Zechariah 8:12, 10:9.

N° 26 cotton

Gossypium herbaceum L. Cotton has been grown in Asia since the 7th. Century BCE for yarn, textile and medicine. Cotton gins for combing the cotton and removing seeds were known in northern India in 1,000 BCE. In the early Christian period

AUTUMN CROCUS   CROCUS NUDIFLORUS

CHABATZELETH - ROSE   Judges 180

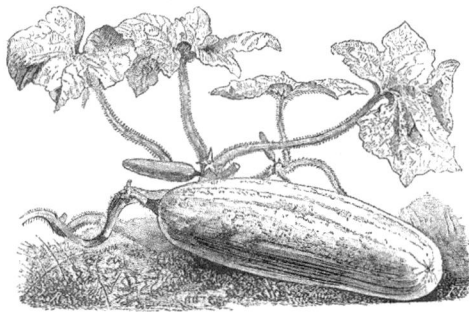

CUCUMBER.—(*Cucumis sativus.*)

cotton textile was being traded as far as China and Romans considered it a luxury, as silk. The textile milled from it is light, cool and absorbant. Cotton seeds were also regarded as a foodstuff in the Middle East in biblical times.

Esther 1:6. Isaiah 19:9. Proverbs 7:16. Revelation 18:12 (WYC).

Nº autumn **crocus**

Crocus sativus L., Autumn crocus, saffron crocus, saffron, is cultivated from the Western Mediterranean to India for its dried stigmas which are the source of the spice saffron. As a food flavouring and colouring and golden yellow textile dye it is highly valued. The properties of the plant have been known since the 7th. Century BCE. Saffron and turmeric (*Curcuma longa* L.) are sometimes interchanged in the Bible. See also **Nº 94 spicery**.

Hosea 14:5 (MSG). Isaiah 35:1. Proverbs 7:17 (LXX). Song of Solomon 2:1, 4:14.

Nº 27 **cucumber**

Cucumis sativus L., the common, or garden cucumber. *Cucumis melo* L. is the muskmelon. See also **Nº 60 melon**.

Baruch 6:69-70 (KJVA). Epistle of Jeremy 1:70 (LXX). Isaiah 1:8. Jeremiah 10:5. Numbers 11:5.

Nº 28 **cumin**

Cuminum cyminum L., cumin or *jeera* (Hindi), is a small drought-tolerant plant known to have been cultivated in the Near East from the 2nd. Millennium BCE. Cumin seeds and an essential oil from the seeds are strongly flavoured (*ie.*, hot) and used typically in curries. It has medicinal uses. See also **Nº 48 herbs**.

Isaiah 28:25-27. Matthew 23:23.

CUMMIN —(*Cuminum cyminum.*)

Nº 29 **cypress and gopher wood**

Cupressus sempervirens L., the Mediterranean or Italian cypress. Cypress is a durable scented wood, smooth-grained, lightweight and water resistant. Its uses range from framework construction to quality furniture-making, to firewood. The identity of gopher wood is unknown. See also **Nº 35 fir**.

2 Chronicles 2:8, 3:5. Ezekiel 27:6, 31:8. Genesis 6:14 (also gopher wood). Isaiah 14:8, 37:24, 41:19, 44:14, 55:13, 60:13. 1 Kings 5:8, 10, 6:15, 34, 9:11. 2 Kings 19:23. Psalm 104:17. Song of Solomon 1:17, 4:14. Zechariah 11:2.

BRANCH OF CYPRESS-TREE.—(*Fir-tree of Scripture.*)

N° darnel

Lolium temulentum L., known as darnel or cockle, is commonly found growing with wheat. *Agrostemma githago* L. is common corn cockle [*qv.*]. *Cephalaria syriaca* (L.) Schrad. is Syrian scabious. Any of these could have been the plant in the Parable of the Tares in Matthew 13:30.

Job 31:40. Matthew 13:25-27, 29-30, 36, 38-40.

N° date palm

Phoenix dactylifera L. Date palms have been cultivated in the Middle East and Egypt for food, building material and a fermented beverage since the 4th. Century BCE and 6th. Century BCE in Arabia.

1 Chronicles 16:3 (date cake). 2 Chronicles 28:15 (City of Palms). Deuteronomy 34:3. Exodus 15:27. Ezekiel 40:26, 31, 34, 37, 41:18-19, 25-26. Genesis 43:11 (TYN). Jeremiah 40:10, 12. Joel 1:12. Judges 1:16, 3:13, 4:5 (Palm of Deborah). 1 Kings 6:29, 32, 7:36. Kings II 16:1-2 (LXX). Leviticus 23:40. Nehemiah 8:15. Numbers 33:9. Psalm 92:12. 2 Samuel 6:19 (date cake). Song of Solomon 5:11, 7:78 (all fig.).

N° 30 desert vegetation

The Middle East is characterized by desert and there are references throughout the Bible to hardship and privation, usually in a figurative sense, in such inhospitable terrain. A blooming desert is a metaphor for hope and a better life. Here are six thornless species common in Middle Eastern desert terrain. See also **N° retem; N° thistles; N° 100-109 thorns.**

Ochradenus baccatus Del., taily weed. It has sweet edible fleshy berries. The shrub is grazed. It has medicinal uses.

Haloxylon salicornicum (Moq.) Bunge ex Boiss., *rimth* (Ar.) has multiple uses including grazing for animals, the making of soap and the roots being used as fuel. The stems and ash are used medicinally.

Haloxylon scoparium Pomel. In the northern Sahara it is a valuable source of food for camels in times of drought. In Algeria its decline is due to its harvesting for snuff. The plant has medicinal uses.

DATE PALMS.

Haloxylon persicum Bunge ex Boiss. & Buhse, white saxaul tree, *ghada* (Ar.). This shrub or small tree is particularly useful in stabilizing dunes and preventing further desertification. Its shrinking habitat is due to its traditional use as timber, a source of fuel and overgrazing.

Cistanche tubulosa (Schenk) Wight, desert broomrape, desert hyacinth, yellow broomrape. This is a salt-tolerant parasitic desert plant. It has medicinal uses and is particularly valued in Chinese herbal medicine.

Cynomorium coccineum L., scarlet synomorium, desert thumb, *tarthuth* (Bedouin), is a desert geophyte that exists entirely on the roots of a salt-tolerant host *Cistaceae* (rock-rose [*qv.*]) shrub. The plant is edible and has a long tradition of medicinal use, particularly in China.

Exodus 16:3, 32 (manna). Ezekiel 19:13. Hosea 9:10. Isaiah 16:8, 35:1, 41:19. Jeremiah 9:10, 17:6, 23:10, 48:6. Job 24:5, 30:7, 38:27. Joel 2:22. 1 Kings 19:4 (broom-bush). Psalm 65:12.

Nº dill

Anethum graveolens L. is a strongly aromatic plant whose leaves and seeds have culinary and medicinal uses. See also **Nº 48 herbs**.

Isaiah 28:25, 27. Matthew 23:23.

Nº 31 dove's dung

The common explanation of this reference is that it is the Star-of-Bethlehem (*Ornithogalum umbellatum* L.). The plant, whose bulbs are sometimes known as white field onions, is toxic. It may be a biblical emphasis on the desperation of the Samarians under siege that this (or other) plant was being sold as food at such a high cost.

2 Kings 6:25.

STAR OF BETHLEHEM.
(*Ornithogalum umbellatum.*)

Nº 32 ebony

Diospyros ebenum Koenig, also Ceylon ebony, India ebony. This tree is valuable for its black heartwood, fine grain and durability. Its astringent fruit is edible, if unpalatable. The fruit also has medicinal uses. *Dalbergia melanoxylon* Guill. & Perr. is African ebony.

Ezekiel 27:15. Song of Solomon 3:10 (BBE).

EBONY TREE.—(*Diospyros ebenus.*)

Nº common **fennel flower**

Nigella sativa L. The seeds of this annual of the *Ranunculaceae* family are used to flavour food. The plant has medicinal uses. Common names include black cumin, Roman coriander and black caraway. It is not common fennel (*Foeniculum vulgare* Mill.). See also **Nº 48 herbs**.

Isaiah 28:25, 27.

Nº 33 fig

Ficus carica L., common fig, is one of the first cultivated plants. Evidence dating from early Neolithic (9th. Century BCE) was discovered in the Jordan Valley. This predates the domestication of wheat, barley and legumes. See also **Nº 97** large-fruited **sycamore fig**.

Amos 4:9, 7:14. 1 Chronicles 12:40. Deuteronomy 8:8. Ezekiel 27:17. Hosea 9:10 (fig). Isaiah 28:4, 34:4, 38:21 (poultice). James 3:12. Jeremiah 5:17, 8:13, 24:1-3, 5 (fig.), 8 (fig.), 29:17 (fig.), 40:10. Joel 2:22. Judith 10:5 (LXX). Kings IV 4:42, 20:7 (LXX). 2 Kings 18:31, 20:7 (poultice, also cake). Luke 6:44, 13:6-7, 9, 12. Mark 11:114. Matthew 7:16, 21:19. Micah 7:1. Nahum 3:12, 17. Nehemiah 13:15. Numbers 13:23-24, 20:5. Proverbs 27:18. Revelation 6:13. 1 Samuel 25:18, 30:12. 2 Samuel 16:1-2. Song of Solomon 2:13. Tobit 1:7 (GNTA).

Specific to the fig tree: Haggai 2:19. Hosea 2:12. James 3:12. Joel 1:7, 12. John 1:48, 50. Luke 13:6, 21:29. Mark 11:12-14, 19-21, 13:28. Matthew 21:18-22, 24:32. Micah 4:4. Nahum 3:12. Revelation 6:13. Zechariah 3:10.

BRANCH OF FIG-TREE.

N° 34 fitches

Fitch is a corruption of vetch of which bitter vetch (*Vicia ervilia* [L.] Willd.) was one of the first domesticated crops in the Near East. It is another name for common fennel flower. See **N° 12 bitter herbs; N° common fennel flower**.

Ezekiel 4:9. Isaiah 28:25-27.

N° 35 fir

Firs are a genus (*Abies*) of a group of an evergreen coniferous species of the *Pinaceae* family that continue to be of great economic importance. The lumber is easily worked and has multiple uses when protected from weather. One species in the Middle East is the Cilician fir (*Abies cilicica* [Antoine & Kotschy] Carrière) of Syria, Lebanon and Turkey. Many of the firs provide pitch which has practical and medicinal uses. See also **N° 29 cypress and gopher wood; N° 74 pine**.

2 Chronicles 2:8, 3:5. Ezekiel 27:5, 31:8, 55:13. Isaiah 14:8, 37:24, 41:19, 44:13, 55:13, 60:13, 69:13. 1 Kings 5:8, 10, 6:15, 34, 9:11. 2 Kings 19:23. Nahum 2:3. Psalm 104:17. 2 Samuel 6:5. Song of Solomon 1:17. Zechariah 11:2.

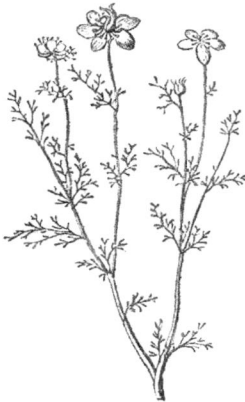

FITCHES —(*Nigella sativa*)

N° 36 flax

Linum usitatissimum L., cultivated flax, also known as common flax and linseed. It is an important crop grown for food, (linseed) oil, fibre and medical use. The fibre has wide application in the making of clothing accessories, rope, bow strings, sacking, sails *etc*. The textile produced is linen which is more durable than cotton and of better quality.

Thymelaea hirsuta (L.) Endl., hairy spurge flax, shaggy sparrow-wort, was used as a fibre source for rope-making by Bedouin. It is probably the plant referred to in Samson and Delilah (Judges) and *mitnan* of 1 Chronicles 4:7, Jeremiah 38:1, Nehemiah 12:19 and Numbers 21:19.

Specific to flax: Exodus 9:31. Ezekiel 40:3. Hosea 2:5, 9. Isaiah 19:9, 42:3, 43:17. Joshua 2:6. Judges 15:14, 16:9. Matthew 12:20. Proverbs 31:13.

Specific to linen: 1 Chronicles 4:21, 15:27. 2 Chronicles 2:14, 3:14, 5:12. Daniel 10:5, 12:6-7. Deuteronomy 22:1. Esther 1:6, 8:15. Exodus 25:4, 26:1, 31, 36, 27:9, 16, 18, 28:5-6, 8, 15, 39, 42, 35:6, 23, 25, 35, 36:8, 35, 37, 38:9, 16, 18, 23, 39:2, 5, 8, 24, 27-29. Ezekiel 9:2-3, 11, 10:2, 6-7, 16:10, 13, 27:7, 16, 40:3, 44:17-18. Genesis 41:42. Hosea 2:5, 9. Isaiah 3:23, 19:9. Jeremiah 13:1. John 11:44, 19:40, 20:5-7. Judges 14:12-13. Leviticus 6:10, 13:47, 48, 52, 59, 16:4, 23, 32. Luke 16:19, 23:53, 24:12. Mark 14:51, 15:46. Matthew 27:59. Proverbs 31:22, 24. Revelation 15:6, 18:12, 16, 19:8, 14. 1 Samuel 2:18, 22:18. 2 Samuel 6:14.

N° 37 frankincense

Boswellia sacra Flückiger-Dupiron is commonly known as the frankincense or olibanum tree. This small deciduous tree is milked for its sap by cutting into the bark two or three times a year. The sap coagulates into an aromatic resin known as frankincense or olibanum. It is used in incense, perfumery and medicine. The resins come from many parts of Arabia and Africa and have different characteristics. It has been traded for at least four thousand years. Some researchers suggest the olibanum (from the Hebrew word) of the Old Testament is from *B. serrata* Roxb. ex Colebr. sourced in India. The best quality frankincense is Omani from *B. sacra* Flückiger-Dupiron. *B. papyrifera* (Del.) Hochst. is Sudanese frankincense. See headings **N° 7 balm of Gilead** and **N° 8 balsam** for general balm, resin and gum references.

1 Chronicles 9:29. 2 Chronicles 28:25. Exodus 30:34. Ezekiel 6:13 (RHE). Genesis 43:11 (LXX). Isaiah 43:23, 60:6, 66:3. Jeremiah 6:20, 17:26, 41:5. Leviticus 2:1-2, 15, 16, 5:11, 6:15, 24:7. 111 Maccabees 5:2, 10, 45 (LXX). Matthew 2:11. Nehemiah 13:5, 9. Numbers 5:15. Revelation 18:13. Sirach 24:15, 39:14, 50:8 (LXX). Song of Solomon 3:6, 4:6, 14.

FRANKINCENSE.
(*Boswellia thurifera.*)

ARBOUR COVERED WITH A GOURD.

N° 38 gourd

The genus *Lagenaria* of climbing gourd-bearing vine is a very early cultivated plant species in Asia (possibly the first) and known in the Middle East for thousands of years. The bottle gourd, or calabash *Lagenaria siceraria* (Molina) Standl. in particular provided shade and food. Its mature, dried casings were used as drinking vessels, containers for liquids, for decoration and for making musical instruments.

2 Chronicles 4:3 (RSV). Isaiah 1:8 (WYC). Jonah 4:6-7, 9-10. 1 Kings 6:18, 7:24. 2 Kings 4:39. Numbers 11:5.

N° 39 wild gourd

In 2 Kings 4:39 the MS author refers to the wild gourd story where the fruit collected and added to a broth is not the edible gourd of the previous entry.

Jeremiah 2:21 (fig.). Jonah 4:6-10. 1 Kings 6:18. 2 Kings 4:39.

Notes on the Botany of the Bible

Entries Nos. 40 - 55

N° 40 galbanum

Ferula gummosa Boiss. The resinous gum from this plant is obtained through incisions at the base of the stalks. It gives a celery-like flavour to food and has medicinal properties. It was used in anointing oils by the Hebrews and in embalming by the Egyptians. See headings N° 7 balm of Gilead and N° 8 balsam for general balm, resin and gum references.

Exodus 30:34.

N° 41 gall

The word gall is used in the Bible to convey bitterness. It refers to gall, the gallbladder, sometimes liver, or to bitterness in plants. Wormwood [*qv.*] (*Artemisia judaica* L.) and poppy (*Papaver rhoeas* L.) are suggested as likely plants. See also N° 47 hemlock.

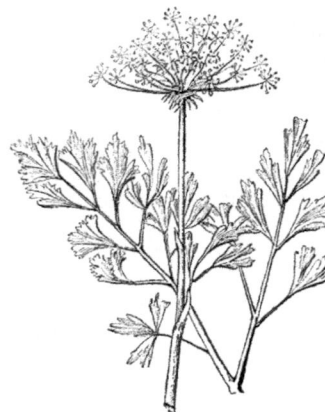

GALBANUM.—(*Polylophium officinale.*)

Amos 6:12. Deuteronomy 29:18, 32:32 (serpent venom). Jeremiah 8:14, 9:15, 23:15. Job 16:13, 20:16 (serpent venom), 20:25 (liver). Hosea 10:4. Lamentations 3:15, 19. Matthew 27:34. Proverbs 5:4. Psalm 69:21.

N° 42 garlic

Allium sativum L. has been cultivated since 3,000 BCE for culinary, medicinal and insecticidal use. The flowering stems and leaves are also used in cooking and have a milder flavour than the bulbs. The Numbers verse shows the Israelites reminiscing over this and other vegetables. See also N° 48 herbs; N° 72 onion.

Numbers 11:5.

GARLIC.
(*Allium sativum.*)

N° European grape

Vitis vinifera L. is one of the oldest fruit crops. Seeds have been found at early Bronze Age sites at Jericho (3,200 BCE) and at other ancient sites in the Levant. Apart from its fruit (eaten fresh and dried) it also provides juice for wine-making, an oil from its seeds and Cream of Tartar. It has medicinal uses. See also N° 111 vine.

Amos 9:13. 1 Corinthians 9:7. Deuteronomy 23:24, 24:21, 28:39, 32:14, 32. Exodus 22:29 (juice). Ezekiel 15:6, 18:2. Genesis 40:10-11, 49:11. Habakkuk 3:17 (NIV). Hosea 9:10. Isaiah 5:2, 4, 17:11, 18:5, 24:13, 32:10, 62:9, 63:3, 4, 6, 8 (fig.), 65:8. Jeremiah 6:9, 8:13, 25:30, 31:29-30, 48:32-33, 49:9. Job 15:33. Joel 1:5, 11, 3:13. Judges 8:2, 9:12-13, 27, 13:14. Leviticus 19:10, 25:5, 26:5. Luke 6:44, 20:10. 1 Maccabees 6:34. Mark 12:1. Matthew 7:16, 21:33. Micah 4:4, 6:15, 7:1. Nehemiah 5:11, 13:15. Numbers 6:3-4, 13:20, 23-24, 30 (juice), 20:5. Obadiah 1:5. Psalm 80:12. Revelation 19:15, 14:18-19. 1 Samuel 8:15. Song of Solomon 2:13, 7:8, 12.

N° 43 grass and hay

References to meadow and grassland are often used figuratively to offer desolation and poverty (drought, thorn bushes, wild animals, cities reduced to wasteland), or a land of plenty (lush pasture, abundant cattle and sheep) through faith in God.

Daniel 4:15. Deuteronomy 32:2. Genesis 1:11-12, 30, 2:5, 9:3, 41:2, 18. Isaiah 9:18, 15:6, 19:7, 30:23, 40:6-8, 24, 51:12. Job 5:25, 6:5, 38:27, 40:15, 22. Joel 1:19-20. John 6:10. Mark 6:39. Proverbs 27:25. 1 Peter 1:24. Psalm 37:2, 72:16, 129:6. Revelation 9:4. 2 Samuel 23:4 (fig.).

Specific to grassland, pasture and meadow: Amos 1:2. Ben Sira 24:42 (RHE). 1 Chronicles 4:39-41, 5:16, 6:55, 57-60, 64, 66-81, 13:2, 17:7. 2 Chronicles 11:14, 31:19. Daniel 4:15, 23. 2 Esdras 9:19 (fig.). Ecclesiastes 10:7 (fig.). Exodus 15:13 (fig.), 22:5. Ezekiel 25:5, 27:8, 34:13-15, 18-19, 23, 31, 36:5 (all fig.), 48:17. Genesis 13:6, 24:63, 65, 29:7, 30:31, 37:2, 12, 41:2, 18, 47:4. Hosea 4:16, 9:13, 13:6 (all fig.). Isaiah 5:17, 11:7, 13:20, 14:30, 17:2, 27:10, 30:23, 32:14, 20, 33:20, 34:13, 35:7, 37:27, 40:11, 44:4, 49:9, 61:5, 63:14, 65:10, 25 (most verses fig.). Jeremiah 6:2-3, 7:32, 23:1, 3, 25:36, 33:12, 46:19, 49:19-20, 50:7, 11, 19, 44-45 (all verses fig.). Jeremias 10:21, 25, 23:1, 3, 27:7, 19, 45 (LXX most verses fig.). Job 1:14, 5:25, 6:5, 8:11, 18:17, 24:2, 39:4, 8. Joel 1:18. John 10:9 (fig.). Joshua 14:4 21:2-3, 8, 11, 13-19, 21-39, 41-42. Judges 20:33. 1 Kings 4:23. Lamentations 1:6 (fig.). Leviticus 25:34. Luke 15:4 (fig.). Malachi 4:2 (fig.). Micah 2:12, 5:8, 7:14 (all fig.). Nehemiah 3:15 (LXX). Numbers 22:4, 23:14, 32:4, 35:2-5, 7. Psalm 23:2, 37:3, 20, 65:12, 72:16, 74:1, 79:13, 95:7, 100:3 (all fig.). 1 Samuel 6:18, 17:15. 2 Samuel 7:8. Song of Solomon 1:3, 7-8, 6:2 (all fig.). Zechariah 10:1, 11:4, 9 (all fig.). Zephaniah 2:6-7, 14, 3:13 (all fig.).

Specific to hay: Amos 2:13, 7:1. 1 Corinthians 3:12. Deuteronomy 11:15. Genesis 24:25, 32. Isaiah 11:7, 15:6, 33:11, 65:25. Job 5:26, 6:5. Judges 19:19. Micah 4:12. Proverbs 27:25.

N° 44 grove

Groves are associated with idols and early worship in the open air. If relating to trees or crops these are usually specified. Acacia Grove (or Shittim) in Numbers 33:49 was so-named because of the extensive acacias on the east bank of the Jordan. Elm (*Ulmus minor*) is mentioned in Isaiah. See also N° **acacia**; N° **19 cedar of Lebanon**; N° **date palm**; N° **68 nuts**; N° **69 oak**; N° **71 olive**; N° **75 pomegranate**.

Acts 1:12 (Olive Grove). Amos 4:9 (olive). 1 Chronicles 14:14 (balsam), 27:28 (olive). Deuteronomy 6:11 (olive), 11:30 (oak), 28:40 (olive). Ecclesiastes 2:6. 2 Esdras 16:28-29 (olive). Exodus 23:11 (olive). Genesis 13:18 (oak), 14:13 (oak), 18:1 (oak), 27:39. Hosea 5:2 (Acacia Grove), 14:6 (cedar). Isaiah 1:29 (oak), 41:19, 60:13 (elm). Jeremiah 17:2. Jeremias 4:29 (LXX). John 18:1, 3, 26 (all olive). Joshua 2:1, 3:1 (both acacia), 24:13 (olive). Judges 15:5 (olive). 2 Kings 5:26 (olive). Mark 14:32 (olive). Matthew 26:36 (olive). Micah 6:5 (Acacia Grove), 7:14. Nehemiah 5:11, 9:25 (both olive). Numbers 24:6 (palm), 25:1, 33:49 (both acacia). Psalm 105:33. 1 Samuel 8:14 (olive). Song of Solomon 6:11 (nut). Zacharias 12:11 (pomegranate) (LXX). Zechariah 1:8, 10-11 (birch).

N° Gum Tragacanth Milkvetch

Astragalus gummifer Labill. This small woody evergreen shrub has many medical, culinary and material uses. The gum obtained from its root and stem is used principally as a thickening agent in food and in printing. It can be burnt as an incense. *Astragalus bethlehemiticus* Boiss. is Bethlehem milkvetch. See headings **N° 7 balm of Gilead** and **N° 8 balsam** for general balm, resin and gum references.

Genesis 37:25, 43:11 (NAS).

N° Tournefort's **gundelia**

Gundelia tournefortii L. is a small perennial plant, all parts of which are edible except for the spiny edges of the leaves. It is sold in markets in the Near East. The stem and undeveloped flower buds are cooked like globe artichokes. It is known as galgal, tumbleweed or tumblethistle. Its Arabic name is *akkoub* or *akoub*.

Isaiah 17:13. Judges 9:14-15. Proverbs 2:13. Psalm 83:13.

N° 45 hazel

Corylus avellana L., hazel, hazelnut or common filbert. The seeds are a valuable source of food. Parts of the tree have medicinal uses. See also **N° 68 nuts**.

Genesis 30:37.

N° 46 heath

See **N° 51 Juniper**.

Jeremiah 17:6, 48:6.

N° 47 hemlock

Conium maculatum L. All parts of this plant, especially the seeds, are poisonous and can be lethal to humans and livestock. It grows wild across Europe and is not readily distinguishable from common cow parsley (Queen Anne's lace). It has medicinal uses. See also **N° 41 gall**; **N° 117** white **wormwood**.

Amos 6:12. Hosea 10:4.

N° henna

Lawsonia inermis L. is cultivated for its fragrant flowers and orange-red dye obtained from its leaves. It is used for dyeing cloth and hair, for staining nails, hands and feet. It has medicinal uses. See also **N° 16 Camphire**.

Song of Solomon 1:14, 4:13, 7:11.

N° 48 herbs

Many plants, flowers, vegetables, spices and tree by-products are described in the Bible by a few Hebrew words which are translated simply as 'herb.' Likely herbs are rocket (*Eruca vesicaria* subsp. *sativa* [Mill.] Thell.), Judean sage (*Salvia judaica* Boiss.), garland chrysanthemum (*Glebionis coronaria* [L.] Tzvel.), lettuce (*Lactuca sativa* L.) and common dandelion (*Taraxacum officinale* [Weber] ex Wigg.). See also **N° 12 bitter herbs; N° 94 spicery**.

Culinary herbs: **N° 4 anise; N° 10 bay tree; N° capers; N° 24 coriander; N° 28 cumin; N° dill; N° common fennel flower; N° 42 garlic; N° 50 hyssop; N° lemon grass; N° 62 mint; N° 64 mustard; N° 72 onion; N° 78 purslane; N° 82 rue.**

Amos 7:2. Daniel 4:15, 25, 33, 5:21. Deuteronomy 11:10, 29:23, 32:2. Exodus 9:22, 25 10:12, 15, 12:8. Genesis 1:11-12, 29-30, 2:5, 3:18, 9:3. Hebrews 6:7. Hoshea 10:4 (OJB). Isaiah 15:6, 18:4, 37:27, 42:15, 66:14. Jeremiah 2:22 (boreth), 12:4, 14:5-6, 50:11. Job 5:25, 8:12, 30:4 (salt herbs), 38:27. 1 Kings 21:2. 2 Kings 4:39, 19:26. Luke 11:42. Malachi 3:2. Mark 4:32. Matthew 6:30, 13:26, 32, 23:23. Micah 5:7. Numbers 22:4. Proverbs 15:17, 19:12, 27:25. Psalm 37:2, 72:16, 90:5, 92:7, 102:4, 11, 104:14, 105:35, 147:8. Romans 14:2. 2 Samuel 23:4. Song of Solomon 4:14 (fistula). Wisdom 16:12 (LXX). Zechariah 10:1.

HUSK-TREE.—(Ceratonia Siliqua.)

N° bristly hollyhock

Alcea setosa (Boiss.) Alef. Hollyhocks are a genus of the *Mavaceae*, or mallow family. There are two species common in the Near East today. The flower buds of *A. setosa* are edible and the plant has medicinal uses. *Malva nicaeensis* All. is bull mallow and *M. sylvestris* L. common mallow. The references below are to mallow in general. See also **N° 57 mallows**.

Job 6:6, 24:24, 30:4.

N° 49 husks

A husk or hull is the inedible protective outer layer of a seed. The MS author refers to *Ceratonia siliqua* L., the carob tree or locust bean tree. It is pictured left as the husk tree. See **N° carob**.

Luke 15:16 (husks, also pods).

N° 50 hyssop

Hyssopus officinalis L. is a herbaceous shrub with pink or blue flowers. It has medicinal uses. The Hebrew word of which hyssop is the translation is *ezov* or *ezob*. However, the biblical description does not match that of *H. officinalis* L. An alternative suggestion is *Origanum syriacum* L., Bible hyssop or Syrian Oregano. This plant is highly valued in the Middle East as a culinary herb and for its essential oil.

Exodus 12:22. Hebrews 9:19. John 19:29. 1 Kings 4:33. Leviticus 14:4, 6, 49, 51-52. Melachim Alef 5:134 (OJB). Numbers 19:6, 18. Psalm 51:7.

N° Christ's thorn jujube

Ziziphus spina-christi (L.) Desf. This is a medium-size thorn tree once predominant across the Mediterranean grassland of the Near East. Its fruit is edible. Of many Hebrew words for thorn, that in Isaiah 7:19 and 55:13 is interpreted as referring to this particular tree. It is revered by Muslims as the lote-tree in the Quran.

Paliurus spina-christi Miller, the Jerusalem thorn or garland thorn is also associated with the crucifixion story. The fruit is edible

BRANCH OF HYSSOP.

31

and the tree has medicinal uses. The references below are to the Crown of Thorns. See also **Nº 100-109 thorns**.

John 19:2, 5. Mark 15:17. Matthew 27:29.

Nº wild jujube

Ziziphus lotus (L.) Lam., also known as lotus jujube, lotus tree and wild jujube, is a small deciduous thorny shrub that can form extensive dense thickets. Its fruit is edible. It is associated with the lote-tree of the Quran, as is the closely-related *Z. spina-christi* (L.) Desf. See also **Nº 100-109 thorns**.

CHRIST'S THORN (PALIURUS SPINA-CHRISTI)
KOTZ - THORNS See Page 212
See overleaf

JUNIPER (JUNIPERUS SABINA)
ARAR HEATH See Page 240
See overleaf

Nº 51 juniper

The MS author cites *Juniperus sabina* L. (savin juniper, entry **Nº 46 heath**). This is a small shrub whose habitat is typically over 1,000 metres. All parts are poisonous though it has medicinal and insecticide uses. Also relevant to the Meditteranean is *J. phoenicea* L. (Phoenician juniper) and *J. excelsa* M.Bieb. (Greek or Crimean Juniper). Juniper is an evergreen that can grow to 20 metres and is common in mountainous areas (above 800 metres) in the Near East. Historically the bark of the larger species has been used for roofing, timber and fuel.

2 Chronicles 2:8, 3:5. Ezekiel 27:5, 31:8. Isaiah 14:8, 37:24, 41:19, 55:13, 60:13. Jeremiah 48:6. Job 30:4. 1 Kings 5:10, 6:34, 19:4-5. 2 Kings 19:23. Nahum 2:3. Psalm 104:17, 120:4. Zechariah 11:2.

LÔT, OR LADANUM.

Nº 52 ladanum

Cistus ladanifer L., labdanum or common gum cistus. The seeds can be ground and added to flour as a flavouring. A resin is obtained from the stem that is used as a commercial flavouring. Historically, resin has also been collected from the bush as a sweet 'manna.' This is also used in cosmetics and perfumery. It has medicinal uses. See headings **Nº 7 balm of Gilead** and **Nº 8 balsam** for general balm, resin and gum references.

Genesis 37:25, 43:11 (DBY).

Nº 53 leek

Allium ampeloprasum L., nom. cons. is the wild leek. Its bulb can be eaten cooked or raw and its flowers are used to flavour cooked food. It has medicinal uses similar to that of garlic. *Allium kurrat* Schweinf. ex K.Krause is the Egyptian leek. *Trigonella foenum-graecum* L. is fenugreek or cultivated trigonella.

Numbers 11:5.

LEEK.—(*Allium porrum.*)

Nº lemon grass

Cymbopogon citratus (DC.) Stapf, lemon grass or oil grass, is a tropical herbal plant. Its leaves have culinary and medicinal uses. *C. martinii* (Roxb.) W.Watson (palmarosa) of the same genus, gives an essential oil valuable for its scent and for household and medicinal uses. It has anthelminthic and antifungal properties. It is also used as an insect repellent in stored grain and beans. *C. schoenanthus* (L.) Spreng. is known as geranium grass. Like the other grasses in the species it has fragrant foliage and grows in a temperate climate. See also **Nº 48 herbs**.

Nº 54 lentil

Lens culinaris Medik. This plant was domesticated as early as 7,000 BCE making it a food staple and one of the oldest crops. The dried seeds can be ground and added to bread. Seeds can be eaten cooked, raw or sprouted and young seedpods can be cooked like green beans. The seeds have medicinal uses. See also **Nº 11 bean; Nº 77 pulse**.

Ezekiel 4:9. Genesis 25:34. 2 Samuel 17:28, 23:11.

LENTILES.—(*Ervum lens.*)

MADONNA LILY - LILIUM CANDIDUM

SHUSAN - LILY

Nº 55 lily

Lilium candidum L., white lily or Madonna lily. The bulb when cooked is sweetish and rich in starch. It can be cooked in the same way as potato. The plant has medicinal uses. See also **Nº 56 Lily of the field**.

2 Chronicles 4:5. Exodus 25:33. Hosea 14:5. Isaiah 35:1-2. 1 Kings 7:19, 22, 26. Luke 12:27. Matthew 6:28. Psalm 45:1, 59:17, 60:1, 69:1, 80:1. Song of Solomon 1:17, 2:2, 11, 16, 4:5, 5:13, 6:2, 31, 7:2.

Notes on the Botany of the Bible

Entries Nos. 56 - 68

N° 56 lily of the field

The MS author suggests a reference to the anemone or poppy in Matthew 6:28 and Luke 12:27. The references below are to lily in general. See also **N° Persian buttercup** (for flower of the field references); **N° 55 lily**; **N° Spanish marigold**; **N° 79-81 roses**.

Ben Sira 39:14, 50:8. 2 Esdras 2:19, 5:24. Hosea 14:5. Isaiah 35:1-2. Judith 10:3. Song of Solomon 1:17, 2:1-2, 16, 5:13, 6:2-3, 7:1-2 (all fig.).

N° madder

Rubia tinctorum L., common madder, dyer's madder, was grown in the Ancient World to provide a red textile dye. *Puah* in Judges 10:1 may mean madder. The references below are to Thyatira, now Akhisar in Turkey, where madder and dyed cloth were produced.

Acts 16:14. Revelation 1:11, 2:18, 24.

N° 57 mallows

This does not relate to the *Malva* genus that includes the common mallow. Biblical references are probably to the Mediterranean saltbush *Atriplex halimus* L. The leaves of this shrub are edible but unpalatable. See also **N° bristly hollyhock**; **N° Mediterranean saltbush**.

Job 6:6, 24:24, 30:4.

MANDRAKE.—(*Atropa mandragora*)

N° 58 malabathron

Malabathron or malabathrum is the name of the leaves of several cinnamon [*q.v.*] trees. Those used in India and Greece for the ointment *oleum malabathri* was probably *Cinnamomum tamala* (Buch.-Ham.) Nees. (Indian bay-leaf). The Greeks flavoured wine with the leaves and the Romans used them as a condiment. Song of Solomon 2:17 may relate to this.

N° 59 mandrake

Mandragora officinarum L. Mandrake has a long association with medicine, superstition and as a love-plant, though all parts of the plant are poisonous except the leaves. Ginseng and other plants have been suggested as that referred to in the verses below.

Genesis 30:14-16. Song of Solomon 7:13.

N° Spanish marigold

Anemone coronaria L. The MS author suggests this is one of the lilies of the field. It grows wild throughout the Near East and is a noted floral attraction in the Spring in Israel. See **N° Persian buttercup** (for flower of the field references); **N° 56 Lily of the field**; **N° 79-81 roses**.

N° 60 melon

Most culinary fruit melons belong to the species *Cucumis melo* L. which includes muskmelon, honeydew and cantaloupe. The watermelon (*Citrullus lanatus* [Thunb.] Matsumura & Nakai) is a trailing vine. Both types were known in the Middle East in biblical times. Melons are one of the oldest domesticated plants. They are appreciated in hot dry climates for their refreshing, delicately scented flesh, food value and medicinal uses. See also **N° 27 cucumber**; **N° watermelon**.

Isaiah 1:8. Jeremiah 10:5. Numbers 11:5.

MELON.—(*Cucumis melo.*)

N° 61 millet

Panicum miliaceum L. is a food staple that has been grown in the Middle East for millennia. It has a short growing season and is drought- and heat-tolerant. Green millet was used as animal fodder. When ripe it was ground for use in bread. See also **N° 25 corn and wheat**; **N° sorghum**.

Ezekiel 4:9, 27:17. Isaiah 28:25. 2 Samuel 17:28.

N° 62 mint

Mentha longifolia (L.) Huds., one of about 18 in the genus and commonly known as horsemint, is a widespread aromatic herb with a slight peppermint smell. It is native to Europe and Asia and parts of Africa. It is used extensively in food and drinks. It also has medicinal and anti-rodent properties. See also **N° 48 herbs**.

Luke 11:42. Matthew 23:23. Song of Solomon 4:14, 7:8.

MILLET.—(*Panicum miliaceum.*)

MINT.—(*Mentha sylvestris.*)

N° 63 mulberry

Morus nigra L., black mulberry, is a deciduous flowering tree widespread throughout the Middle East and Asia. It is valued for its edible fruit which is sweeter than that of the red and white mulberry (*M. rubra* L. and *M. alba* L.).

1 Chronicles 14:14-15. Isaiah 40:20. Luke 17:6 (fig.) (sycamine), 19:4. 1 Maccabees 6:34. Psalm 78:47 (RHE). 2 Samuel 5:23-24. Luke 17:6.

N° 64 mustard

The leaves of *Brassica nigra* (L.) W.D.J.Koch (black mustard) and *Sinapis alba* L. (white mustard) are used in mixed salads. The ground seeds of both species are used to make the condiment paste. Seeds, leaves and oil have medicinal uses. *Sinapis arvensis* L. is field mustard or charlock. See also **N° 48 herbs.**

Luke 13:19, 17:6. Mark 4:31. Matthew 13:31-32, 17:20.

N° 65 myrrh

Commiphora myrrha (Nees) Engl., common myrrh or Somali myrrh, is a medium-size tree of the Arabian Peninsula whose resin has long been used in the Middle East in incense, perfume and medicine. *C. gileadensis* (L.) C.Christ., is the Arabian balsam tree whose common names include Mecca myrrh and Mecca balsam. *C. africana* (Rich.) Engl. is African myrrh. *C. kataf* (Forssk.) Engl., bisabol myrrh, *C. kua* (R.Br. ex Royle) Vollesen, Abyssinian myrrh, *C. myrrha* (Nees) Engl., hesabol myrrh. See headings **N° 7 balm of Gilead** and **N° 8 balsam** for general balm, resin and gum references.

Exodus 30:23 (anointing). Esias 39:2 (LXX). Esther 2:12. Genesis 37:25, 43:11. John 19:39 (embalming). Mark 15:23 (offered to Jesus). Matthew 2:11 (Magi). Proverbs 7:17. Psalm 45:8. Revelation 18:13. Song of Solomon 1:13, 3:6, 4:6, 14, 5:1, 5, 13.

MUSTARD-TREE.

N° 66 myrtle

Myrtus communis L. is an evergreen shrub or small tree common in the Middle East. Its fruit and leaves have culinary uses and its leaves and essential oil have medicinal uses. The plant has a traditional place in Jewish prayer. *Myrica gale* L., known as sweetgate, has similar properties as well as anti-parasitic uses.

Exodus 30:23. Isaiah 41:19, 55:13. Nehemiah 8:15. Zechariah 1:8, 1:10-11.

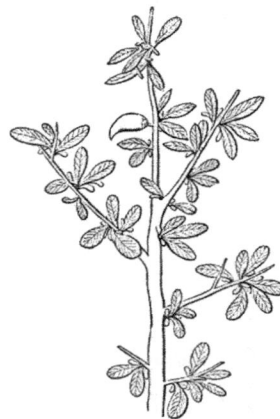

N° cream narcissus

Narcissus tazetta L., cream narcissus or bunchflower daffodil, is a bulb that grows in damp meadows around the Mediterranean. The root has medicinal uses. An essential oil from the flowers is used in perfumery. See also **N° Persian buttercup** (for flower of the field references).

Song of Solomon 2:1.

MYRRH.

N° *Nardostachys jatamansi*

Nardostachys jatamansi (D.Don) DC. is a perennial flowering plant ot the Valerian family native to the Himalayas. In herbal medicine it is known as a calming herb. The incense and essential oil (nard oil) produced from the rhizomes are commonly known as spikenard. This was an important ingredient of Hebrew incense in the Tabernacle. It was a luxury item imported into the Near East, ancient Rome and ancient Greece. The plant has medicinal, culinary and cosmetic uses and its dried leaves are also burnt as incense. See headings **N° 7 balm of Gilead** and **N° 8 balsam** for general balm, resin and gum references.

John 12:3. Mark 14:3. Song of Solomon 1:12, 4:13-14

N° 67 nettles

Urtica dioica L. is the common nettle or stinging nettle. It has culinary uses, the young plant having a spinach-like flavour when cooked. All parts of the plant are used medicinally. Its tough fibre is used to make cloth and paper. *Urtica pilulifera* L., the Roman nettle, is native to Egypt and has similar properties and uses. *Urtica urens* L. is the dwarf nettle or small nettle. See **N° 100-109 thorns** for nettle references in the Bible.

NETTLE.—(*Urtica urens.*)

N° nightshade

Solanum incanum L., nightshade, also thorn apple, bitter apple, Dead Sea apple, Dead Sea fruit-wild potato. It is a herbaceous thorny shrub with small green fruit native to sub-Saharan Africa and the Middle East. Its habitat is mainly as a weed around overgrazed grassland. It has medicinal uses. The fruit is poisonous on the wild form of the tree. It may be the thorn *hedek* described as having leaves that are woolly on the underside. See **N° 100-109 thorns.**

Micah 7:4. Proverbs 15:19.

N° 68 nuts

The MS author cites pistachio and walnut. The pistachio *Pistacia vera* L. is a desert plant that can grow to 10 metres in height in poor saline soils. It is native to Central Asia and the Middle East and its seeds (pistachio nuts) were a common food by the 7th. Millennium BCE. *Pistacia atlantica* Desf. is Atlantic pistachio. See also **N° 2 almond; N° 20 chestnut; N° 45 hazel; N° 114 walnut.**

Exodus 25:33-34, 37:19-20. Genesis 43:11. Luke 13:19 (pine nut). Mark 4:31 (pine nut). Matthew 13:31 (pine nut). Song of Solomon 4:13, 6:11 (walnut).

Notes on the Botany of the Bible

Entries Nos. 69 - 78

Nº 69 oak

Quercus coccifera L., the Kermes oak, is a hardy evergreen shrub that can withstand heavy grazing. It was valuable for the red dye produced from the Kermes insect. Related to this species is *Quercus calliprinos* Webb (Palestine oak or common Israeli oak). Valonia oak or Mt. Tabor oak (*Quercus ithaburensis* Decne.) is larger and once flourished on the Eastern Mediterranean coastal plain. *Quercus infectoria* G.Olivier is Aleppo oak.

Amos 2:9. 1 Chronicles 10:12, 12:10. Deuteronomy 11:30. Ezekiel 27:6. Genesis 12:6, 13:18, 14:13, 18:1, 35:4, 8. Hosea 4:13. Isaiah 1:29-30, 2:13, 6:13, 44:14, 57:5, 61:3. Joshua 19:33, 24:26. Judges 4:11, 6:11, 19, 9:6, 37. 1 Kings 13:14. Psalm 29:9, 56:1. 1 Samuel 10:3. 2 Samuel 18:9-10, 14. Zechariah 11:2.

ABRAHAM'S OAK.

Nº oleander

Nerium oleander L., oleander or rose-bay, is an ornamental evergreen flowering shrub. The whole plant is toxic but has medicinal uses. It is a parasiticide and insecticide. The Hebrew word *habatstseleth* in Song of Solomon 2:1 and Isaiah 35:1 may refer to the oleander. See also **Nº 79-81 roses**.

OLEANDER.

OIL-TREE.—(*Elæagnus angustifolia.*)

Nº 70 oil tree

Elaeagnus angustifolia L., the Oleaster or Russian olive, is thought to be the tree referred to in the verses below. It is a tree or small shrub, often thorny, with edible olive-like fruit.

Isaiah 41:19. Judges 9:9. 1 Kings 6:23, 31-33. Nehemiah 8:15.

Nº 71 olive

Olea europaea L. The olive may have been domesticated as long ago as 8,000 BCE. As with other prime crops and animals in biblical times, olive trees and their produce were a measure of prosperity and well-being. As such, tree and fruit are often used figuratively. It remains an important food and source of high quality oil that is used in cooking, as a preservative and in the pharmaceutical industry.

OLIVE-TREE.—(*Olea europæa.*)

Amos 4:9. 1 Chronicles 9:29, 12:40, 23:29, 27:25, 28, 29:22 (anointing). 2 Chronicles 2:10, 15, 11:11, 23:11 (anointing), 28:15, 31:5, 32:28. Deuteronomy 6:11, 7:13, 8:8, 11:14, 12:17, 14:23, 18:4, 24:20, 28:40, 51, 32:13, 33:24. Ecclesiastes 9:8 (anointing). Exodus 23:11, 27:20, 28:41, 29:2, 7, 23, 36, 40-41, 30:24-25, 31, 31:11, 35:8, 14, 28, 37:29, 39:37, 40:9, 11. Ezekiel 16:9, 13, 18-19, 23:41, 27:17, 32:14 (fig.) 45:13-14, 24-25, 46:5, 7, 11, 14-15. Ezra 3:7, 6:9, 7:22. Genesis 8:11, 27:39 (fig.). Habakkuk 3:17. Haggai 1:11, 2:12, 19. Hosea 2:4-5, 8, 21-22, 9:2, 12:1, 14:6 (fig.). Isaiah 1:6, 17:6 (fig.), 24:13 (fig.), 39:2, 41:19, 57:9. James 3:12, 5:14 (anointing). Jeremiah 11:16-17 (fig.), 31:12, 40:10, 41:8. Job 15:33 (fig.), 20:17, 24:11, 29:6. Joel 1:10, 2:19, 24. John 18:1, 3, 13, 26. Joshua 24:13. Judges 9:8-9 (fig.), 15:5. Judith 10:5, 15:13. Kings II 15:18 (LXX). 1 Kings 1:34, 39, 45 (all three anointing), 5:11, 6:23 (olive wood), 31-33 (olive wood), 17:12, 14, 16, 19:15 (anointing). 2 Kings 4:2, 4-7, 9:1, 3, 6 (both anointing), 5:26, 11:12 (anointing), 18:32, 20:13, 23:20 (anointing). Leviticus 2:1-2, 4-7, 15-16, 5:11, 6:15, 21, 7:10, 12, 8:2, 26, 9:4, 14:10, 12, 15, 21, 24, 26, 21:10, 23:13, 24:2. Luke 7:46, 10:34, 16:6. 2 Maccabees 14:4. Micah 6:7, 15 (both fig.). Mark 6:13. Matthew 6:17, 25:3-4, 8-9. Nehemiah 5:11, 8:15, 9:25, 10:37, 39, 13:5, 12. Numbers 4:9, 16, 5:15, 6:15, 7:1 (anointing), 13, 19, 25, 31, 37, 43, 49, 55, 61, 67, 73, 79, 84, 8:8, 11:8, 15:4, 6, 9, 18:12, 28:5, 9, 12-13, 20, 28, 29:3, 9, 14. Proverbs 5:3 (fig.), 21:17, 20, 27:16. Psalm 52:8, 55:21 (both fig.), 92:10 (anointing), 104:15, 109:18, 128:3 (fig.), 133:2, 141:5 (both anointing). Revelation 6:6, 11:4, 18:13. Romans 11:17, 24 (both fig.). Ruth 2:14 (CJB). 1 Samuel 8:14, 10:1, 16:1, 13. 2 Samuel 1:21. Sirach 24:14 (fig.), 50:10 (fig.). Susanna 1:17 (CEBA). Zechariah 4:2-3, 11-12.

Specific to the Mount of Olives: Acts 1:12. Ezekiel 11:23. John 8:1, 18:1, 3, 26. 1 Kings 11:7. 2 Kings 23:13. Luke 19:29, 37, 21:37, 22:39. Mark 11:1, 13:3, 14:26, 32 (Gethsemane). Matthew 21:1, 24:3, 26:30, 36 (Gethsemane). 2 Samuel 15:23, 30, 32, 16:31. Zechariah 14:4.

ONIONS.—(*Allium cepa.*)

N° 72 onion

Allium cepa L., the onion, was cultivated from the wild species about 5,000 BCE. It is a food staple used in cuisine around the world. It has medicinal uses. See also **N° 48 herbs**.

Numbers 11:5.

N° 73 palm

See *Phoenix dactylifera* L., **N° date palm.**

N° papyrus

Cyperus papyrus L., see **N° 83-88 rushes.**

N° 74 pine

Pinus halepensis Mill., Aleppo pine or Jerusalem pine, is valuable for its resin. *Pinus brutia* Ten., Turkish pine or Calabrian pine, was used in construction, boat-building and as fuel. Both species host an aphid that produces honeydew collected by bees for what is known as pine honey. *Pinus pinea* L. is Italian stone pine. See also **N° 35 fir.**

2 Chronicles 2:8, 3:5. Ezekiel 27:5-6, 31:3, 8 (both fig.). Hosea 14:8 (fig.). Isaiah 6:13, 14:8, 37:24, 41:19, 44:14, 23, 55:13, 60:13. Jeremiah 26:18. Job 8:11. 1 Kings 5:8, 10, 6:15, 34, 9:11. 2 Kings 19:23. Luke 13:19. Mark 4:32. Matthew 13:32. Nahum 2:3. Nehemiah 8:15. Psalm 104:17. Song of Solomon 1:17. Zechariah 11:2.

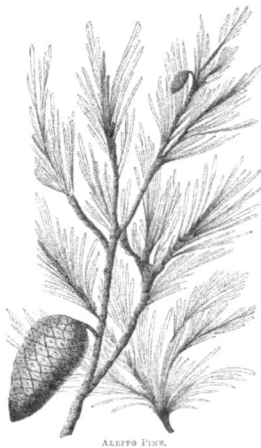

SCOTCH PINE. PINUS SYLVESTRIS

ALEPPO PINE.

N° oriental **plane**

Platanus orientalis L., oriental plane, is well-known as a tree planted for shade. Its leaves and bark are used medicinally and a fabric dye is made from its twigs and roots. The timber, sometimes referred to as lacewood, is used for outdoor furniture. See also **N° 20 chestnut.**

Ben Sira 24:14 (KJVA). Ezekiel 31:8. Genesis 30:37. Isaiah 41:19, 60:13.

N° 75 pomegranate

Punica granatum L., pomegranate, is a small deciduous tree with juicy refreshing fruit. Its fresh seeds can be eaten raw. Use of all parts of the plant

PLANE-TREE.—(*Chesnut-tree of Scripture.*)

POMEGRANATES.

in medicine have been known for at least 3,000 years. A red dye is obtained from the flowers and a black ink from the bark.

Ben Sira 45:9 (RSVA). 2 Chronicles 3:16, 4:11, 13 (all archit.). Deuteronomy 8:8. Exodus 28:33-34, 39:24-26. Haggai 2:19. Jeremiah 52:21-23 (archit.). Joel 1:12. 1 Kings 7:17-18, 20, 40, 42. 2 Kings 25:17 (archit.). Numbers 13:23, 20:5. 1 Samuel 14:2. 2 Samuel 5:23. Song of Solomon 4:3, 13, 6:7, 11, 7:8, 12, 8:2, 5 (all fig.). Tobit 1:7 (CEBA).

N° 76 poplar

Populus euphratica Oliv., Euphrates poplar, is a deciduous tree of the willow family. It is heat- and drought-tolerant and its timber has been used in building, firewood and for paper-making. Its leaves are used for fodder. Its bark has anthelminthic properties. References to the willow in many biblical passages could be to the poplar which is similar in appearance. *Populus alba* L. is white poplar. See also N° **115 willow**; N° **116 willow of Babylon**.

1 Chronicles 14:14-15. Genesis 30:37. Hosea 4:13. Isaiah 15:7 (Ravine of the Poplars), 44:4. Job 40:22. Leviticus 23:14. Psalm 137:2. 2 Samuel 5:23-24.

N° 77 pulse

Pulse is the often dried seed of legumes. It is distinguished from vegetables by the seeds being contained in pods and include peas, beans, lentils, carob, chickpeas (*Cicer arietinum* L.) and vetch. Some are forage legumes grown specifically for livestock to graze. References to pottage are included below. See also N° **11 bean**; N° **54 lentil**.

Bel 1:33 (KJVA). Daniel 1:12, 16 (KJV). Ezekiel 4:9. Genesis 25:29-30, 34. Haggai 2:12. Isaiah 28:25, 27, 44:16. Joshua 5:11. 2 Kings 4:38-40. Leviticus 23:14. Romans 9:21. Ruth 2:14. 2 Samuel 17:28, 23:11.

N° 78 purslane

Portulaca oleracea L., common purslane, is a succulent known in the Middle East since the 7th. Century BCE. It is used as a fresh salad or cooked in stews and soups. It has medicinal uses. See also N° **48 herbs**.

Job 6:6.

GARDEN PEA PISUM SATIVUM
ZEROIM - PULSE

PURSLANE PORTULACA OLERACEA
PURSLANE

Notes on the Botany of the Bible

Entries Nos. 79 - 89

Nº common reed

Phragmites australis (Cav.) Trin. ex Steud., the common reed, is a widespread perennial grass that grows in a watery environment. Its stems can reach six metres in height. It has been of significant economic value in the Middle East for thousands of years in the making of spears, fishing poles, paper, insulation, musical instruments, rudimentary roofing and screens, baskets and mats. Many parts of the plant are edible. It has medicinal uses. See also **Nº 83-88 rushes; Nº calamus**.

Ben Sira 40:16. Exodus 2:3, 5, 30:23. Ezekiel 27:19 (reed spice), 29:6 (fig.), 40:3, 5-8, 41:8, 42:16-20, 45:1-3, 6, 48:8-10, 13, 15-17, 21, 30, 32-35. Genesis 38:28 (TYN), 41:2, 18. Hosea 13:15. Isaiah 9:14 (fig.), 18:2, 19:6-7, 15 (fig.), 35:7, 36:6, 42:3 (fig.), 43:24 (spice reed), 44:4, 58:5. Jeremiah 6:20 (spice reed), 35:7, 51:32. Job 8:11-13, 9:26, 40:16 (LXX), 21, 41:2, 20 (all fig.). Joshua 16:8, 17:9 (both RHE). 1 Kings 14:15 (fig.). 2 Kings 18:21 (fig.). Luke 7:24. 3 Maccabees 2:22, 4:20. Mark 15:19, 36. Matthew 11:7, 12:20, 27:29-30, 48. Psalm 68:30, 114:3, 5. Revelation 11:1, 21:15-16.

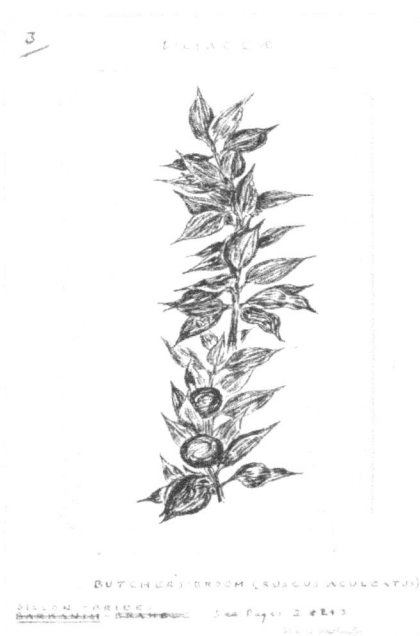

BUTCHER'S BROOM (RUSCUS ACULEATUS)

Nº retem

Retama raetam (Forssk.) Webb., white broom, is a genus of flowering broom. It is a large perennial shrub with white flowers found in desert wadis in the Near East. It was formerly a source of charcoal and grazing for goats. It has medicinal uses. Biblical Rithmah in Numbers 33:18-19 was so-named after the Hebrew word *rotem* (white broom). Biblical references to the MS author's notes on white broom (**Nº 51 Juniper** page 103) are included below.

Calycotome villosa (Poir.) Link, spiny broom or furrowed thorny broom grows in maquis terrain, woodland and shrubland in the Near East. Its small dried flowers are traditionally used with sesame seeds to produce a fragrant oil. See also **Nº 30 desert vegetation**.

Jeremiah 17:6 (*retama* in the Spanish Bible), 48:6. Job 30:4. 1 Kings 19:4-5. Psalm 120:4. Teshayah 14:23 (OJB).

Nº hairy rockrose

Cistus incanus L., hairy rockrose or hairy rock-rose. Some cistus species, including this one exude a gum from their leaves and hairy stems. It was known in the Middle East in the 4th. Century BCE and considered to be the biblical source of ladanum gum/ resin used in perfumes, incense, medicine and the Balm of Gilead [*qv.*]. *Cistus laurifolius* L. is the laurel-leaved rockrose and *Cistus salviifolius* L. the sage-leaved rockrose. See headings **Nº 7 balm of Gilead** and **Nº 8 balsam** for general balm, resin and gum references.

Nº 79-81 roses

Rose in the Bible could refer to various vibrant flowers including the crocus, lily, rockrose, narcissus and tulip, or to the sea-daffodil (*Pancratium maritimum* L.). This last grows along Israel's Mediterranean coastal plain, the Sharon plain. Rose of Sharon, lily of the valley and flower of the field are poetic expressions. In the Wycliffe bible based on Greek texts and printed more than 200 years before the 1611 King James Version the editors translated Rose of Sharon as flower of the field [*qv.*]. The rose has significance in other religions including Islam in which it represents the human soul.

Rosa canina L., the dog rose or wild rose, is a deciduous shrub with small white to pink flowers found across the Middle East. Rose hips have a high Vitamin C content and are used in the making of sweet wine, tea, jams and syrup. Other species include *Rosa phoenicia* L., Phoenician rose, which is also present in the Near East. It is thorny and rambling with small white flowers.

See **Nº** Persian **buttercup** (for flower of the field references); **Nº 56 lily of the field**; **Nº sea-daffodil**; **Nº tulip**. The MS author suggests the three rose references in the Book of Ecclesiasticus are to the oleander [*qv.*].

General references to rose: Ben Sira 24:14, 39:13, 17, 50:8, 51:8. Ecclesiasticus 39:13. 2 Esdras 2:19 (KJVA). Esther 1:6 (LXX). Hosea 2:15. Isaiah 35:1-2, 61:3. 3 Maccabees 7:17 (CEBA). Psalm 65:11-12, 69:1. Song of Solomon 2:1.

See **Nº 100-109 thorns** for bramble and brier references.

ROSE OF SHARON.—(*Narcissus tazetta.*)

Nº 82 rue

Ruta chalepensis L., fringed rue, is a perennial herb native to Eurasia and North Africa. It has medicinal uses. See also **Nº 48 herbs**.

Luke 11:42.

RUE.—(*Ruta graveolens.*)

Nº 83-88 rushes

Rush and bulrush

The terms rush and bulrush in the Bible are believed to refer to the papyrus (*Cyperus papyrus* L., papyrus, papyrus sedge or Nile grass). This hardy perennial sedge can grow to four metres in height and was abundant and widespread in watery habitats in biblical times. It has been an important resource for 5,000 years to the Egyptians particularly in the making of paper. It was also used for boat-making, matting and roofing as well as being a source of fuel and food. Other rushes, canes, reeds, flag and species of water-lily are as follows:

Typha domingensis (Pers.) Poir. ex Steud., southern cattail, a

BULRUSH.

43

PAPYRUS PLANT.—(*Papyrus antiquorum.*)

perennial wetland herb mistakenly referred to as bulrush. All parts except the fibre are edible. The plant has many other uses in thatching, weaving and paper-making. It has medicinal properties.

The MS author in **N⁰ 85** (page 127) suggests *Arundo donax* L., giant cane or giant reed, as that referred to in Isaiah 9:14-15. This prefers full sun and damp soils and can reach six metres in height. Historically it has multiple uses including in Ancient Egypt, the wrapping of the dead in its leaves. Mouthpiece reeds and flutes are made from the cane. It is also a building material and it has medicinal uses. The MS author also mentions that sugar cane (*Saccharum officinarum* L.) was known in Palestine imported from Asia.

Schoenoplectus lacustris (L.) Palla, common club-rush, common clubrush, lakeshore bulrush. This species of club-rush grows in soft silt at the edge of fresh or fresh flowing water. It can reach three-and-a-half metres in height and grow into dense stands. In general it shares the common names rush and bulrush.

Juncus maritimus Lam., sea rush or seaside rush, a sharp-pointed rush common on sandy or silty shorelines and dunes. Cattle avoid browsing the stems because of their spiny tips. The Ancient Egyptians used them as quill pens. Also inhabiting coastlines is *Zostera marina* L., common eel grass or seawrack. It was once found on the Mediterranean shore of Syria and used as a fibre source and as food.

Flag

This is a general word of Egyptian origin used in the Bible to denote reeds, rushes, sedges and weeds. The MS author suggests *Butomus umbellatus* L. (flowering rush, grass rush) and *Cyperus esculentus* L. (shuta sedge, nut grass) as flag. *B. umbellatus* L. grows in a watery environment preferring higher altitudes in warmer climates, as those of the Eastern Mediterranean.

The MS author also cites four aquatic plants common in Palestine but not mentioned in the Scriptures; *Juncus conglomeratus* L. (compact rush), *Nymphaea alba* L. (European white water-lily, white water rose), *Nuphar luteum* (L.) Sibth. & Sm. (yellow water-lily), *Nymphaea lotus* L. (Egyptian white water-lily.) Also found in Egypt is *Nymphaea nouchali*

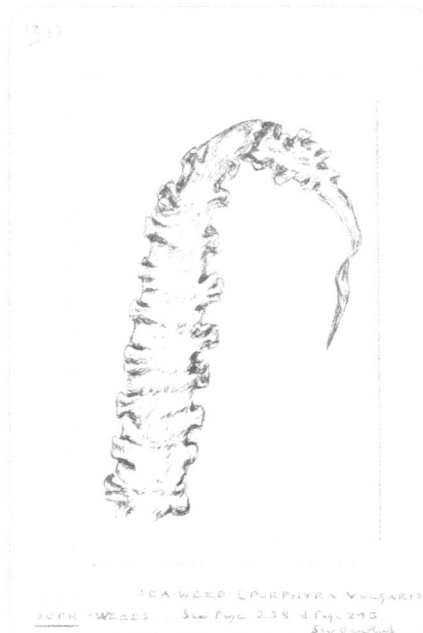

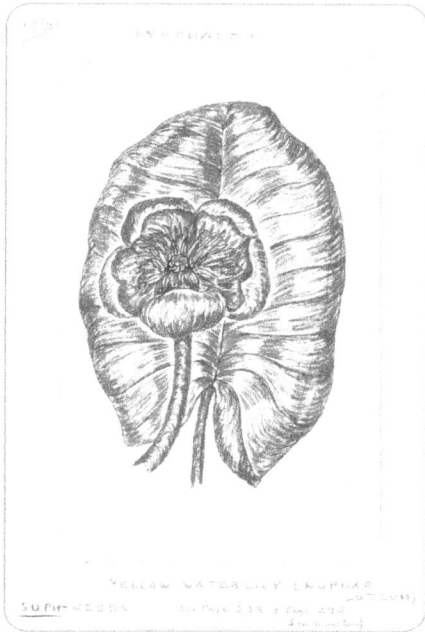

YELLOW WATERLILY (NUPHAR LUTEUM)

SUDD-WEEDS

var. *caerulea* (Savigny) Verdc., the blue water-lily or Egyptian lotus. See also N° **15 calamus**; N° common **reed**.

Specific to bulrush: Exodus 2:3 (papyrus), 2:5. Isaiah 9:14, 18:2, 19:6-7, 15, 35:7, 58:5. Job 8:19, 41:20.

Rushes in general: Isaiah 9:14-15 (fig.), 19:6, 15, 35:7, 18:2, 42:3, 58:5. Job 8:11, 41:2, 20. John 2:15.

Flag in general: Exodus 2:3, 5. Genesis 41:2, 18. Isaiah 19:6. Job 8:11-13 (fig.). Joel 3:18 (LXX). Jonah 2:5 (weeds).

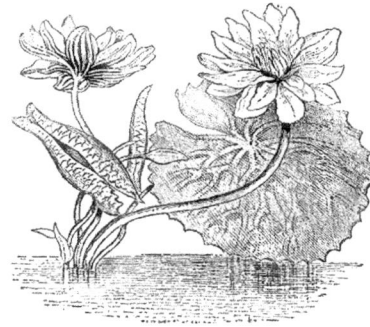

EGYPTIAN LOTUS.

N° 89 rye

Secale cereale L. is a cereal grain and food staple. It is the most hardy cereal and can be grown in more adverse weather and soil conditions than wheat. It is used in the making of bread. Its main consumption in the Middle East was as animal fodder, bedding, thatching and paper-making. See also N° **25 corn and wheat**.

Exodus 9:32. Ezekiel 4:9 (marginalia). Isaiah 28:25.

WHEAT, BARLEY, AND RYE.

Notes on the Botany of the Bible

Entries Nos. 90 - 109

Nº 90 saffron

See Nº autumn **crocus**.

Nº Mediterranean **saltbush**

Atriplex halimus L., Mediterranean saltbush, saltbush, sea purslane, is a drought-tolerant shrub that can survive in alkaline and saline soils. It has been cultivated in the past to sustain grazing animals in harsh environments.

Jeremiah 17:6 (fig.) Job 30:4.

Nº red **sandalwood**

Pterocarpus santalinus L.f., red sandalwood, red sanders, is a small deciduous tree native to India and Western Asia whose fine red aromatic timber has been prized for millennia in the making of high quality furniture. See also **Nº 1 algum**, almug tree.

2 Chronicles 2:8, 9:10-11. 1 Kings 10:11-12.

Nº *Schoenoplectus lacustris*

See **Nº 83-88 rushes**.

Nº sea-daffodil

Pancratium maritimum L., sea-daffodil, sand daffodil, sand lily, inhabits beaches and sand dunes of the Mediterranean and Black Sea. It may be the plant referred to as the Rose of Sharon because it grows along Israel's Sharon plain. See also **Nº** Persian **buttercup** (for flower of the field references); **Nº 79-81 roses**.

SHITTAH-TREE.—(*Acacia Seyal.*)

Nº 91 shittah tree

See **Nº acacia** for acacia and *shittim* references.

Nº drug **snowbell**

Styrax officinalis L., the storax tree, snowdrop bush, official storax. The white flowers of this deciduous shrub have a citrus fragrance. Branches and stems produce a fragrant resin known as storax that is used in cosmetics and perfumery. It has medicinal uses. It could be an ingredient of stacte [*qv.*]. See headings **Nº 7 balm of Gilead** and **Nº 8 balsam** for general balm, resin and gum references.

Genesis 30:37 (LXX), 43:11 (RHE). Ben Sira 24:15, 21 (LXX).

N° 92 soap

The MS author cites *Salsola kali* L. (prickly saltwort, common saltwort, Russian thistle) and *Sarcocornia fruticosa* (L.) A.J.Scott, (shrubby samphire). The latter is also referred to as *Salicornia fruticosa* L. Similarly useful in soap-making was *Salsola inermis* Forssk. (spineless saltwort). *Salicornia* species are perennial herbs whose habitat is salt marshes. They are a foodstuff, ingredient of medicine and source of soda ash in glass and soap-making.

Suaeda palaestina Eig. & Zohary, Palestinian sea-blite, seepweed or common reaumuria, also grows on Mediterranean coastal salt marshes. It has been similarly harvested for its soda ash.

Hosea 2:17. Isaiah 1:25. Jeremiah 2:22 (MSG, soaps), 2:22 (DBY, potash), 2:22 (RHE, borith). Job 9:30. Malachi 3:2 (OJB). Proverbs 25:20. Psalm 26:6.

N° sorghum

Sorghum bicolor (L.) Moench. is a grass species with very small grains known in the Middle East and Egypt as a drought-resistant crop that provides food for human and animal consumption. *Dochan*, the Hebrew word for millet could also include sorghum, one of its common names being great millet. See also **N° 25 corn and wheat**; **N° 61 millet**.

N° 93 spikenard

See N° *Nardostachys jatamansi*.

N° 94 spicery

The MS author uses this term for gums and resins. See headings **N° 7 balm of Gilead** and **N° 8 balsam** for general balm, resin and gum references. See also **N° 17 cassia**; **N° 21 cinnamon**; **N° autumn crocus**; **N° 48 herbs**.

1 Chronicles 9:29-30, 14:14 (BBE). 2 Chronicles 2:4, 9:1, 9, 24, 13:11. Daniel 2:46 (BBE). Esias 39:2 (LXX). 16:14, 32:27. Esther 2:12. Exodus 25:6, 30:7-8 (BBE), 23-24 (NIRV), 25 (LEB), 27 (BBE), 34-35 (NLT), 31:8 (BBE), 11, 35:8, 15, 28, 37:25 (BBE), 29, 39:37 (RHE), 38, 40:27-28 (mostly WYC). Ezekiel 16:19 (MSG), 24:10, 27:17-19, 22. Genesis 2:12, 37:25, 43:11, 50:2, 26 (all WYC). Isaiah 3:24, 28:27, 39:2, 43:24, 60:6 (BBE). Jeremiah 6:20, 34:5. Job 41:31 (BBE). John 19:39-40. 1 Kings 10:2, 10, 15, 25. 2 Kings 20:13 (WYC). Leviticus 4:7 (YLT), 16:12 (YLT), 13 (WYC), 24:7 (BBE). Luke 11:42 (GW), 23:56, 24:1. Mark 15:23 (NIRV), 16:1. Matthew 2:11, 23:23, 27:34. Numbers 4:16 (YLT), 7:14, 20, 26, 32, 38, 44, 50, 56, 62, 68, 74, 80, 86, 16:7, 17-18, 40, 46-47, 24:6 (NCV) (all others BBE). Proverbs 7:17, 9:2, 5 (WYC), 23:30 (NIRV). Psalm 45:8 (BBE), 69:21 (NIRV), 75:8. Revelation 18:13. 2 Samuel 5:23 (BBE). Sirach 24:14. Song of Solomon 1:12 (BBE), 3:6, 4:10, 13-14, 16, 5:1, 13, 6:2, 8:14.

STACTE.

N° 95 stacte

Stacte (*nataf* in Hebrew) is one of the ingredients of Temple incense (see Exodus 30:34). It is a well-documented gum resin collected from 'weeping' cuts in a tree or bush but its botanical source is unknown. It could be gum from a shrub of the *Styrax* genus. The Syrians used it in perfumery and in medicine according to Pliny. See headings N° **7 balm of Gilead** and N° **8 balsam** for general balm, resin and gum references.

Ben Sira 24:15. Exodus 30:34. Ezekiel 27:19. Genesis 37:25 (WYC), 43:11 (LXX). Kings III 10:25 (LXX). Psalm 45:8.

N° oriental **sweetgum**

Liquidambar orientalis Mill., oriental sweetgum, oriental sweetgum, Turkish sweetgum or storax, is a deciduous tree native to the eastern Mediterranean. It is valuable for the resin tapped from its wood and inner bark. This has wide usage in food flavouring, in chewing gum, perfumery, cosmetics and medicine. Its bark is burnt as an incense. See headings N° **7 balm of Gilead** and N° **8 balsam** for general balm, resin and gum references.

SYCOMORE FIGS.

SYCOMORE-TREE. —(*Ficus sycomorus.*)

N° 96 **sycamine**

See N° **63 mulberry**.

N° 97 large-fruited **sycamore fig**

Ficus sycomorus L., sycamore fig, also known as fig-mulberry, common cluster fig and sycomore, is an ornamental tree that can grow to 20 metres in height. It is known for its attractive wood grain and as a source of food. This species of fig has been grown in Egypt since 3,000 BCE. See also N° **33 fig**.

Psalm 78:47.

N° athel **tamarix**

Tamarix aphylla (L.) Karst., athel tamarisk, is a deciduous shrub or tree of hot desert wadis in Western Asia

BRANCH OF TEIL-TREE, OR TEREBINTH-TREE.

and North-east Africa. Its twigs give a manna-like substance that is chewed or mixed with water to make a sweet drink. It is possibly the *eshel* tree planted by Abraham in the Book of Genesis. The references below are to tamarisk. *Tamarix nilotica* (Ehrenb.) Bunge, is Nile tamarisk. This species is salt-tolerant, good for sand stabilisation and has medicinal uses.

1 Chronicles 10:12 (NKJV). Genesis 21:33. Isaiah 44:4. Jeremiah 17:6, 48:6 (both fig.) (CJB). 1 Samuel 22:6, 31:13.

48

N° 98 tares

See N° darnel.

N° 99 teil tree

Pistacia terebinthus L., see next heading.

N° terebinth

Pistacia terebinthus L., terebinth, Eastern turpentine tree or Cyprus turpentine, is a small deciduous tree whose fruit, leaves and oil are edible. The oil from the seeds is sweeter than almond oil. Resin is obtained from incisions in the bark. It has medicinal uses. See headings **N° 7 balm of Gilead** and **N° 8 balsam** for general balm, resin and gum references.

1 Chronicles 10:12. Deuteronomy 11:30. Ezekiel 6:13. Genesis 12:6, 13:18, 14:13, 18:1, 35:4, 8, 43:11. Hosea 4:13. Isaiah 1:29-30, 6:13, 44:14. Joshua 19:33, 24:26. Judges 4:11, 6:11, 19, 9:6, 37. 1 Kings 13:14, 1 Samuel 10:3, 17:2, 19, 21:19. 2 Samuel 18:9-10, 14. Sirach 24:16 (CEBA).

TAMARISK-TREE.

N° thistles

Thistles are considered a weed or invasive weed in agricultural land. Because of their spines they are not generally tolerated on waste ground and roadsides though some species are grown for decoration. Many species have edible young stems and oil can be extracted from their seeds. The whole plant with spines macerated or removed has been used for animal fodder. The oil and other parts of some thistles have extensive medicinal properties. The botanist Harold Moldenke (d. 1996) estimated 125 species of thistle grow in the Holy Land.

Centaurea iberica Trevir. ex Spreng., Iberian knapweed, Iberian star-thistle, is a biennial shrub whose habitat ranges from South-eastern Europe to South-western Asia. Its leaves are edible. It has medicinal properties.

Scolymus maculatus L., spotted golden thistle, is an annual of Mediterranean Europe. Its roots and young leaves are edible.

TEIL-TREE, OR TEREBINTH-TREE.—(*Pistacia Terebinthus.*)

Scolymus hispanicus L., Spanish golden thistle, common golden thistle, is a herbaceous biennial. Its habitat is Mediterranean woodland and shrubland. The whole plant can be eaten when young. It has medicinal uses.

Notobasis syriaca (L.) Cass., Syrian thistle, is an annual of semi-desert regions of the Mediterranean and Middle East to Western Asia. It has edible shoots.

Echinops spinosissimus subsp. *spinosissimus*, viscous globe-thistle, spiny globe-thistle. In the Middle East it is also known as the Egyptian medicinal plant. It frequents semi-arid habitats and exudes a gum that can be chewed. It has medicinal properties.

Silybum marianum (L.) Gaertn., holy thistle, Saint Mary's thistle or milk thistle. Its habitat ranges from Mediterranean woodland to extreme desert. The plant's young fleshy stems are a good food source. It has a long history of medicinal use.

GLOBE ARTICHOKE (CYNARA SCOLIMUS)
MERORIUM - BITTER HERBS (see Page 364 (see Drawing 138)

YELLOW SPOTTED THISTLE (SCOLYMUS MACULATUS)
CHOACH - THISTLE see Page 2 & 242

Saussurea lappa (Decne.) C.B.Clarke, costus root or *kutha* (Hindi). The dried root of this Himalayan perennial herb of the thistle family was imported into the Middle East for its medicinal value and high quality oil used in Temple incense. See also **N° desert vegetation** and the following heading.

General thistle references: 2 Chronicles 25:18 (fig.). Genesis 3:18 (fig.) Hebrews 6:8 (NAS), 12:15 (fig.) (MSG). Hosea 10:8 (fig.). Isaiah 9:18, 17:13, 34:13 (all fig.). 2 Kings 14:9 (fig.).

N° 100-109 thorns

The Near East (specifically the Holy Land and Israel) has been referred to as a land of thorns. It is partly the geography that includes desert and a climate that is hot and dry for much of the year. In modern times it is also because of a prolonged mis-management of natural resources. The Near East was relatively verdant in biblical times, *ie.*, two to three millennia past. Thorns, thistle and other scrub particularly when protected by spines adapt to ground wasted by over-grazing, tree-felling and dwindling rainfall.

Faidherbia albida (Delile) A.Chev., (apple-ring acacia, ana tree and winter thorn), has leaves and starch-rich pods important as animal feed and forage. Seeds and pods have been eaten by humans during famine. Its timber is used in construction, its bark in tanning and its thorny branches as protective fencing. The bark has medicinal uses.

Sarcopoterium spinosum (L.) Spach., thorny burnet, pricky burnet, is a perennial bush of the *Rosaceae* common in the Middle East. It has small red flowers, flexible stems and thorns up to four inches long and is thought to be more likely the thorny shrub of the Crown of Thorns. It has medicinal uses.

Alhagi maurorum Medik., camelthorn, camelthorn bush, Caspian manna, is a species of legume, perennial with long thorns. It is common in the Middle East thriving in dry rocky habitats and is regarded as a noxious weed. It produces a sweet manna and has medicinal uses.

Rhamnus lycioides subsp. *graeca* (Boiss. & Reuter) Tutin, Mediterranean buckthorn is a thorny, poisonous, deciduous or evergreen plant resistant to overgrazing. It has medicinal uses. A yellow dye has been produced from its leaves.

There are more than 70 species of the box-thorn genus *Lycium* (desert thorn or wolfberry). These flowering shrubs, not all of which are thorny have a long tradition of use in medicine in the Far East, particularly *Lycium barbarum* L. (matrimony vine), from where they were traded by the Greeks and Romans. *L. europaeum* L. grows in the Near East in Mediterranean maquis and wadis. Its ripe fruit is edible.

Ononis spinosa L., spiny restharrow. Root leaves and flowers of this perennial meadow plant are edible and have medicinal uses.

Acanthus hirsutus subsp. *syriacus* (Boiss.) Brummitt, Syrian bear's breech, is a perennial herb with particularly sharp thorns that deter grazing. It is widespread across the Middle East in dry open rocky terrain and on waste ground. Some authorities consider this plant to be the biblical nettle. *Acanthus spinosus* L., spiny bear's breech, is a perennial shrub whose habitat is woodland scrub and stony hillsides. It has medicinal uses.

Zilla spinosa (L.) Prantl, spiny zilla, is a perennial shrub that grows to one-and-a-half metres in height in habit ranging from Mediterranean woodland to extreme desert. It has medicinal uses including the removal of thorns from skin. Its chickpea-like fruit can be ground into flower but is fibrous.

Rubus sanctus Schreb., holy bramble, blackberry, is a deciduous shrub that grows from Europe to West Asia in open woodland, shrubland, dunes and wasteland. Its fruit is edible. See also **Nº 14 burning bush**; **Nº 30 desert vegetation**; Nº Christ's thorn **jujube**; Nº wild **jujube**; Nº **nightshade**; **Nº 70 oil tree**; **Nº retem**.

SALTWORT . SALSOLA KALI

BOKITH - SOPE .....

Specific to bramble and briar: Ezekiel 2:6, 28:24, 34. Esias 55:13 (LXX). Genesis 3:18, 22:13 (WYC). Hebrews 6:8. Hosea 9:6, 10:8. Isaiah 5:6, 7:19, 23-25, 9:18, 10:17, 27:4, 32:13, 34:13, 55:13. Job 5:5 (NLT), 30:7 (DBY), 31:40. Joshua 23:13 (NLT). Judges 8:7, 16, 9:14-15. Luke 6:44. Matthew 7:16. Micah 7:4. Psalm 58:9, 80:8. 1 Samuel 13:6 (MSG). Song of Solomon 2:2.

Specific to nettle: Ecclesiastes 7:6 (fig.). Ezekiel 2:6. Hosea 9:6, 10:8 (WYC, both fig.). Isaiah 34:13, 55:13 (both fig.). Job 30:7, 31:40 (fig.). Proverbs 24:31. Zephaniah 2:9 (fig.).

General thorn references, most of which are figurative: Acts 7:30, 35. Baruch 6:70-71. 2 Corinthians 12:7. 2 Chronicles 25:18, 33:11. Ecclesiastes 7:6-7. Epistle of Jeremy 1:70-71 (LXX). 2 Esdras 16:32-33, 77-78. Exodus 3:2-4, 22:6. Ezekiel 2:6, 28:24. Ezra 4:15 (MSG). Genesis 3:18, 26:35. Hosea 2:6, 9:6, 10:8, 13:14 (NAS). Isaiah 5:5-6, 7:19, 23-25, 9:18, 10:17, 27:4, 32:13, 33:12, 34:13, 41:19, 55:13. Jeremiah 4:3, 12:13. Job 5:5, 30:7, 31:40, 40:21-22, 41:2. Joel 3:18. John 19:2, 5. Joshua 23:13. Judges 2:3, 8:7, 16, 9:14-15. 1 Kings 11:25 (MSG). 2 Kings 14:9 (BBE). Kings II 23:6 (LXX). Luke 6:44, 8:7, 14, 20:37. Mark 4:7, 18, 12:26, 15:17. Matthew 7:16, 13:7, 22, 27:29. Micah 7:4. Nahum 1:10. Numbers 33:55. Proverbs 15:19, 22:5, 24:31, 26:9. Psalm 32:4, 58:9, 68:9, 118:12. Sirach 24:15 (CEBA), 28:24. 1 Samuel 13:6 (LEB). 2 Samuel 23:6-7. Song of Solomon 2:1-2. Zephaniah 2:9.

Notes on the Botany of the Bible

Entries Nos. 110 - 117

N° 110 thyine wood

Tetraclinis articulata (Vahl) Mast., see **N° 8 balsam**.

N° tulip

Tulipa montana Lindl. is a perennial bulb giving a small red flower with central black interior. It grows in rocky terrain to 3,000 metres from West Asia to Iran. The root is edible when cooked or it can be ground to supplement flour. *Tulipa agenensis* Redouté (Sharon tulip), is a Middle East species. There are thought to be 150 species of *Tulipa*, many being cultivars. See **N° Persian buttercup** (for flower of the field references).

N° 111 vine

Vitis vinifera L. is a species of vining plant native to the Mediterranean region and cultivated across South-West Asia, North Africa and Central Europe. It was domesticated at least as early as 3,000 BCE in the Middle East and became important economically for the production of its fruit, dried fruit, fruit juice and the fruit's fermentation into the making of wine. The expansion of Islam caused the decline of vineyard agriculture from the 7th. Century CE. See also **N° European grape** and the following heading.

THE GRAPE VINE.

Specific to vine, vineyard: Acts 28:3. Amos 4:9, 5:11, 17, 9:13-14 (OJB). Ben Sira 33:16 (GNTA). 1 Chronicles 27:25, 27. 2 Chronicles 26:10. 1 Corinthians 9:7. Deuteronomy 6:11, 8:8, 20:6, 22:9, 23:24, 24:21, 28:30, 39, 32:32. Ecclesiastes 2:4. 1 Esdras 4:16 (LXX). 2 Esdras 16:43 (LXX). Exodus 22:5, 29, 23:11, 16. Ezekiel 15:2, 5, 28:26. Genesis 9:20, 40:10, 49:11. Habakkuk 3:17. Haggai 1:11, 2:19. Hosea 2:12, 15, 10:1, 14:7. Isaiah 1:8, 3:14, 5:1-7, 10, 7:23, 16:8-10, 17:10-11, 18:5, 24:7, 13, 27:2, 32:12, 33:4, 36:16-17, 37:30, 61:5 (vine-dressers), 65:21. Jeremiah 5:10, 17, 6:9, 8:13, 12:10, 18:15, 31:5, 32:15, 35:7, 9, 39:10, 48:32, 49:9, 52:16 (vine-dressers). Job 15:33, 24:6, 18. Joel 1:7, 10, 11 (vine-dressers), 12, 2:22, 3:18. John 15:1 (vine-dresser). Joshua 24:13. Judges 8:2, 9:27, 11:33, 14:5, 15:5-6, 21:10, 20-21. Judith 2:17. 1 Kings 4:25, 21:1-2, 6-7, 15-16, 18. 2 Kings 5:26, 18:31-32, 19:29, 25:12. Leviticus 19:10, 25:3-5, 11. Luke 13:6, 7

CALOTROPIS TREE
CALOTROPIS GIGANTEA
GEPHEN SEDOM - VINE OF SODOM Jud. Cap 23 4

(vine-dresser), 20:9-10, 13-16. 1 Maccabees 3:56, 14:12. Malachi 3:11. Mark 12:1-2, 7 (vine-dressers), 8-9. Matthew 20:1-2, 4, 7-8, 21:28, 33-35, 38-41 (vine-dressers). Micah 1:6, 4:4, 7:1. Nahum 2:2 (NIV). Nehemiah 5:3-5, 11, 9:25. Numbers 13:23, 16:14, 18:27, 20:5, 17, 21:22, 22:24. Obadiah 1:5. Proverbs 24:30, 31:16. Psalm 37:20, 78:47, 105:33, 107:37. Revelation 6:6, 14:18. 1 Samuel 8:14-15, 22:7. Song of Solomon 1:6, 14, 2:12-13, 15, 6:11, 7:12, 8:11-12. Zechariah 3:10, 8:12. Zephaniah 1:13.

N° 112 wild grapes

Vitis vinifera subsp. *sylvestris,* wild grape, is a widespread plant around Europe to the Black Sea and North Africa. It is the progenitor of the cultivated variety. It grows in woodland by streams and up pine trees. It is considered important as a potential means of improving the genetic structure of the cultivated vine in specific environments. See also N° European **grape** and the preceding heading.

N° 113 Vine of Sodom

The tree or plant first referred to in the Deuteronomy verse below remains unknown. Bitterness and discomfort metaphorically in the Bible are conveyed through words such as gall, bile, thistle, thorn and weed. *Calotropis procera* (Ait.) Ait. fil. (apple of Sodom, Dead Sea apple, giant milkweed) has a milky sap that is poisonous to humans and animals and is regarded as a weed in many places around the world. *Citrullus colocynthis* (L.) Schrad. (vine of Sodom, bitter apple, wild gourd) is a climbing desert vine. It has small, hard bitter fruit. Its seeds are edible and have medicinal uses.

Deuteronomy 32:32.

N° 114 walnut

Juglans regia L., Persian walnut, common walnut, California walnut, is a large deciduous tree. It is a valuable foodstuff with a high quality seed (nut) that can be eaten raw or pressed for its oil. Its leaves have insect repellent properties and can be used to make wine. Its wood is prized in furniture-making for its decorative grain. Many parts of the tree have medicinal uses. See also N° 68 **nuts.**

Genesis 30:37, 43:11 (both LXX). Song of Solomon 6:11.

WALNUT-TREE.--(*Juglans regia.*)

N° watermelon

Citrullus lanatus (Thunb.) Matsumura & Nakai, watermelon, is a sprawling annual plant. It is grown for its fruit, the centre of which is juicy and refreshing and a rind which is edible when cooked. It is more often pickled or used in fruit preserves. It has been cultivated in Egypt since at least the 2nd. Millennium BCE. See also N° 60 **melon.**

N° emmer wheat

Triticum turgidum L. subsp. *dicoccum* (Schrank) Thell., cultivated emmer wheat or hulled wheat, was the first domesticated form in the western Fertile Crescent from 7,800 BCE. Its cultivation spread to the Caucasus, Northern India, the Balkans and Danube. In other areas it has been superceded by naked wheats. See **N° 25 corn and wheat** for specific biblical references to wheat.

N° 115 willow

Salix acmophylla Boiss. This species of willow is a shrub or small tree that grows in the Middle East and as far as Pakistan. Its habitat is ravines, wadis and proximity to irrigation channels. Its bark has medicinal uses. *Salix alba* L., white willow, is a medium to large deciduous tree native to Europe across to Central Asia. Its stems are used in basket-weaving and wood in charcoal manufacture. The medicinal properties of its bark was known to the Sumerians, Assyrians, Ancient Greeks and Egyptians. See also **N° 76 poplar.**

Ezekiel 17:5. Isaiah 15:7, 44:4. Job 40:22. Leviticus 23:40. Psalm 137:2-3.

N° 116 willow of Babylon

The trees growing along the Euphrates River in Babylon referred to in the Bible as *gharab* and translated as willows of Babylon, are the Euphrates poplar (*Populus euphratica* Olivier). See **N° 76 poplar.**

WILLOW-TREE.—(*Salix babylonica.*)

N° wolfberry

Lycium genus, see **N° 100-109 thorns.**

N° 117 white wormwood

Seriphidium herba-alba (Asso) Soják, white wormwood, is a strongly aromatic perennial shrub that grows on the dry Mediterranean steppes. It is liked by grazing animals. *Artemisia judaica* L., wormwood, is a similarly aromatic species of Artemisia that grows commonly in the Middle East. Its habitat is wadis and stony desert plains. Both species have medicinal uses. As with the Vine of Sodom [*qv.*] its references in the Bible imply bitterness. See **N° 12 bitter herbs.**

Amos 5:7, 6:12 (both OJB). Deuteronomy 29:18. Jeremiah 9:15, 23:15. Lamentations 3:15, 19. Proverbs 5:4. Revelation 8:11.

WORMWOOD.—(*Artemisia Absinthium.*)

Index of plants by common name

NB. This index is based on the list of 206 species in Dr. Włodarczyk's 2007 paper (see endnote [2] page 10.)
* indicates agreed species (95) in the Bible.

Common Name	Scientific Name
a	
acacia, umbrella thorn acacia	*Vachellia tortilis* var. *raddiana* (Savi) Kyal. & Boatwr.*
agarwood	*Aquilaria agallocha* (Lour.) Roxb.*
sweet **almond**	*Prunus dulcis* D.A.Webb*
aloe vera, Barbados aloe	*Aloe vera* (L.) Burm. f.
aloes, ling-aloes	*Aloe succotrina* Lam.*
jointed **Anabasis**, *ajrem* (Ar.)	*Anabasis articulata* (Forssk.) Moq.
apple of Sodom	*Calotropis procera* (Ait.) Dryand.
crab **apple**, European crab apple	*Malus sylvestris* Mill.
apricot, Siberian apricot	*Prunus armeniaca* L.
arar tree, Berber thuya, Medit. sandarac-cypress	*Tetraclinis articulata* (Vahl) Mast.
Syrian **ash**	*Fraxinus angustifolia* subsp. *syriaca* (Boiss.) Yalt.
b	
balanites, Egyptian balsam	*Balanites aegyptiaca* (L.) Delile
common **barley**	*Hordeum vulgare* L.*
six-row **barley**	*Hordeum hexastichon* L.
two-row **barley**	*Hordeum distichon* L.
broad **bean**, fava bean, horse bean	*Vicia faba* L.
bushy **bean-caper**	*Tetraena dumosa* (Boiss.) Beier & Thulin
bitter herbs, false sow-thistle	*Reichardia tingitana* (L.) Roth
box, common box, American boxwood	*Buxus sempervirens* L.
holy **bramble**	*Rubus sanctus* Schreb.*
spiny **broom**, furrowed thorny broom	*Calycotome villosa* (Poir.) Link
white **broom**, retem	*Retama raetam* (Forssk.) Webb*
desert **broomrape**, desert hyacinth, yellow broomrape	*Cistanche tubulosa* (Schenk) Wight
thorny **burnet**, pricky burnet, brushwood	*Sarcopoterium spinosum* (L.) Spach.
Asiatic **buttercup**, Persian buttercup	*Ranunculus asiaticus* L.*
c	
camelthorn, camelthorn-bush, Caspian manna	*Alhagi maurorum* Medik.
giant **cane**, giant reed	*Arundo donax* L.
capers	*Capparis spinosa* L.*
carob	*Ceratonia siliqua* L.*
castor bean, castor oil plant	*Ricinus communis* L.*
southern **cattail**	*Typha domingensis* Pers.*
Lebanon **cedar**, cedar of Lebanon	*Cedrus libani* A.Rich.*
Syrian **cephalara**, Syrian scabious	*Cephalaria syriaca* (L.) Schrad.

Palestinian **chamomile**	*Cota palaestina* Reut. ex Unger & Kotschy*
chickpea	*Cicer arietinum* L.
chicory, succory	*Cichorium intybus* L.
wild **chicory**, wild endive, dwarf chicory	*Cichorium pumilum* Jacq.
garland **chrysanthemum**, crown daisy, Chop-Suey Greens	*Glebionis coronaria* (L.) Tzvel.
cinnamon	*Cinnamomum verum* J.Presl*
Chinese **cinnamon**	*Cinnamomum cassia* (L.) J.Presl*
citron, citron melon	*Citrus medica* L.
common **club-rush**, common tule, true bulrush	*Schoenoplectus lacustris* (L.) Palla
coriander	*Coriandrum sativum* L.*
common **corn-cockle**, corncockle	*Agrostemma githago* L.
costus, kuth (Hindi)	*Saussurea lappa* (Decne.) C.B.Clarke
Levant **cotton**	*Gossypium herbaceum* L.*
Autumn **crocus**	*Crocus sativus* L.*
cumin, *zeera* (Hindi)	*Cuminum cyminum* L.*
Mediterranean **cypress**, Italian cypress	*Cupressus sempervirens* L.*

d

common **dandelion**	*Taraxacum officinale* (Weber) ex Wigg.
darnel, cockle	*Lolium temulentum* L.*
date palm	*Phoenix dactylifera* L.*
dill	*Anethum graveolens* L.*

e

African **ebony**, African blackwood	*Dalbergia melanoxylon* Guill. & Perr.
ebony, Ceylon ebony, India ebony	*Diospyros ebenum* J. Koenig ex Retz.*
common **eel grass**, seawrack	*Zostera marina* L.
elephant tree, Sudanese frankincense	*Boswellia papyrifera* (Del.) Hochst.
grey **elm**, downy elm, hoary elm	*Ulmus minor* subsp. *canescens* (Melville) Browicz & Ziel.
Cretan **eryngo**, field eryngo	*Eryngium creticum* Lam.

f

common **fennel flower**, black cummin	*Nigella sativa* L.*
fenugreek, cultivated trigonella	*Trigonella foenum-graecum* L.
common **fig**	*Ficus carica* L.*
large-fruited sycamore **fig**, fig-mulberry, sycomore	*Ficus sycomorus* L.*
Cilician **fir**	*Abies cilicica* (Antoine & Kotschy) Carrière*
flax, common flax, linseed	*Linum usitatissimum* L.*
hairy spurge **flax**, shaggy sparrow-wort	*Thymelaea hirsuta* (L.) Endl.
Indian **frankincense**, Indian olibanum tree	*Boswellia serrata* (Roxb.) ex Colebr.
frankincense, olibanum tree	*Boswellia sacra* Flückiger-Dupiron

g

galbanum	*Ferula gummosa* Boiss.
garlic, cultivated garlic	*Allium sativum* L.*
viscous **globe-thistle**	*Echinops spinosissimus* subsp. *spinosissimus*

bottle **gourd**, calabash — *Lagenaria siceraria* (Mol.) Standl.
common **grape vine**, European grape — *Vitis vinifera* L.*
geranium **grass**, camel grass — *Cymbopogon schoenanthus* (L.) Spreng.
Gum tragacanth milkvetch, tragacanth — *Astragalus gummifer* Labill.*

h
black **hawthorn**, Mediterranean buckthorn — *Rhamnus lycioides* subsp. *graeca* (Boiss. & Reuter) Tutin

hemlock, poison hemlock — *Conium maculatum* L.*
Egyptian **henbane** — *Hyoscyamus muticus* L.
golden **henbane**, henbane — *Hyoscyamus aureus* L.
henna tree — *Lawsonia inermis* L.*
bristly **hollyhock** — *Alcea setosa* (Boiss.) Alef.

i
yellow **iris**, yellow flag, water flag — *Iris pseudacorus* L.
common **ivy**, English ivy, European ivy — *Hedera helix* L.

j
Judas tree — *Cercis siliquastrum* L.
Christ's thorn **jujube**, Syrian Christ-thorn — *Ziziphus spina-christi* (L.) Desf.*
lotus **jujube**, lotus, lotus tree — *Ziziphus lotus* (L.) Lam.*
Greek **juniper** — *Juniperus excelsa* M.Bieb.
Phoenician **juniper** — *Juniperus phoenicea* L.

l
laurel, bay laurel, sweet bay, bay tree — *Laurus nobilis* L.
laurustinus, laurustinus viburnum, laurestine — *Viburnum tinus* L.
Egyptian **leek**, salad Leek — *Allium kurrat* Schweinf. ex K.Krause
leek, garden leek — *Allium ampeloprasum* L., nom. cons.
lemon grass, palmarosa, Indian geranium — *Cymbopogon martinii* (Roxb.) W.Watson*
lentil, common lentil — *Lens culinaris* Medik.*
lettuce — *Lactuca sativa* L.
white **lily** — *Lilium candidum* L.

m
madder, dyer's madder — *Rubia tinctorum* L.*
bull **mallow**, French mallow — *Malva nicaeensis* All.
common **mallow**, garden mallow — *Malva sylvestris* L.*
mandrake — *Mandragora officinarum* L.*
Spanish **marigold** — *Anemone coronaria* L.*
mastic tree — *Pistacia lentiscus* L.
cantaloupe **melon** — *Cucumis melo* L.*
Bethlehem **milkvetch** — *Astragalus bethlehemiticus* Boiss.
proso **millet**, common millet, broomcorn — *Panicum miliaceum* L.
silver **mint**, grey mint, horsemint — *Mentha longifolia* (L.) Huds.*
acacia **mistletoe** (suggested) — *Plicosepalus acaciae* (Zucc.) D.Wiens & Polhill
black **mulberry** — *Morus nigra* L.*

white mulberry	*Morus alba* L.
mullein (variety)	*Verbascum sinaiticum* Benth.
black mustard	*Brassica nigra* (L.) W.D.J.Koch*
field mustard, charlock	*Sinapis arvensis* L.
white mustard	*Sinapis alba* L.
myrrh, herabol myrrh	*Commiphora myrrha* (Nees) Engl.
myrrh tree, Abyssinian myrrh	*Commiphora kua* (R.Br. ex Royle) Vollesen
African myrrh	*Commiphora africana* (Rich.) Engl.
bisabol myrrh, bdellium of Bombay	*Commiphora kataf* (Forsk.) Engl.
Mecca myrrh, balm of Gilead, Arabian balsam tree	*Commiphora gileadensis* (L.) C.Christ*
myrtle	*Myrtus communis* L.*

n
cream narcissus	*Narcissus tazetta* L.*
dwarf nettle, small nettle	*Urtica urens* L.*
Roman nettle	*Urtica pilulifera* L.*
nightshade, thorn apple, Dead Sea apple	*Solanum incanum* L.*

o
Kermes oak	*Quercus coccifera* L.*
Valonia oak	*Quercus ithaburensis* Decne.*
oleander	*Nerium oleander* L.*
olive	*Olea europaea* L.*
onion	*Allium cepa* L.*
Syrian oregano, Syrian marjoram, hyssop	*Origanum syriacum* L.*

p
papyrus, papyrus sedge, Egyptian paper plant	*Cyperus papyrus* L.*
Aleppo pine	*Pinus halepensis* Mill.*
Italian stone pine, parasol pine, pignolia-nut pine	*Pinus pinea* L.*
Turkish pine, Calabrian pine	*Pinus brutia* Ten.*
Atlantic pistachio, Mount Atlas mastic tree, cashew	*Pistacia atlantica* Desf.
green-almond pistachio, pistachio nut	*Pistacia vera* L.
oriental plane	*Platanus orientalis* L.*
pomegranate	*Punica granatum* L.*
Euphrates poplar	*Populus euphratica* Oliv.*
white poplar	*Populus alba* L.*
common poppy, corn poppy, field poppy	*Papaver rhoeas* L.
common purslane, garden purslane, little hogweed	*Portulaca oleracea* L.

r
red-squill, sea-squill, sea-onion	*Drimia maritima* (L.) Stearn
common reed	*Phragmites australis* (Cav.) Trin. ex Steud.*
rocket, arugula	*Eruca vesicaria* subsp. *sativa* (Mill.) Thell.
hairy rockrose	*Cistus incanus* L.*
laurel-leaved rockrose	*Cistus laurifolius* L.
sage-leaved rockrose, Gallipoli rose	*Cistus salviifolius* L.

climbing wild **rose**	*Rosa phoenicia* Boiss.*
dog **rose**, wild rose	*Rosa canina* L.*
rue, fringed rue	*Ruta chalepensis* L.*
flowering **rush**, grass rush	*Butomus umbellatus* L.
sea **rush**, seaside rush	*Juncus maritimus* Lam.

s

Judean **sage**	*Salvia judaica* Boiss.
Mediterranean **saltbush**, shrubby saltbush	*Atriplex halimus* L.*
common **saltwort**, prickly saltwort, Russian thistle	*Salsola kali* L.
unarmed **saltwort**, spineless saltwort	*Salsola inermis* Forssk.
perennial marsh **samphire**, perennial saltwort, perennial glasswort	*Sarcocornia fruticosa* (L.) A.J.Scott
red **sandalwood**	*Pterocarpus santalinus* L.f.*
saxaul (var.)	*Haloxylon salicornicum* (Moq.) Bunge ex Boiss.
saxaul (var.)	*Haloxylon scoparium* Pomel
white **saxaul tree**	*Haloxylon persicum* Bunge ex Boiss. & Buhse
Palestinian **sea-blite**, seepweed, common reaumuria	*Suaeda palaestina* Eig. & Zohary
sea-daffodil, Carolina spiderlily	*Pancratium maritimum* L.*
senna pods	*Senna alexandrina* Mill.
drug **snowbell**	*Styrax officinalis* L.*
sorghum	*Sorghum bicolor* (L.) Moench*
common **sow-thistle**	*Sonchus oleraceus* L.
spikenard, nard, *Jatamansi* (Hindi)	*Nardostachys jatamansi* (D.Don) DC.*
Narbonne **Star-of-Bethlehem**	*Ornithogalum narbonense* L., nom. cons.
Pyrenees **Star-of-Bethlehem**, grass lily	*Ornithogalum umbellatum* L.
Iberian **star-thistle**, Iberian knapweed	*Centaurea iberica* Trevir. ex Spreng.*
sweet flag, calamus	*Acorus calamus* L.
oriental **sweetgum**, storax	*Liquidambar orientalis* Mill.*
scarlet **synomorium**, desert thumb	*Cynomorium coccineum* L.
Syrian Bear's Breech	*Acanthus hirsutus* subsp. *syriacus* (Boiss.) Brummitt

t

taily weed	*Ochradenus baccatus* Delile
athel **tamarisk**, athel tree	*Tamarix aphylla* (L.) Karst.*
Nile **tamarisk**	*Tamarix nilotica* (Ehrenb.) Bunge
terebinth, Eastern turpentine tree	*Pistacia terebinthus* L.*
Spanish golden **thistle**, Spanish oyster plant	*Scolymus hispanicus* L.
holy **thistle**, Saint Mary's thistle, milk thistle	*Silybum marianum* (L.) Gaertn.*
spotted golden **thistle**	*Scolymus maculatus* L.*
Syrian **thistle**	*Notobasis syriaca* (L.) Cass.*
umbrella **thorn acacia**	*Vachellia tortilis* (Forssk.) Galasso & Banfi
Christ's **thorn**, Jerusalem thorn	*Paliurus spina-christi* Mill.
winter **thorn**, apple-ring acacia	*Acacia albida* Delile
Tournefort's gundelia	*Gundelia tournefortii* L.*
tulip	*Tulipa montana* Lindl.*
Sharon **tulip**, sun's-eye tulip	*Tulipa agenensis* Redouté
common **turmeric**, Indian-saffron	*Curcuma longa* L.

v

vine of Sodom, wild gourd, bitter apple, bitter
  cucumber, desert gourd

Citrullus colocynthis (L.) Schrader*

w

walnut, common walnut, California walnut

Juglans regia L.*

blue water-lily Egyptian lotus

Nymphaea nouchali var. *caerulea* (Savigny) Verdc.

European white water-lily

Nymphaea alba L.

Egyptian white water-lily

Nymphaea lotus L.

watermelon

Citrullus lanatus (Thunb.) Matsumura & Nakai*

common wheat, bread wheat

Triticum aestivum L.

durum wheat, macaroni wheat

Triticum turgidum L. subsp. *durum* (Desf.) Husn.*

emmer wheat, hulled wheat

Triticum turgidum L. subsp. *dicoccum* (Schrank) Thell.

willow

Salix acmophylla Boiss.*

white willow

Salix alba L.*

wolfberry

Lycium europaeum L.*

wormwood

Artemisia judaica L.

white wormwood

Seriphidium herba-alba (Asso) Soják*

z

spiny zilla

Zilla spinosa (L.) Prantl

Index of plants by scientific name

NB This index is based on the list of 206 species in Dr. Włodarczyk's 2007 paper (see endnote [2] page 10.)
* indicates agreed species (95) in the Bible. Plants without a page number have not been discussed in this book.

Cephalaria syriaca (L.) Schrad.	24	Syrian **cephalara**, Syrian scabious
Ceratonia siliqua L.*	19	carob
Cercis siliquastrum L.	17	Judas tree
Cicer arietinum L.	41	chickpea
Cichorium intybus L.	17	chicory, succory
Cichorium pumilum Jacq.	17	wild **chicory**, wild endive, dwarf chicory
Cinnamomum cassia (L.) J.Presl*	19	Chinese **cinnamon**
Cinnamomum verum J.Presl*	21	cinnamon
Cistanche tubulosa (Schenk) Wight	24	desert **broomrape**, desert hyacinth, yellow broomrape
Cistus incanus L.*	42	hairy **rockrose**
Cistus laurifolius L.	42	laurel-leaved **rockrose**
Cistus salviifolius L.	42	sage-leaved **rockrose**, Gallipoli rose
Citrullus colocynthis (L.) Schrader*	53	vine of Sodom, wild gourd, bitter apple, bitter cucumber, desert gourd
Citrullus lanatus (Thunb.) Matsumura & Nakai*	53	watermelon
Citrus medica L.	21	citron, citron melon
Commiphora africana (Rich.) Engl.	36	African **myrrh**
Commiphora gileadensis (L.) C. Christ*	36	Mecca **myrrh**, balm of Gilead, Arabian balsam tree
Commiphora kataf (Forsk.) Engl.	36	bisabol **myrrh**, bdellium of Bombay
Commiphora kua (R.Br. ex Royle) Vollesen	36	**myrrh tree**, Abyssinian myrrh
Commiphora myrrha (Nees) Engl.	36	**myrrh**, herabol myrrh
Conium maculatum L.*	30	**hemlock**, poison hemlock
Coriandrum sativum L.*	21	coriander
Cota palaestina Reut. ex Unger & Kotschy*	20	Palestinian **chamomile**
Crocus sativus L.*	23	Autumn **crocus**
Cucumis melo L.*	35	cantaloupe **melon**
Cuminum cyminum L.*	23	cumin, *zeera* (Hindi)
Cupressus sempervirens L.*	23	Mediterranean **cypress**, Italian cypress
Curcuma longa L.	23	common **turmeric**, Indian-saffron
Cymbopogon martinii (Roxb.) W.Watson*	33	**lemon grass**, palmarosa, Indian geranium
Cymbopogon schoenanthus (L.) Spreng.	33	geranium **grass**, camel grass
Cynomorium coccineum L.	24	scarlet **synomorium**, desert thumb
Cyperus papyrus L.*	43	**papyrus**, papyrus sedge, Egyptian paper plant

d

Dalbergia melanoxylon Guill. & Perr.	25	African **ebony**, African blackwood
Diospyros ebenum J. Koenig ex Retz.*	25	**ebony**, Ceylon ebony, India ebony
Drimia maritima (L.) Stearn		**red-squill**, sea-squill, sea-onion

e

Echinops spinosissimus subsp. *spinosissimus*	50	viscous **globe-thistle**
Eruca vesicaria subsp. *sativa* (Mill.) Thell.	30	rocket, arugula
Eryngium creticum Lam.	17	Cretan **eryngo**, field eryngo

f

Ferula gummosa Boiss.	28	galbanum

Ficus carica L.*	25	common **fig**
Ficus sycomorus L.*	48	large-fruited sycamore **fig**, fig-mulberry, sycamore
Fraxinus angustifolia subsp. *syriaca* (Boiss.) Yalt.	15	Syrian **ash**

g

Glebionis coronaria (L.) Tzvel.	30	garland **chrysanthemum**, crown daisy, Chop-Suey Greens
Gossypium herbaceum L.*	22	Levant **cotton**
Gundelia tournefortii L.*	30	**Tournefort's gundelia**

h

Haloxylon persicum Bunge ex Boiss. & Buhse	24	white **saxaul** tree
Haloxylon salicornicum (Moq.) Bunge ex Boiss.	24	**saxaul** (var.)
Haloxylon scoparium Pomel	24	**saxaul** (var.)
Hedera helix L.		common **ivy**, English ivy, European ivy
Hordeum distichon L.	16	two-row **barley**
Hordeum hexastichon L.	16	six-row **barley**
Hordeum vulgare L.*	16	common **barley**
Hyoscyamus aureus L.		golden **henbane**, henbane
Hyoscyamus muticus L.		Egyptian **henbane**

i

| *Iris pseudacorus* L. | 19 | yellow **iris**, yellow flag, water flag |

j

Juglans regia L.*	53	**walnut**, common walnut, California walnut
Juncus maritimus Lam.	44	sea **rush**, seaside rush
Juniperus excelsa M.Bieb.	32	**Greek juniper**
Juniperus phoenicea L.	32	**Phoenician juniper**

l

Lactuca sativa L.	30	**lettuce**
Lagenaria siceraria (Mol.) Standl.	27	bottle **gourd**, calabash
Laurus nobilis L.	16	**laurel**, bay laurel, sweet bay, bay tree
Lawsonia inermis L.*	30	**henna tree**
Lens culinaris Medik.*	33	**lentil**, common lentil
Lilium candidum L.	33	white **lily**
Linum usitatissimum L.*	26	**flax**, common flax, linseed
Liquidambar orientalis Mill.*	48	oriental **sweetgum**, storax
Lolium temulentum L.*	21	**darnel**, cockle
Lycium europaeum L.*	51	**wolfberry**

m

Malus sylvestris Mill.	15	crab **apple**, European crab apple
Malva nicaeensis All.	31	bull **mallow**, French mallow
Malva sylvestris L.*	31	common **mallow**, garden mallow
Mandragora officinarum L.*	34	**mandrake**

Mentha longifolia (L.) Huds.*   35   silver **mint**, grey mint
Morus alba L.   35   white **mulberry**
Morus nigra L.*   35   black **mulberry**
Myrtus communis L.*   36   **myrtle**

n

Narcissus tazetta L.*   36   cream **narcissus**
Nardostachys jatamansi (D.Don) DC.*   36   **spikenard**, nard, *Jatamansi* (Hindi)
Nerium oleander L.*   38   **oleander**
Nigella sativa L.*   25   common **fennel flower**, black cummin
Notobasis syriaca (L.) Cass.*   49   Syrian **thistle**
Nymphaea alba L.   44   European white **water-lily**
Nymphaea lotus L.   44   Egyptian white **water-lily**
Nymphaea nouchali var. *caerulea* (Savigny) Verdc.   44   blue **water-lily**, Egyptian lotus

o

Ochradenus baccatus Delile   24   **taily weed**
Olea europaea L.*   38   **olive**
Origanum syriacum L.*   31   Syrian **oregano**, Syrian marjoram, hyssop
Ornithogalum narbonense L., nom. cons.   Narbonne **Star-of-Bethlehem**
Ornithogalum umbellatum L.   25   Pyrenees **Star-of-Bethlehem**, grass lily

p

Paliurus spina-christi Mill.   31   Christ's **thorn**, Jerusalem thorn
Pancratium maritimum L.*   46   **sea-daffodil**, Carolina spiderlily
Panicum miliaceum L.   35   proso **millet**, common millet, broomcorn
Papaver rhoeas L.   28   common **poppy**, corn poppy, field poppy
Phoenix dactylifera L.*   24   **date palm**
Phragmites australis (Cav.) Trin. ex Steud.*   42   common **reed**
Pinus brutia Ten.*   40   Turkish **pine**, Calabrian pine
Pinus halepensis Mill.*   40   Aleppo **pine**
Pinus pinea L.*   40   Italian stone **pine**, parasol pine, pignolia-nut pine
Pistacia atlantica Desf.   37   Atlantic **pistachio**, Mount Atlas mastic tree, cashew
Pistacia lentiscus L.   16   **mastic tree**
Pistacia terebinthus L.*   49   **terebinth**, Eastern turpentine tree
Pistacia vera L.   37   green-almond **pistachio**, pistachio nut
Platanus orientalis L.*   40   oriental **plane**
Plicosepalus acaciae (Zucc.) D.Wiens & Polhill   14   acacia **mistletoe** (suggested)
Populus alba L.*   41   white **poplar**
Populus euphratica Oliv.*   41   Euphrates **poplar**
Portulaca oleracea L.   41   common **purslane**, garden purslane, little hogweed
Prunus armeniaca L.   15   **apricot**, Siberian apricot
Prunus dulcis D.A.Webb*   15   sweet **almond**
Pterocarpus santalinus L.f.*   46   red **sandalwood**
Punica granatum L.*   40   **pomegranate**

q

Quercus coccifera L.*	38	Kermes **oak**
Quercus ithaburensis Decne.*	38	Valonia **oak**

r

Ranunculus asiaticus L.*	18	Asiatic **buttercup**, Persian buttercup
Reichardia tingitana (L.) Roth	17	**bitter herbs**, false sow-thistle
Retama raetam (Forssk.) Webb*	42	white **broom**, retem
Rhamnus lycioides subsp. *graeca* (Boiss. & Reuter) Tutin	52	black **hawthorn**, European **buckthorn**
Ricinus communis L.*	20	**castor** bean, castor oil plant
Rosa canina L.*	43	dog **rose**, wild rose
Rosa phoenicia Boiss.*	43	climbing wild **rose**
Rubia tinctorum L.*	34	**madder**, dyer's madder
Rubus sanctus Schreb.*	51	holy **bramble**
Ruta chalepensis L.	43	**rue,** fringed rue

s

Salix acmophylla Boiss.*	54	willow
Salix alba L.*	54	white **willow**
Salsola inermis Forssk.	47	unarmed **saltwort**, spineless saltwort
Salsola kali L.	47	common **saltwort**, prickly saltwort, Russian thistle
Salvia judaica Boiss.	30	Judean **sage**
Sarcocornia fruticosa (L.) A.J.Scott	47	perennial marsh **samphire**, perennial saltwort, perennial glasswort
Sarcopoterium spinosum (L.) Spach.	50	thorny **burnet**, pricky burnet
Saussurea lappa (Decne.) C.B.Clarke	50	**costus**, *kutha* (Hindi)
Schoenoplectus lacustris (L.) Palla*	44	common **club-rush**, common tule, true bulrush
Scolymus hispanicus L.	49	Spanish golden **thistle**, Spanish oyster plant
Scolymus maculatus L.*	49	spotted golden **thistle**
Senna alexandrina Mill.		**senna pods**
Seriphidium herba-alba (Asso) Soják*	54	white **wormwood**
Silybum marianum (L.) Gaertn.*	50	holy **thistle**, Saint Mary's thistle, milk thistle
Sinapis alba L.	36	white **mustard**
Sinapis arvensis L.	36	field **mustard**, charlock
Solanum incanum L.*	37	**nightshade**, thorn apple, bitter apple, Dead Sea apple
Sonchus oleraceus L.	17	common **sow-thistle**
Sorghum bicolor (L.) Moench*	47	**sorghum**
Styrax officinalis L.*	46	drug **snowbell**
Suaeda palaestina Eig. & Zohary	47	Palestinian **sea-blite**, seepweed, common reaumuria

t

Tamarix aphylla (L.) Karst.*	48	athel **tamarisk**, athel tree
Tamarix nilotica (Ehrenb.) Bunge	48	Nile **tamarisk**
Taraxacum officinale (Weber) ex Wigg.	30	common **dandelion**

Tetraclinis articulata (Vahl) Mast.	16	**arar tree**, Berber thuya, Mediterranean sandarac-cypress
Tetraena dumosa (Boiss.) Beier & Thulin	19	bushy **bean-caper**
Thymelaea hirsuta (L.) Endl.	26	hairy spurge **flax**, shaggy sparrow-wort
Trigonella foenum-graecum L.	33	**fenugreek**, cultivated trigonella
Triticum aestivum L.	21	common **wheat**, bread wheat
Triticum turgidum L. subsp. *durum* (Desf.) Husn.*	54	durum **wheat**, macaroni wheat
Triticum turgidum L. subsp. *dicoccum* (Schrank) Thell.	22	emmer **wheat**, hulled wheat
Tulipa agenensis Redouté	52	Sharon **tulip**, sun's-eye tulip
Tulipa montana Lindl.*	52	**tulip**
Typha domingensis Pers.*	43	southern **cattail**

u

Ulmus minor subsp. *canescens* (Melville) Browicz & Ziel.	29	grey **elm**, downy elm, hoary elm
Urtica pilulifera L.*	37	Roman **nettle**
Urtica urens L.*	37	dwarf **nettle**, small nettle

v

Vachellia tortilis var. *raddiana* (Savi) Kyal. & Boatwr.*	14	umbrella **thorn acacia**
Verbascum sinaiticum Benth.		**mullein** (variety)
Viburnum tinus L.		**laurustinus**, laurustinus viburnum, laurestine
Vicia faba L.	17	broad **bean**, fava bean, horse bean
Vitis vinifera L.*	28	common **grape vine**, European grape

z

Zilla spinosa (L.) Prantl	51	spiny **zilla**
Ziziphus lotus (L.) Lam.*	32	lotus **jujube**, lotus, lotus tree
Ziziphus spina-christi (L.) Desf.*	31	Christ's thorn **jujube**, Syrian Christ-thorn
Zostera marina L.	44	common **eel grass**, seawrack

General subject index

NOTES ON THE BOTANY
OF THE BIBLE

X For Nos
see Below

1 Sandal Wood
2 Also Ling Aloes
3 No information concerning Bdellium procurable save that it was a spice
4 + in Number (1) Lettuce (2) Endive (3) Chicory (4) Artichoke x
↓ No of Illustrated Card
↓ (5) Dandelion

5 Acacia Nilotica
6 Star-of-Bethlehem
7 Scarlet Anemone
8 Polyanthus Narcissus
9 Autumn Crocus
10 Oleander

11 Papyrus
12 Flowering Rush
13 Reed
14 Yellow Iris
15 General Term
16 Sugar Cane

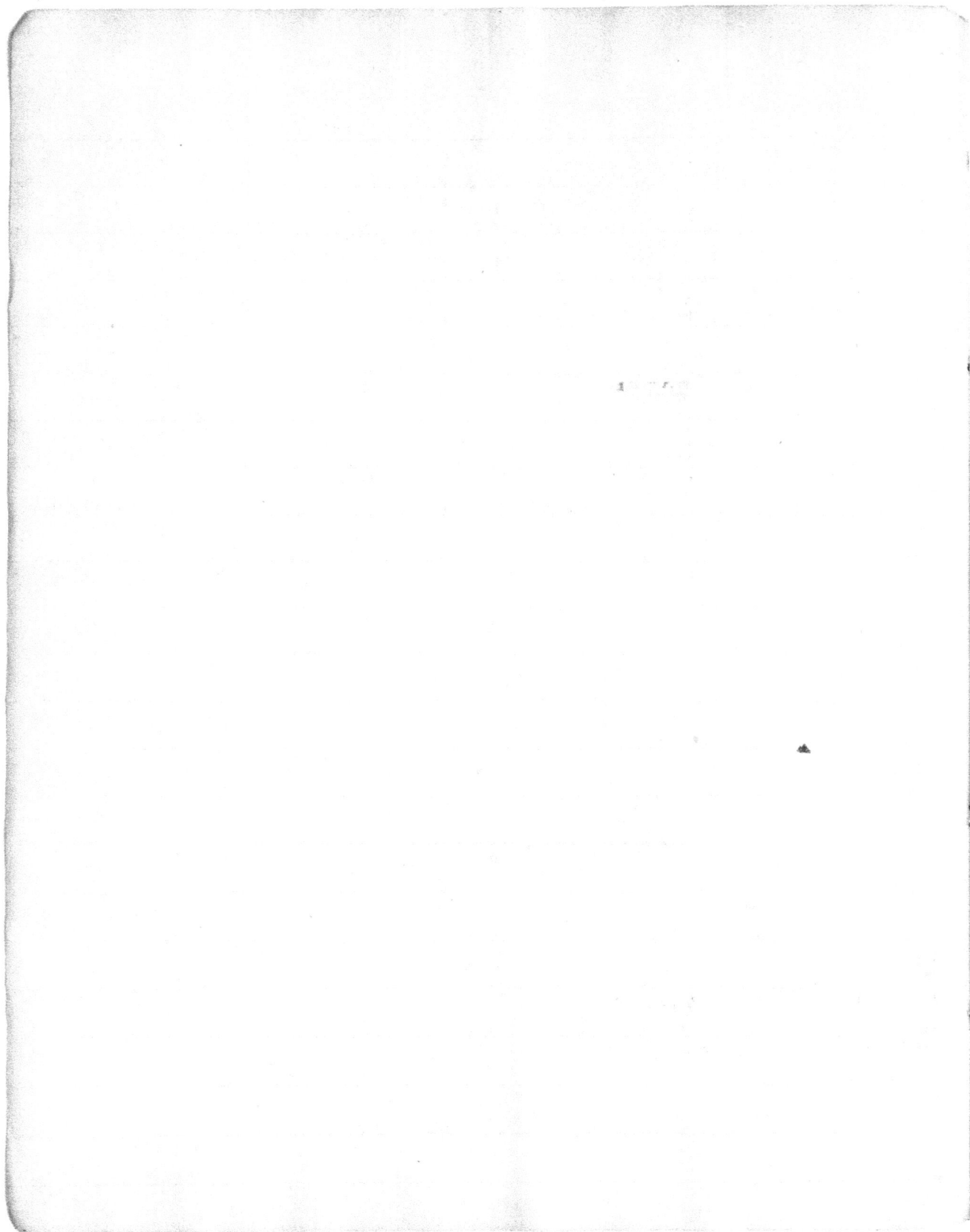

ALGUM-TREE & ALMUG-TREE

ALMUS
~~ALGUM~~ 1 Kings 10.11 +12
~~ALMUG~~ 2 Chron 9.10 +11
ALSUM

Species Illustrated   WHITE-SANDALWOOD
(SANTALUM ALBUM)

Two Hebrew words not translated — ALMUG in Chron & ALGUM in Kings. Two different kinds of timber used in the building of the Temple

ALGUM Brought from Lebanon where it grew with the Cedar & the Fir. Used in the building of the Temple. It is not known what tree was intended

ALMUG Brought by Hiram's navy from Ophir with gold & precious stones & used for pillars & terraces, also musical instruments.   It was a precious wood close & hard grained.
       Probably the Red Sandal Wood of India (Pterocarpus santalinus) which is fine grained very heavy & of a brilliant red colour & is today highly esteemed in the East for the construction of musical instruments.   Or it may have been the White Sandal Wood (Santalum Album) also a native of India, the wood of which is richly fragrant & used in the manufacture of cabinets caskets etc

No 2   ALMOND

ALMOND (Sháked)
Gen 43.11 : Ex 25.33-35
Num 17   Ecc 12   Jer 1.11

AMYGDALIS COMMUNIS

} Selected References. Mentioned
also many times elsewhere in Scripture

Illustrations —
2 Flowers
2B Fruit

= The word of the Lord came unto me saying Jeremiah what seest thou ? And I said
I see the rod of an almond tree (Sháked) Then said the Lord unto me Thou hast
well seen : for I will hasten (Sháked) my word to perform it " Jer 1.11

The Almond is indigenous in the Mediterranean region, is native of Palestine & is cultivated in all semi-tropical countries.   The flowers appear before the leaves (in very early spring) hence its Hebrew name SHAKED "HASTEN" or "WATCH" There is a play on the meaning of the word in Ju 1.11.
The Almond is often mentioned in the Scripture. Jacob sent Almonds as part of his gift to Joseph (Gen 43.11) The bowls of the golden-candlestick were modelled from the flowers (Ex 25. 33 to 35)
Aaron's rod was of this tree (Num 17) In the description of an old man in Ecclesiasticus 12 the white hairs of age are figured by the Almond — The white blossoms covering the tree in January & February. The flowers are fragrant, pink & white. The fruit a drupe, green & downy. The Almond of commerce being the stone.   The chief varieties are Sweet & Bitter Almonds. Oil of Almonds being the essential juice compressed from the Bitter Almond. The characteristic odour of the Almond denotes the presence of Prussic Acid & many fatal cases of poisoning have occured from the consumption of the Oil of Bitter Almonds.

No 3   ALOES & LING-ALOES

ALOES (Ahâlim)
         Ps 45.8: Prov 7.17: Cant 4.19: John 19.39
LING ALOES Num 24.6
Lignum Aloes = Wood Aloes

Species Illustrated ALOE VULGARIS (3)
              (3A)   YUCCA FILAMENTOSA
(Illustrative of The BOTANICAL ALOE)

ALOES A spice employed mixed with Myrrh Cassia & Cinnamon as a perfume to give an odour to garments & in the embalming of the dead. A foreign product — probably the gum of the Eagle Tree (Aquilaria agallocha) native of India. The Aloes of Scripture have no connection with the Aloe of Medicine Aloe Vulgaris. Medicinal Aloes being the dried juices of this plant

LING-ALOES A vigorous native tree used by Balaam as a figure of the prosperity of Israel
         The name signifies Wood Aloes & was possibly given because of some resemblance to some character of the Aloe of India. There is no indication as to what tree is intended

Aloe Vulgaris is a ldivecious plant bearing a cluster of long narrow stout acutely toothed leaves from
Jordan Almonds, the finest Sweet Almonds are brought from Malaga

Aloes (continued)

the centre of which rises a stout flower stem to the height of four feet bearing numerous pendant tubular dark red flowers. As already noted the dried juices of this plant are the Aloes of medicine. The Yucca is closely related to ~~the~~ Aloe vulgaris & to the Agave, the American Aloe called the Century Plant because it is reputed to blossom once in a hundred years. What realy happens is that the plant will grow for many years – twenty, thirty, fifty, may be in actuality a hundred, then it will send up an immense flower-stalk to a height of five or six feet bearing hundreds of flowers. This effort exausts the plant & after seeding it dies. ✱ The Yucca possesses this same ~~character~~ character to but in an even greater degree producing more & larger flowers. The Yucca however is remarkable in that it is fertilised by a single insect only — the Yucca Moth (Pronuba yuccasella) This moth is confined to Mexico the native home of the Yucca. The Yucca has been introduced into Europe & though it will thrive in Britain & produce a multitude of flowers & so much honey that it drops from the flowers & darkens the ground beneath yet it cannot set a single seed owing to the absence of this moth. Only in Mexico of all the world can it mature it's seed & reproduce it self.
✱ The Aloe flowers frequently, produces a moderate spike, & does not die after flowering

No 4   ANISE

ANISE (ΑΥΗΘΟΥ) Matt 23.23   DILL (ANETHUM GRAVOLENS) (Illustrated)

Mentioned only once in Scripture when the Lord rebuked the Pharisees for their scrupulous attention to trifles whilst neglecting greater & important matters. Incorrectly translated ANISE. It is the DILL & is so suggested in the R.V. margin. A small white-flowered Umbelliferous plant grown for the sake of it aromatic fruit which are used in medicine & as a condiment. These are somewhat flattened & slightly winged & from them the Dill Water of ~~medicine~~ medicine is produced.
The Talmud requires that the seeds & stem leaves pay tass

No 5   APPLE

APPLE (Tappúach)   APRICOT (PRUNUS ARMENIACA)   Species Illustrated
Prov 25.11 Cant 2.3 : 2.5 : 7.8 : 8.5 : Joel 1.2   (5) APRICOT (FRUIT)
Apple Tree occurs four times in the Song & once in Joel & Apple once illustratively (5A) QUINCE (FRUIT)
in Proverbs. The tree was a familiar one & afforded a grateful shade. The fruit was fragrant & golden. In both the Authorised & Revised Versions & also the New Translation the tree is given as "Apple" without comment but the Apple does not fit the description, is not much cultivated in Palestine & when cultivated is not a success ✱. Quince, Orange, & Citron have also been suggested but ~~like~~ the Apple do not answer the description. The Quince ✪ although a native of Palestine & fragrant bears a green or brown fruit which is astringent & unpleasant to the taste until cooked. The Orange was not introduced into the Holy Land until after the Captivity. The Citron ✶ although the foliage is dense & the fruit fragrant & golden does not bear an edible fruit. The fruit being sour & unpleasant & only used when candied. The Apricot fulfils all the requirements of the test. It grows to a height of thirty feet & carries a dense head of glossy leaves which shine silvery in the sunlight, fragrant white flowers & a fragrant, sweet, smooth, golden fruit & is abundantly cultivated

✱ The fruit being small woody & lacking in flavour. ✪ This is considered by some authorities to be the Apple of Joel but the same word is translated "Apple" in the Song & Proverbs & the Quince does not fit the description. The Quince bears large white flowers in Spring succeeded by a fragrant pear-shaped greenish brown fruit. This fruit which is the size of a small pear is astringent & woody to the palate when raw but edible when cooked & for it's sake the tree has long been cultivated. The foliage is broad in proportion to it's length, indeed it is almost round. The tree attains a height of some twenty feet. ✶ See No 22 for Notes on the Citron in it's connections with the Scriptures.

Apple (continued)

throughout Palestine. The tree must have been cultivated in Palestine from an early date as it's name was given to a number of places as early as the time of Joshua. (Josh 12.17:15.34+53: 17.8)

No 6 ASH

ASH

PINE (Oren) Isa 44.14   PINE   Species Illustrated SCOTCH PINE (PINUS SYLVESTRIS) (FRUIT)

Only once mentioned in Scripture. Occurring in Isa 44.14 as a tree from which idols were made. The tree intended cannot be the Common Ash which does not occur in Palestine. The LXX translate it Pine. It is given as "Pine-tree" in the R.V. & as "Pine" in the N.T. (here with a foot-note "or Mountain Ash"). The Aleppo Pine (Pinus halepensis) is frequent in Palestine & is no doubt the tree intended. The Scotch Pine (Pinus sylvestris) also occurs on the mountain ranges & may be intended. The Manna Ash (Fraxinus ornus) has been suggested by some. This tree bears crowded white blossoms & pinnate leaves with serrated edges. It superficialy resembles the Rowan which carries the alternate name of Mountain Ash. This tree may be intended by the note "Mountain Ash" in the N.T. It's Arabic name is ARAN. The Rowan is not known to occur in Palestine.

No 7   BALM-OF-GILEAD   (Illustrated)

SPICES (BOSEM) Ex 3.23: Cant 5.1+13:6.2.   BALSAMADENDRON GILEADENSE
BALM (TZORI) Gen 37.25: 4.3.11 Ezek 27.17 Jer 8.22: 46.11: 51.8

Two words signify BALM in the Scripture. (1) BOSEM translated SPICES (2) TZORI translated BALM. It was a fragrant resin much esteemed as possessing great healing virtues & was obtained from the Balsamodendron Gileadense a small tree with smooth bark & bearing scanty dark green evergreen foliage, small crimson or white flowers & a reddish-flesh pulpy fruit containing a fragrant yellow seed. The balm is obtained from the bark by incission, from the green nut, & an inferior quality from bruising & boiling the young stems. The gum is yellow, very tenacious, & has a fragrant resinous scent. It is still valued for it's fragrance & as an external remedy for wounds & internally for stomachic complaints. It was formerly cultivated in Palestine but is not found there today. It is cultivated still at Mecca & grows wild in Somali-land.
It is suggested in the margin of the R.V. (Gen 37.25) that the Balm was Mastic, & it is held by some that the Balm of Gen 43.11 was also Mastic as it is very doubtful whether the true Balm of Gilead had at that early date been introduced into Palestine

No 8   BALSAM

BALM Gen 37.25: 43.11   MASTIC (PISTACIA LENTISCUS) (Illustrated)
MASTICK-TREE (Susannah 54) "Under a Mastic Tree" marg. Greek Upsilon schinon 54

The name Mastic occurs only in the Apocrypha (Hist of Sus vose 54) but it is supposed by many to be the tree from which the Balm of Gen 37.25 & 43.11 was obtained as it is very doubtful whether at that early date the true Balm of Gilead had been introduced into Palestine. The Mastic is a small evergreen tree, very bushy, with thick crooked branches & reaching a height of some twelve feet. The leaves are pinnate & the flowers which are small & green & inconspicuous are clusted in tufts near the juncture of the leaves. The fruit is a red berry about the size of a Hawthorn fruit & remains on the tree through the winter. The resin is obtained from incissions in the bark made in dry weather in summer & autumn. This has been a commercial commodity from the earliest times, it is considered very valuable for the teeth, hence it's name signifying "to chew" or "masticate". It is chiefly used as a varnish & is only slightly fragrant. A spirit is distilled from the berries. It is common in all the Mediterranean countries & is found frequently on the hills

Balsam (continued)

along the plains of Palestine where it is indigenous.

No 9   BARLEY

BARLEY (Seôrah)   HORDEUM DISTICHUM (Illustrated)

Ex 9.31 & 32 Numb 5.15 Ruth 1.22 : 2.23 : 2 Sam 21.9 : 2 Chron 2.10 Hos 3.2 Ez   4.9 — 12 : 13.9
Kριθαὶ John 6.9 — Note Selected Reference Mentioned also many times elsewhere in Scripture

The common food in Palestine of men, horses, asses & draught oxen. Cultivated from the earliest times. Oats were unknown. The Promised Land was a land of Barley (Deut 8.8) The Barley harvest extends from March to May according to locality. Barley is the most cultivated of Cereals, having both a more northerly & southerly range than Wheat. It bears drought better & will thrive in a much lighter soil, reaches maturity earlier, requires less heat to ripen it, but will thrive under tropical conditions. But Barley bread is much inferior in nutritive qualities to Wheaten & is therefore employed in various portions of Scripture to signify inferiority or poverty

No 10   BAY — TREE

BAY — TREE (Ezrach) Ps 37.35.   LAUREL (LAURUS NOBILIS) (Illustrated)

Here the word EZRACH is translated BAY — TREE elsewhere it signifies a native in contrast to a stranger or foreigner. Both the R.V. & N.T give "a green tree in it's native soil" Apparently the reference in the Psalms is not to any particular kind of tree but to a vigorous tree growing luxuriantly in it's native soil. If a specific tree is intended it must be an evergreen & the Sweet Bay has the appearance about it of luxuriance well fitting the idea of prosperity & vigour conveyed by the Psalmist. The Laurel is a native of Palestine. It is not common generally but frequent in locality — in wooded dales in the North & West. The foliage is aromatic, the flowers are borne in clusters, are greenish white & small, & the succeeding fruit is a black drupe. A fragrant is extracted from it's foliage in the Orient.

BDELLIUM

BDELLIM (Bedôlach) Gen 2.12 : Numb 11.7.   Mentioned only in the two passages noted above. There is doubt as to what is intended. Some authorities consider it to be a precious stone, others the fragrant gum of a Balsamodendron. The N.T. gives the following note — "A fragrant resin as generally understood"

No 11   BEANS

BEAN (Pol) 2 Sam 17.28 Ezek 4.9   COMMON — BEAN (FABA VULGARIS) Illustrated (Fruit)

Beans were extensively cultivated in Palestine as an article of food & used both as a vegetable or a flour. The flour mixed with a little wheaten flour being much used by the poor to make a coarse bread. They were gathered with the Wheat harvest. The Common Bean was the species commonly cultivated. Note Peas ✳ Lentils ✳ & Vetches were also cultivated.

No 12   BITTER HERBS

BITTER HERBS (MORORIM) Ex 11.8 : Numb 9.11
BITTERNESS   Lam 3.15

The Bitter herbs were eaten with the Paschal Lamb & according to tradition were five in number Lettuce, Endive, Chicory, Artichoke & Elecampane ✳ The same word is translated "Bitterness" in Lam 3.15. No specific plant is intended by the word.

Illustrations — LETTUCE 12
             CHICORY 12 B
             ENDIVE 12 A
GLOBE — ARTICHOKE 12 C
    ELECAMPANE 12 D

✳ Or some claim Nettles others Mint.   Note 2 Sam 17.28 Mentioned amongst the provisions brought to David in the wilderness — Ezek 4.9 Mentioned as an ingredient in the making
✳ See No   ✳ See No

Bitter-Herbs (continued)

LETTUCE (LACTUCA SATIVA) Lettuce has been cultivated from an early date for the sake of it's succulent leaves which are eaten raw as salad. If left uncut the plant will throw up a branching flower stem to a height of some two or three feet. The small flower-heads consist of a few yellow strap-shaped florets & are succeeded by a pappus-bearing fruit. The flowers open in July & August & the plant is of annual duration. The Lettuce is not found in a wild state & does not establish itself as an escape from cultivation. Some consider that it is a cultivated form of the Prickly Lettuce (L Scariola) an acrid prickly plant with erect branches & foliage — The upper leaves of which are sagittate & clasping the stem. This plant is found rarely in waste places in Britain. All species of Lettuce secrete a milky juice & the Garden Lettuce yields such a juice from the roots which has narcotic properties similar to Opium.

ENDIVE (CICHORIUM ENDIVA) Related to the Chicory & cultivated for it's foliage which blanched is used as a Winter salad. If the plant is allowed to develope naturally it will throw up a stout stem to a height of three or four feet. The majority of the leaves will then form a rosette upon the ground from which the stem will spring. Few leaves will be found on the stem & these will be lobed & clasping the stem. This stem is tough & wiry & much branched. The flowers are attached to the stem without the intervention of a flower stalk. The florets are strap-shaped & broad & of a light blue, pink or white hue. They appear in July. The whole plant resembles the Chicory in miniature.

CHICORY (CICHORIUM INTYBUS) Chicory is sometimes cultivated for the sake of it's leaves which when blanched as in the Endive can be used as a salad. For this purpose it has been appreciated & cultivated from the earliest times. Today however it's esteem as a salad has depreciated & it is usualy cultivated for the sake of it's large fleshy tap-root which is roasted & blended with coffee. It is extensively cultivated for this purpose especialy in Germany. The Succory is a stiff-looking plant with upright grooved stems branching at an angle & alternately. The radical leaves are long, narrow, & coarsely toothed, those which occur on the stem are scattered alternate & linear, lobed at the base & clasping the stem. The flowers are bright blue & open from July to October. They are large & conspicuous & very pleasing. The plant abounds in a milky juice & the stem is tough & wiry. The flowers spring directly from the stem, have no flower stalk, & are usualy borne in pairs. The Chicory occurs frequently in waste places in chalky districts of Britain.

GLOBE ARTICHOKE (CYNARA SCOLYMUS) A species of Thistle bearing purple flowers. It has been cultivated from an early date for the sake of it's flower-heads — the fleshy base of the involucrum of these being the Artichoke employed as a vegetable. It is commonly cultivated in Palestine where it is indigenous *

* The so called JERUSALEM ARTICHOKE is a species of Sunflower — HELIANTHUS TUBEROSUS. It received it's name of Artichoke from the resemblance of it's flavour to that of the Globe Artichoke, but in this plant it is the tubers which are cooked & eaten. It is commonly cultivated in Britain where it will grow freely in any soil & produce an abundance of tubers. It is quite capable of establishing itself in waste places & by the side of roads but although it forms many flower-buds the flowers rarely or never open in Britain — the plant is semi-tropical (a native of Brazil) & does not usually open its flowers earlier than November or December & in this country the first cuts it down whilst yet in bud. The tubers however are hardy & the plant easily retains its footing. The name "Jerusalem" is an error & the plant does not occur in Palestine despite the fact that the soup made from its tubers is called "Palestine Soup." It was introduced into New England from Brazil at a early date & was from thence introduced into England about 1617

Bitter-Herbs (continued)

ELECAMPANE (INULA HELENIUM) The foliage of this plant has been employed raw as a salad from early times in the East & is still ~~appreciated for this~~ purpose by the Arabs in Palestine. In Europe the Elecampane had formerly a medical reputation being employed as a tonic it's candied rhizome being valued for diseases of the lungs. It was extensively cultivated for these purposes in earlier times but today it is little valued & it's cultivation has ~~declined~~ practically ceased. The Elecampane is a very coarse looking plant reaching a height of some five or six feet. The leaves are large — the radical ones often over a foot in length, oblong saw-toothed, wrinkled, downy beneath, with long stalks. The stem leaves are sessile & heart-shaped. The flower heads are solitary, terminal, three or four inches across, & of a bright yellow. The involucre is leafy. — The leaf-like bracts are broadly ovate & downy. The flowers appear in July & continue to open till August. The Elecampane occurs frequently in Palestine, in Britain it occurs infrequently in meadows, quarries, & woods. It is indigenous but usualy when found it is a escape from cultivation.

No13   BOX
"TEASSHUR" —BOX Isa 4.19 : 60.13.| BUXUS LONGIFOLIA (Illustrated)
"ASSHUR" — ASHURITES Ezek 27.6 — * The company of the Ashurites have made thy benches of ivory (A.V) * They made the benches of ivory inlaid in boxwood *(N.T) "Box-wood" also in the R.V.
The Box is twice mentioned in Isaiah as a forest tree in conjunction with the Fir & Pine. Some think that the Juniper is meant. Both grow on Lebanon. The Box of Palestine is Buxus longifolia. It resembles the Common Box but the leaves are longer. It reaches a height of twenty feet & is found on Mount Lebanon & the Galilean Hills. That Box is realy intended is borne out by the R.V where "ASSHUR" in Ezekiel 27.6 translated ASHURITES is translated Box-wood (ASSHUR is considered by many authorities to be a contraction of TEASSHUR) The N.T also gives Box-wood with a note "Or Larch". The art of inlaying with ivory was practised by the Phoenicians & Box-wood was generally used. It is still employed in Palestine for making combs, spoons, & other small articles

No14   BURNING BUSH
"SENEH" BUSH Ex 3.2 & Deut 33.16   Species Illustrated — ACACIA NILOTICA
         THORN-BUSH (N.T) *
Seneh denotes some specific species of bush, the Hebrew generic name for bush being another word. The N.T. gives "Thorn-bush" The word is only found in the passages telling of Jehovah appearing to Moses in the bush. A small thorny Acacia (Acacia nilotica) occurs frequently in the Arabian Peninsula. It is the SÛNT of Egypt. It is very similar to it's near relative the SHITTAH — TREE (Acacia seyal) but is smaller & closer in growth

No15   CALAMUS
"Kaneh" CALAMUS (Ezek 27.19 *   LEMON-GRASS (ANDROPOGON SCHŒNATHUS)
"Kaneh hattôb" SWEET-CANE Jer 6.20 * & Isa 43.24   Species Illustrated —
"Keneh" CALAMUS * Cant 4.14   (15) LEMON-GRASS
"Keneh bosem" CALAMUS Ex 30.23 *   (15.A) SWEET-SEDGE
Calamus — A chief spice which with Myrrh & Cinnamon was a perfuming ingredient. It was imported into Palestine from a far country & sold in the markets of Tyre. The Sweet Cane of Isa 43.24 & Jer 8.20 is thought by some to be the SUGAR CANE but more probably it is the Calamus. If so it not a sweet-cane
* Note "Bramble" N.T. But this cannot be so. The Bramble does not occur in the desert
# With the note "or Myrrh" in the N.T. * Translated "Sweet Camphire" in the N.T. * Trans

Calamus (continued)

in the same sense as is the Sugar-Cane but sweet in the sense of aromatic. Calamus was probably the Lemon Grass of India (Andropogon schœnanthus) which has a strong sweet odour especially in stems & roots. Some consider that it was the Sweet Sedge (Acorus calamus) introduced into Palestine from India. The whole of this plant is aromatic especially the long underground root. It is an aquatic plant with somewhat the habit of a Sedge. The leaves are radial & sword-shaped with wavy margins, fragrant when bruised. The flowers are perfect & (as in iroides) in d spadesc. The spathe is leaf-like. The stamens six. The ovary three-chambered & superior. The stems, as the leaves, are fragrant when bruised & the rhizome is very fragrant & is employed in perfumery. The Sweet Sedge is indigenous in England but very rare save in parts of Norfolk. It supplied the "rushes" which in former days were strewn before the introduction of carpets into England

No 16 CAMPHIRE

"COPHER" – CAMPHIRE Cant 1.14 : 4.13 : HENNA (LAWSONIA ALBA) (Illustrated)

Camphire is an old form of Camphor & is given in the A.V through an error in the similarity of the Hebrew name "Copher". The plant intended is the Henna (Lawsonia alba) as given in the R.V & the N.T. It is a small shrub reaching a height of about eight feet with dark bark, pale green foliage (the same hue as the foliage of the Lilac) & bearing large clusters of small, very fragrant, white & yellow flowers. It has been valued for its fragrance from antiquity, & likewise from remote ages it has been famous as a cosmetic. The young leaves & stems are reduced to a powder which is mixed with hot water in a paste. It is used to give a reddish-orange stain to the nails, palms of the hand, & soles of the feet. It cannot be removed with soap & checks perspiration. The stain has been found on Egyptian mummies. The Henna is found in North Africa, Egypt & India & still maintains in Palestine at Engedi only.

No 17 CASSIA No 18 CASSIA IRIS FLORENTINA

CINNAMOMUM/CASSIA Species Illustrated No 17 CINNAMOMUM CASSIA

"KIDDAH" – CASSIA Ex 30.24 : Ezek 27.19 .✳- No 18 IRIS FLORENTINA

"KETZIOTH" – CASSIA Ps 45.8 .✳

Cassia was one of the ingredients of the holy anointing oil. There is some doubt as to the plant from which it was obtained. The LXX believed it to be a Flag. The Florentine Iris (Iris Florentina) has a fragrant rhizome resembling Violets in odour. This dried & ground forms the ORRIS ROOT of commerce used today chiefly in perfumery & as an ingredient of tooth-pastes. If the LXX is correct in their assumption Cassia was the Orris root. The Florentine Iris bears large handsome white flowers in early summer. The R.V gives in the margin "Costus" which is obtained from the Root (Aplotaxis lappa) an aromatic rooted Composite found on the mountains of India & used today as an ingredient in the incense used in Chinese temples. Two words are translated CASSIA (see above) & it has been suggested that Kiddah is Costus & Ketzioth is Orris. Other authorities claim that Cassia was the bark of Cinnamomum cassia a relative of the Cinnamon & native of India. The dried bark of this tree is used today under the name of "cassia" it is coarser & more pungent than Cinnamon. The tree reaches a height of thirty feet. The flowers are small, white & arranged in racemes. The foliage is oblong-lanceolate & triplicostate. The spice is the inner bark dried & ground.

-✳- R.V. Marg in "Costus" Produced from an Indian Composite Aplotaxis lappa & Rendered "Cassia" without comment in the N.T
✳ It has been suggested that this is "Orris" & See Cinnamon No 1 & Calamus /Cane No 58
& "Sweet Myrtle" in the N.T. Ex 30.23 & Cant 4.14 rendered Calamus in the N.T without comment

No 19   CEDAR-OF-LEBANON

"EREZ" — CEDAR   CEDRUS LIBANI (Illustrated)

Lev 14.4 : Numb 19.6 : 1Kings 5 6 7 : Ezra 3.7 : 2 Kings 19.9 : Ps 92.12 : 114.16 : Isa 2.13.
Ezek 17.23 : 31.3 & 6 : Amos 2.9 : Zech 11.1 & 2 — Selected References. Mentioned also many times
~~elsewhere in Scripture~~ elsewhere in Scripture. THE SMELL OF LEBANON (Cant 4.11)

Cedar is applied in Scripture generically to the whole Pine family & specifically to the Cedar
of Lebanon. The Cedar of Leviticus & Numbers was probably a species of aromatic Juniper found
around Sinai, the Cedar of Lebanon not occurring in the desert. Elsewhere Cedar denotes the
Cedar of Lebanon, a noble tree, the prince of the vegetable Kingdom in Palestine & consequently
used as the symbol of grandeur, loftiness, might, glory, & ever increasing expansion. Though
it grows rapidly it produces a durable, firm, compact, & strongly fragrant wood. It lives to
a great age (300 to 800 years). It was used in the construction of the three temples, in
Solomon's palace, by David in the King's House, & the dome of the Church of the Holy Sepulchre
in Jerusalem is today of Cedar. The Cedar is found in Palestine only on Lebanon but
it also grows on the Taurus Mountains in Cyprus & on the Atlas Mountains in Africa.

No 20   CHESTNUT

"ARMÔN" — CHESTNUT Gen 30.37 :   ORIENTAL PLANE (PLANTANUS ORIENTALIS)
        Ezek 31.8 :   PLANE-TREE Ecclus 24.14.   (Illustrated)

Translated "Chestnut" in the A.V, rendered "Plane Tree" by the LXX & given in the R.V. In the N.T.
given "Maple" with the note "or Plane". There is no doubt that "Plane" is the correct ~~rendering~~
as the Chestnut does not occur in Palestine whereas the Oriental Plane though of local
habit is frequent by the streams mingling with the Willow & the Poplar. It is a vigourous
tall & noble tree. The leaves are palmate, richly cut, & of a refreshing light green hue.
The flowers are in clusters of pendulous rounded balls. The fruit is globular. The name
"Armôn" signifies "naked" & it is characteristic of the Plane Tree that it annualy sheds it's
outer bark. In Ecclesiasticus 24. 14 Wisdom is compared to "A plane-tree by the water". The
Oriental Plane is ~~cultivation~~ common cultivation in Britain as an ornamental tree especially by the sides of roads.
It was held sacred by the Greeks.

No 21   CINNAMON

"KINAMÓN" — CINNAMON   CINNAMONIUM ZEYLANICUM (Illustrated) ✳
         Ex 30.23 Prov 7.17 Cant 4.14 Rev 18.13

A sweet spice, one of the chief ingredients of the holy anointing oil (Ex 30.23) & used as a perfume
(Prov 7.17) It is the very aromatic inner bark of the Cinnamon Tree a member of the Laurel
Family closely affiliated to the Cassia Tree. The tree is a native of Ceylon & the islands of the
Indian Ocean. It makes a height of thirty feet & bears large oval prominently ribbed leaves which
when bruised have the flavour of Cloves. The flowers are small & white. The tree is pollarded to
induce the growth of numerous upright shoots from which the bark is peeled. The inner bark dried
& ground being the Cinnamon of commerce. Oil of Cinnamon is obtained by boiling the ripe fruit
& an inferior quality from the outer bark & foliage.

No 22   CITRON

         CITRUS MEDICA   (Illustrated)

"Ye shall take ye on the first day the boughs of goodly trees" (Margin "Fruit") Lev 23.40 : A.V.
     "The fruit of goodly trees" Lev 23.40 : R.V.

✳ See Cassia No 17 & Malabathron No 58

Citron (continued)

"And ye shall take on the first day the fruit of beautiful trees" Lev 23.40 : N.T. Citron is not mentioned by name in the Scripture, but the instruction "Take ye on the first day the boughs of goodly trees (Lev 23.40) ("Fruit" Margin in A.V. Text R.V & N.T) is taken by the Chaldean paraphrase & by the Rabbi's to mean "Fruit of the Citron Trees" & likewise considered by Josephus & so accepted by the Jews today who use the Citron fruit at the celebration of the Feast of Tabernacles. Indeed this fruit is used regularly in the services of the synagogue, being handed round & smell by the worshipers when departing when they thank God for all His good gifts. The Citron is a native of India & is the commonest of the Orange Family in Palestine where it was introduced at an early date. The flowers are numerous, conspicuous, & of a pale purple hue. The flowering season lasts several months. The foliage is deep green & larger than that of the Orange. The Fruit is oblong, much larger than that of the Lemon, fragrant & of a pale orange, almost golden, colour, but sour & unpleasant to the palate & only used as a conserve. The tree is spiny. The candied fruit is in frequent use as a ~~confection~~.

No 23   COCKLE

BAOSHAH — COCKLE Job 31.40   CORN COCKLE (GITHAGO SEGETUM)
   Marg in "Noisome weeds" "Tares" N.T (Text)   Species Illustrated (23) CORN COCKLE
                                                                   (23A) SKUNK CABBAGE
                                                          (Illustrative of a Foetid Arum ✳)

This word occurs only once in the Scripture & is translated "Cockle" in the A.V & R.V ⸭. The plural occurs in Isaiah 5.2 where it is rendered "Wild Grapes" ✳ The Cockle (Githago segetum) is a common cornfield weed in Palestine as in Britain. It is a handsome, downy, narrow-leaved plant with large, solitary pink flowers. It reaches a height of three feet. The stems are wiry & the seeds are large & difficult to seperate from corn. It is quite possible for the Cockle to come up instead of Barley but the Hebrew word signifies something with a putrid smell & the Margin of both the A.V. & N.T. gives "noisome weeds". There are several Arums common in cornfields in Palestine of a most offensive odour & it has been suggested that one of these is intended. Such would certainly fit the description

No 24   CORIANDER

GAD — CORIANDER Ex 16.31 Numb 11.7   CORIANDRUM SATIVUM (Illustrated)
Only twice mentioned in the Scripture & each time as the seed which the Manna resembled in appearance. The Coriander is an Umbelliferous plant with white blossoms & small, globular, aromatic fruits. The seeds are of a spicy flavour & are grey-white in colour. They are used in confectionary & for flavouring curries, & in the East to flavour bread & to give a spice to sweet-meats. The Coriander is cultivated for its fruit in England, & in Palestine & Egypt where it is very common as a wild plant in cornfields & upon agricultural land it has been cultivated from a very early date

No 25   CORN (The Cereals) & WHEAT

CHITTAH — WHEAT   Species Illustrated WHEAT (~~TRITICUM~~ AESTIVUM)
Gen 30.14 : 20 : 40.9 & 10 : 49.11 Numb 8.23 : 20.5 Deut 8.7 & 8 : Ps 78.47 : 80.9 & 13 : 105.33 Cant 2.15 Isa 16.8 & 11 : Amos 9.13 : Mic 4.4 : Zech 3.10 : John 15.16 & 8 — Selected References. Mentioned also many Wheat of Minnith — Ezek 27.17.   times elsewhere in Scripture

✳ The SKUNK CABBAGE (SYMPOCARPUS FÆTIDUS) is ~~an American~~ plant & does not occur in Palestine & does not occur in Palestine. It is included merely as an illustration of a foetid Arum
⸭ Marg in "Noisome weeds" "Tares" in the text N.T without comment ✳ For fuller details of this see Wild Grape No

Corn + Wheat (Illustrated)

CORN — The Cereals WHEAT, BARLEY ✳ MILLET ☀ and SPELT ✴

Ex 22.6. Lev 24 : 2.16. Josh 5.11 + 12 : Ruth 3.2 Selected References
There are several words to CORN in Hebrew —(1) DAGAN (Corn) Numb 18 27 (2) KAMAH (Standing Corn)
+ dating } Judges 15.5 (3) BAR (Winnowed Corn) Gen 41.49 : Prov 11.26

(4) SHIBBOLEH (Ear-of-Corn) Gen 41.5 Ruth 3.2. Wheat Barley Millet + Spelt are the Cereals grown in
Palestine, Oats are unknown.

WHEAT — The most important + most valued of all the Cereals. It has been cultivated from
the earliest times. It was the principle grain of Mesopatamia in Jacobs time (Gen 30.14) It
was the chief cereal of Egypt + Syria. The many-eared variety usualy (but incorrectly)
called "Mummy Wheat" cultivated in Egypt in Jacob's time (Gen 41.5 + 22) + depicted on
monuments is still, though not frequently, cultivated there. Wheat was one of the blessings
of the Promised Land (Deut 8.8) + from the days Solomon to the destruction of Jerusalem
Palestine was a Wheat exporting country. The Wheat harvest is April to June according
to locality — two months after the Barley Harvest. Thus the Wheat being later than the Barley
escaped destruction in the plague of hail. It was threshed by being trodden out by oxen
(Deut 25.4) pressed out with a wooden wheel, or threshed with a Flail (Isa 28.27) winnowed
with a fan   + sifted

No 26   COTTON
"CARPUS" — GREEN (COTTON?) ✚   GOSSYPIUM HERBACEUM (Illustrated)
"White green + blue hangings" (Esth 1.6) "Hangings of white + blue cotton"
Cotton is not mentioned by name in the A.V. or N.T. but it is introduced three times in the
margin in the R.V. In Esther 1.6. the description of the hangings of the King's palace should
read "white + blue cotton". The Cotton plant is a native of India + as Ahsuerus reigned
from India to Ethiopia he would have access to the substance which has been employed
there from a very early date. It is considered doubtful as to whether the R.V. marginal
rendering "Cotton" for "Fine Linen" in Exodus is correct as it is very dubious as to whether
the Egyptians were acquainted with Cotton at that early period, though it was introduced
into Egypt before the Grecian Conquest (B.C.333) Today it is extensively cultivated
both there + in Palestine. The flowers are yellow + the seeds are surrounded by a white
fleecy fibrous substance from which the Cotton of commerce is derived. It is the most
valuable of all textile substances. The Cotton plant belongs to the Order Malvaceae.
"White cloth" in Isaiah 19.9 is rendered "Cotton" in the R.V. margin

No 27   CUCUMBER
"KISHUIM" — CUCUMBERS Numb 11.5.   CUCUMIS SATIVUS (Illustrated)
"MIKSHAH" — GARDEN OF CUCUMBERS Isa 1.8.
The Cucumber with the Melon + Pumpkin has long been extensively cultivated in Egypt. It was with
the Melon mourned for by the Israelites in the wilderness where these cool + refreshing fruits would
have been especially welcome. Two species of Cucumber are cultivated in Egypt + Palestine —
(1) Cucumis chate with a large fruit + un-serrated leaves. (2) The Common Cucumber (Cucumis sativus)

✳ See No 9   ☀ See No   ✴ See No
✚ The Hebrew word "CARPUS" has been turned into a common word both in Greek + Latin, "Κάρπασος"
"Carbasus" — "Cotton or Awnings" from which it would seem obvious that the word signified "Cotton"

Cucumber (continued)

the species cultivated in Britain. Thus of course it does not require to be grown in hot-houses but is cultivated in fields often being planted after the Barley has been reaped on the same ground. The fruit is smaller than ~~hot~~ when hot-house grown but the crop is very large. The Cucumber is of very common cultivation in Palestine & forms an important item of the food of the poor in summer. "Cucumber" is mentioned only once in Scripture (Numb 11.5) In Isa 1.8 the desolation of Israel is compared to a "lodge in a garden of cucumbers" (also mentioned only once) This was the outlook of the watchman & was a crude wooden hut raised on four poles.

No 28   CUMMIN

"CAMMON" CUMMIN Isa 28. 25 & 27   CUMINUM SATIVUM (Illustrated)
"ΚΥΜ ΙΝΟΝ" - CUMMIN Matt 23.23

An Umbelliferous plant cultivated for it's aromatic seeds which are used in the East as a condiment, bruised to mix with bread, stewed or boiled with meat, & also as a medicine. The leaves resemble the Fennel long & narrow the flowers are usually yellow occassionally white. The fruit resembles that of the Carroway but is larger & of a lighter colour. It is ridged, the ridges being covered with prickley hairs. The essential oil is contained in six channels. The seeds were beaten out with a rod as described in Isaiah 28.25 - 27 being too tender to be threshed like corn. The Saviour charged the Scribes & Pharisees with punctiliously tithing the Cummin (which was only inferentially included in the Levitical Law) along with Mint & Anise, whilst omitting the weightier matters of the Law (Matt 23.23)

No 29   CYPRESS & GOPHER WOOD

"TIRZAH" - CYPRESS - Isa 44.14 (Holm Oak RV & CUPRESSUS SEMPERVIRENS (Illustrated) N.T.)
"GOPHER" Gen 6.14.

"Tirzah" Mentioned only once where it is the material used for making an Idol. Translated ~~Cypress~~ "Cypress" in the A.V & "Holm Oak" in the R.V. & N.T. By some thought to be the Syrian Juniper (Juniperus excelsa) which is frequent on Lebanon. The Hebrew signifies a hard-grained wood. The Cypress is frequent in Palestine on the mountain ranges & in the neighbourhood of towns. The perpendicularly branched variety especially is commonly planted in cemeteries throughout the East — it is the ~~funereal~~ funereal tree. The wood is very tough, compact & durable & it is considered by many authorities that the GOPHER-WOOD of which the Ark was built (Gen 6.14) was Cypress. Gopher is an untranslated Hebrew word & is not found anywhere else in Scripture. The R V gives "Cypress" in the margin for "Fir" in Isaiah 37.24; 40.19 etc

---

No 30   DESERT VEGETATION

Species Illustrated - Desert Euphorbia (Euphorbia   ) Illustrative of Desert Vegetation. The Desert Euphorbia is a native of Africa & does not occur in Palestine.

Desert vegetation is distinctive & characteristic. It is usually woody with small foliage & numerous thorns (often exuding gummy matter & very frequently aromatic) as the Acacia & Myrrh, or it is fleshy, storing water in it's distended tissues (almost invariably armed with sharp thorns) as the Cacti & the Desert Euphorbias. The arid regions of Palestine & the eastern desets of surrounding countries abound in such plants. The most notable are the Acacia ✳ ("the root out of a dry ground" of Isa 53.2) & the Myrrh ✱ Various species of Cactus have been

✳ See No 91   ✱ See No 65

Desert Vegetation (continued)

introduced & established themselves firmly in locality, the most formidable being the Prickly Pear which has over-run all the warmer parts of Europe & Eastern Asia & is very troublesome in Palestine ✳. All originated in America & are of recent introduction. None existed in the Eastern Hemisphere in Biblical times

No 31 — DOVE'S DUNG

"CHIRYONIM" – DOVE'S DUNG 2 Kings 6.25.   STAR-OF-BETHLEHEM
                                              (ORNITHOGALUM UMBELLATUM) (Illustrated)

"Dove's Dung" is mentioned as being used as food in the siege of Samaria (1 Kings 6.25) it is a literal translation of the Hebrew word "Chiryonim". Some have suggested that the word should not be taken literally but is the name of some plant of a nauseous character not ordinarily used as food. It has been suggested that the root of the Star-of-Bethlehem was the substance intended. The Generic name being Ornithogalum — signifying "Bird's Milk" & the thought being borne out by the fact that a species of Salsola is called "Sparrow's Dung" by the Arabs today, but there is no real authority to give the word any other than it's literal meaning. The Star-of-Bethlehem is a very common plant in Palestine. It bears large, erect, white & green flowers in April & May. The leaves have a white stripe running along the main-vein from the base to the apex. The root is bulbous. The Star-of-Bethlehem is not infrequent in England. It is found in the neighbourhood of houses & is not indigenous. The young stems of an allied species — the Spiked Star-of-Bethlehem (O. pyrenaicum) are sometimes cooked & eaten. ✳

No 32 — EBONY

"HOBNIM" – EBONY Ezek 27.15   DIOSPYRUS EBENUS (Illustrated)

Mentioned only once — in Ezekiel as a costly artical brought to the markets of Tyre by the merchants of Dedan — the inhabitants of Persian Gulf. It is the heart-wood of the Date Plum Tree (Diospyrus ebenus) a large tree native of Ceylon & Southern India. This tree bears simple oval leaves, white flowers, & an edible fruit. The Ebony of commerce is obtained only from the centre of the trunk. The outer wood is white, soft, & valueless, the heart-wood (rarely exceeding two feet in diameter) is jet black, hard, very durable, & capable of a high polish ✳

No 33 — FIG

"TENNAH" – FIG Gen 3.7: Deut 8.8,   FICUS CARICA (Illustrated)
"⊃ΥΚΗ" – FIG Matt 21.19: 24.3 & others: Numb 13.23: 1 Kings 4.25: 2 Kings 18.31: Ps 105.33: Jer 5.17: Jer 8.13: Hos 2.12: Joel 1.8 12: 2.22: Isa 38.21. Selected References.
Three Hebrew words are also used for different kinds of Fig – (1) "BIKURAH" (Early Figs) Isa 28.4: Hos 9.10: (2) PAG" (Green Fig - Unripe Fig) Cant 2.13 (3) "DEBELAH" (Cake of Figs) 1 Sam 25.18: Mic 7.1 30.12: 1 Chron 12.40
The Fig Tree is very frequently mentioned both in the Old & New Testament It is indigenous in Palestine being found wild all over the country & is one of the commonest cultivated fruit trees. It frequently reaches a considerable size, the trunk often being five feet in circumference. The pear-shaped "fruit" is a hollow succulent receptacle containing very many minute flowers attached to its inner surface. These produce the numerous true fruits (commonly called "Seeds") The young Figs appear in February before the leaves: (the latter unfolding

✳ This Cactus has over-run vast areas in Australia, rendering them useless.

✱ Occasionaly the heart wood is mottled & then it is exceedingly valuable.

Fig (continued)

in April or May & falling in November) When the leaves are fully out the fruit should be ripe. When the Lord Jesus cursed the Fig Tree in Matthew 21 it was at the end of March & the fruit does not ripen until May or June, but the tree being in full leaf (a most unusual thing for the time of the year) it might reasonably be expected to be in fruit also.

The foliage is very dense & gives a pleasant shelter from the summer sun. Nathanel was seen of the Lord under the Fig Tree where it's dense foliage screened him from all human observation (John 1.48) The palmate leaves are thick, leathery, & very large.

The Fig is the first tree mentioned in Scripture (Gen 3.7) The Promised Land is described as "A land of Fig trees" (Deut 8.8) & the spies sent to view the land brought back Figs (Numb 13.23) The fruitfulness of the Fig is a sign of the favour of God (Joel 2.22) & the smiting of the Fig Tree one of God's threatened judgements upon the land To "sit every man under his vine & fig tree conveys the fullest idea of peace, security, & prosperity — typical of the Millenium. Three Hebrew words are used for different kinds of Fig. —

(1) BIKURAH "Early Figs" — The first ripe Figs. Isa 28.4: Hos 9.10: Mic 7.1

(2) PAG "Green Figs" — The unripened Autumn fruit which remains on the tree through the winter. Cant 2.13

(3) DEBELAH "A cake of dried Fig" — The main crop dried & pressed into cakes for winter use. Mentioned frequently in the Old Testament as a staple article of food (1 Sam 25.18: 30.12: 1 Chron 12.40) It is in this condition that they are commonly imported into this country.

The Fig possesses medical qualities & is still frequently used in the East in the manner described in Isaiah 38.21.

No 34   FITCHES

"KETZACH" – FITCHES Isa 28.25&27   NIGELLA SATIVA (Illustrated)

The Fennel Flower (Nigella sativa) a small annual plant of the Order Ranunculaceæ very common in the East in a wild state & much cultivated for its numerous black seeds (from which it receives its alternative name of "Black Cummin" given in the Margin of the R.V.) which are pungent & are used in Palestine, Syria, & Egypt as a condiment & sprinkled over cakes & bread as Carraway seeds are used in confectionary in Britain. The plant is too small to bear the threshing instrument & the seed is "beaten out with a staff (Isa 28.25&27) The foliage is very much divided & the flowers are yellow. The seed-vessels are globular, swollen, capped with fern-like horns & divided into six cells. An allied species Nigella orientalis also found wild in Palestine where it is very abundant bears blue flowers. Its seeds are used in the same manner but are inferior in pungency. They are also used to adulterate Pepper.

The Hebrew word "CUSSEMETH" is erroneously translated "Fitches" in Ezekiel 4.9. In every other place where the word occurs it is translated "Rye" (Spelt, see No) which is the correct rendering.

No 35   FIR

"BEROSH" – FIR-TREE 1 Kings 5.10 Cant 1.17   2 Sam 6.5   Species Illustrated STONE PINE (PINUS PINEA)(FRUIT)
"BEROTH"   Isa 37.24: 40.13: 41.19: 50.13: Ezek 27.5: 31.8: Hos 14.8: Nah 2.3.

Translated "Fir" in the A.V. in the LXX rendered indifferently "Pine" "Cypress" & "Juniper" Fir in the R.V. with "Cypress" in the Margin & "Cypress" in the N.T. save Hos 14.8 where it is

Fir (continued)

translated "Fir" & Nahum 2.3 where it is rendered "Spear" with the Note "Vi' 'Cypress'"
Often mentioned appreciatively in connection with the Cedar of Lebanon. Its timber was greatly
valued & applied to many uses. Hiram sent it to Solomon for the construction of the Temple where
where it was used for floors ✳ & the outer doors ✱ It was used for rafters (Cant 1.17) for the
decks of ships (Ezek 27.5) for spear shafts ✱ & for musical instruments — harps in particular
(2 Sam 6.5) The Fir-tree is mentioned as one of the blessings & a symbol of the fruitfulness of
the Millenial earth (Isa 41.19; 55.13) Several species of Fir & Pine occur in Palestine. Pinus
maritima is found on the coast but is not frequent. Pinus halepinus is found on the mountains & is
probably the "Fir" of Scripture being inferior only to the Cedar in stateliness & utility.
The Stone Pine (Pinus pinea) is extensively cultivated & is frequently found in a wild state. It
is notable for the umbrella-like form it assumes. The large seeds are cooked eaten by the Arabs ✳
This might be the "Fir" of Scripture. Pinus Carica predominates in the Taurus mountains & several
species of Juniper occur which attain to a considerable size any of which might be the tree
intended. The Cypress is frequent in the highlands & is by some authorities considered to be
indisputably the "Fir" of Scripture. ▪ This view is borne out by the R.V & the N.T. The
R.V. giving "Cypress" in the margin as an alternative to "Fir" & the N.T. giving "Cypress" in the
text.   The forests of Palestine have been wantonly & indiscriminately destroyed over
wide areas during the course of the ages ☼ & the various species of Pine still persisting on
the mountain ranges were much more abundant at an earlier date.

No 36 — FLAX

"PISHTAH"-FLAX   LINUM SATIVUM   Illustrated

Ex 9.31; Josh 2.6; Prov 31.13; Hos 2.9; Matt 12.20

LINEN   Gen 41.42; Ex 39.27 & 28; Prov 7.16; Ezek 44.17; Matt 27.59; Mark 15.46; Luke
TOW   Judges 16.9; Isa 1.31; 43.17   23.53; Rev 15.6

Flax is the earliest material known to have been cultivated & manufactured for clothing purposes
purposes. Linen cloth is found enwrapping the oldest mummies of Egypt & the cultivation
of Flax & the various processess in the manufacture of Linen is depicted in the sculptures
in Egyptian temples. Flax was cultivated in Egypt & Canaan before the Israelitish
settlement (Josh 2.6). Linen was used for the robes of the priests (Ex 27.20), for the curtains
& hangings of the Tabernacle (Ex 26) & for lamp wicks (Isa 43.3). The body of the Lord
was wrapped in linen cloth (John 19.40). Flax is an annual plant with very narrow leaves
& bright blue flowers which open in May & June. The stem contains very many tough fibres
from which Linen is made & for the sake of which the plant is cultivated. The
seeds contain a mild & soothing oil — the "Linseed Oil" of medicine & commerce. Flax is
found not infrequently in a wild state in Britain but it is originally an escape from
cultivation & this is also the case in Palestine & indeed in every country where Flax is
cultivated — it easily adapts itself but it is not to be indigenous in any country
The Flax was full-grown & in flower when smitten by the plague of hail (Ex 9.32)

✳ 2 Chron 3.5. In the N.T. "And the great house he boarded with cypress wood" Which would seem to indicate Floors
in the A.V. "And the greater house he cieled with fir-tree" Which tells that the ceilings were of Fir-wood
✱ 1 Kings 35.10) The folding doors. ✱ This is the significance of Nahum 2.3 "The fir-trees shall
be terribly shaken" rendered in the N.T. "The spears are brandished"
✳☀ Also used in the same manner in France & Egypt ☼ The destruction of the forests being
a contributary cause of the diminished rainfall of Palestine which has reduced the land to such
a state of barreness.

No 37   FRANKINCENSE

"LEBONAH" ~ FRANKINCENSE   FRANKINCENSE-TREE (BOSWELLIA SERRATA
     Ex 30·34 : Rev 2.1 : Neh 13.5: Cant 3.6 : Jer 6.29   (Illustrated)

"Αλβανος" FRANKINCENSE Matt 2.11 : Rev 15.13

Frankincense – One of the ingredients of the incense (Ex 30·34) It was added to the Meat Offering (Lev 2·2), put upon the Shewbread (Lev 24.7), & was one of the gifts presented by the wise men to the Lord Jesus (Matt 2.11). It was a fragrant gum obtained from a tree not native of Palestine, & was brought into the Holy Land from Arabia & Africa (Jer 6.29). Frankincense is the gum resin of the Frankincense Tree (Boswellia serrata) a native of Somali-land & found also (though infrequently) in Arabia. The gum dries into white brittle flakes very bitter to the taste & almost odourless. When ignited however it emits a very powerful & very fragrant odour. The tree rather resembles the Rowan in appearance. The leaves are large, glossy, compound & serrated. The flowers are small, white, star-like, emitting a lemon perfume & arranged in dense clusters. The gum is obtained from incisions made in the bark. There is a species of Boswellia (Boswellia glabra) native of the uplands of India which also produces a fragrant resin which is used with, or instead of, the gum of Boswellia serrata in the incense used by the Roman & Greek Churches but the FRANKINCENSE of Scripture is exclusively the fragrant gum of Boswellia serrata

No 38   GOURD

"KIKAYON" ~ GOURD Jonah 4.5 to 11 *   Species Illustrated GLOBE CUCUMBER
A climbing Gourd of rapid growth & decay, having large leaves,   (CUCUMIS PROPHETARUM)
& trained over arbours in the East as a pleasant shelter from the summer sun. The Bottle Gourd (Cucurbita Pepo) is used for this purpose & also the Globe Cucumber (Cucumis prophetarum) Jonah's Gourd was obviously one of these. Both the R.V & the N.T. give "Gourd" in the text but the former gives "Palma Christi" (which is the Castor Oil Plant) in the margin & the latter a note "Some think it is the Castor Oil plant". The Castor Oil Plant is a large shrubby perennial reaching a height of from twelve to fifteen feet. It bears large palmate leaves with serrated edges, & large spikes of small flowers. From the seeds Castor Oil is produced It occurs in a wild state throughout the East & is extensively cultivated for its seeds. This could not possibly be the gourd of Jonah as it is not an arbour plant nor could it wither so quickly in the manner described * The quickly growing Gourds with their soft watery & slender stems will collapse as quickly if attacked by worms or grubs in the root or
                 stem.

No 39   "WILD GOURD

"PAKKNOTH" ~ WILD GOURD 2 Kings 4.38 & 40   COLOCYNTH (CITRULLUS COLOCYNTHUS) Illustrated
"PEKKAIM" ~ KNOPS 1 Kings 6.18 : 7.24. (R.V. Margin GOURDS, N.T. Text COLOCYNTHS)

"Then one went out into the fields to gather herbs & found a wild vine & gathered from it his lap full of wild colocynths, & came & shred them into the pot of pottage for they did not know them" (2 Kings 4.38. N.T. WILD GOURDS – the poisonous fruit of a wild vine gathered by the young prophet who was sent out by Elisha to gather vegetables. He gathered noxious gourds instead of wholesome species

* R.V. Margin "Palma Christi" N.T. Note "Some think it is the Castor Oil Plant"

* The Vegetable Marrow is a cultivated form of this plant – The fruit being greatly developed.
* The whole incident being a natural process God caused the plant to grow, the worm to attack it, & the plant to perish – The plant must therefore have been one which would die quickly after being attacked by grubs otherwise the significance of the passage is destroyed. One would not limit the power of God all things are possible with Him. A miracle might have no natural explanation [Continued at foot of next page]

Wild Gourd (continued)

(as the Wild Melon). He shredded the fruit, not knowing what it was, & cooked it, & when the pottage was served it was detected as poisonous by it's bitter taste. The Wild Gourds were Colocynths as given in the N.T. They are spherical Gourds about the size of a Grape-Fruit with a bright orange rind, very tempting in appearance but with a nauseous bitter pulp, & evidently poisonous. The Colocynth of medicine is obtained from the dried pulp & the seeds. The plant is very common in the deserts of Palestine & is abundant around Gilgal. It is not found in fertile regions. It trails along the ground with long slender stems furnished with long straggling tendrils & bearing large shiny deeply indented leaves. It bears numerous bright yellow flowers of which the Pistillate are succeeded by an abundance of fruit. This plant would be unknown to a stranger from Bethel but would be reminiscent of the various edible Gourds with which he would be acquainted & it would betray it's poisonous nature by it's bitter taste. Thus the Colocynth accords perfectly with the narrative. It is thought by some that the Vine of Sodom (Deut 32.32) ✳ is the same plant. The knops carved in Cedar wood ornamenting Solomon's temple were probably shaped as Gourds ✳ The Hebrew word "PeKKaim" translated "knop" being the masculine of "PaKKnoth" & the graceful form of the Colocynth fruit would be eminently suitable for decoration

No 40   GALBANUM

"CHELBENAH" – GALBANUM Ex 30.34   GALBANUM OFFICINALE (Illustrated)

A sweet spice used in the mixing of the holy incense. There is a substance today called Galbanum which is a yellow resin obtained from a Syrian plant Galbanum officinale & another gum of the same name obtained from India & Persia. This last is a dark yellow resin which emits a pungent & somewhat disagreeable odour when burnt & is used to ward off mosquitoes. There is some doubt as to the plant from which it is obtained. It has been suggested Ferula galbanifera. It would scarcely seem that the Indian Galbanum could be the Galbanum of Scripture. The Syrian product is more likely

No 41   GALL

"ROSH" – GALL Deut 29.18 : 32.32 : Ps 69.21 : Jer 8.14 : 9.15 : L 5 Species Illustrated   CORN-POPPY
HEMLOCK Hos 10.4 : POISON Deut 32.33 : Job 20.16 : 23.15   PAPAVER RHEAS
✳
"Χολη" – GALL Matt 27.34 : Acts 8.23

A poisonous bitter herb possibly Colocynthus or it may be the Poppy which is very frequent in cornfields & on cultivated land throughout Palestine. ✳ The juice of the Poppy is bitter & poisonous. From the juice of the White Poppy (Papaver somniferum). ✳ Opium is produced. Gall is the translation of the Hebrew "Rosh", twice translated "Poison" (Deut 32.33 : Job 20.16) ✳ & once Hemlock "(Hos 10.4) ✳ It is mentioned often by other with Wormwood. It was from the descriptions of the Scripture a rapidly growing weed of cultivated ground & was very bitter & poisonous. Some have thought that some other plant than than either the Colocynth or Poppy was intended as the Colocynth is not found on cultivated ground whilst the Poppy does not bear berries & it has been considered that from Deut 32.32 "Their grapes are grapes of Gall" some berry bearing plant was intended

---

✳ See No   for notes on "The Vine of Sodom" ✳ Rendered "Gourds" in the Margin of the A.V & "Colocynths" in the text of the N.T. ✳ In these Scriptures it denotes the venom of serpents ✳ See Below. ✳ This species does not apparantly occur in a wild state in Palestine ✳ See No 47 for Notes on the Hemlock ✳ Papaver Rhœas is as frequent in Palestine as Britain occurring in identical localities. The scarlet flowers are

[continued from foot of previous page] but when God uses natural means natural processes follow

No 42   GARLIC

"SHOOM" – GARLIC Numb 11.5   ALLIUM SATIVA (Illustrated)

Mentioned as one of the vegetables which the Israelites had enjoyed in Egypt & after which they lusted in the wilderness. It is akin to the Onion ✳ & much cultivated & appreciated in Southern Europe though in England although cultivated it has nothing like the popularity of the Onion or the Leek. The Garlic with the Onion & the Leek is amongst the most anciently cultivated vegetables & was given divine honours by the Egyptians. It bears in June white flowers with an Onion-like scent, they are comparitively few & are gathered in a terminal head & interspersed with bulbils which drop off with the withering of the flowers & grow into new plants. These bulbils often sprout whilst still on the plant. The root usualy consists of a number of small bulbs clustered together. The whole plant smells strongly of Onion. There are ten species of Garlic occuring in a wild state in Britain but Allium sativa is not amongst them. A number of garlics are native of Palestine & are of frequent occurrence including Allium sativa which is also very commonly cultivated as a vegetable there

No 43   GRASS & HAY

THREE HEBREW WORDS are translated GRASS in the A.V.   Species Illustrated RYE GRASS

(1) "YEREK" Numb 22.4 ✳ — A generic name for green herbage

(2) "DESHER" Gen 1.2 ✳ Signifying "GRASS" in it's true Botanical sense   See Note Below

(3) "CHATZIR" Isa 35.7 : 40.8 d 7 : 51.1 ✳ A generic term for edible herbage ⎱ distinguished from other herbage ⎰ mentioned also many times its entire in Scripture

✳ Selected references

"CHATZIR"-HAY ▬▬▬ Prov 27.25 : ▬ Isa 15.6

▬▬▬ "CHASHAH" – CHAFF Isa 5.24 : 33.11 ■ ("Dried Grass" N.T.)

The Grasses of Palestine may be divided into three groups — GROUP 1 Those of the bare limestone downs of Judea. Short & close, springing up following the rains & withering after a short period. Mostly species native of Arabia & N. Africa. Group 2 The grasses of the maritime plains. Tall & luxuriant in spring but seeding quickly & withering though continuing to grow from below as an after-grass, & providing herbage most of the year. These answer most nearly to ours & consist mainly of South European & a few British Species ✳

Group 3 The grasses of the Jordan Valley & the Dead Sea Basin. Tall, rank, rapidly growing, appearing in very early spring & rapidly seeding & withering, leaving the ground bare, save for the dead stems, for the remainder of the year. These are mostly Arabian & some Sicilian & African species.

The notable characteristic of the Grasses of Palestine is the rapidity with which they spring up in the spring & then quickly seed & die. Thus the transitory character of grass is stressed in the Scripture. "For the sun is no sooner risen with a burning heat, but it withereth the grass, & the flower thereof falleth, & the grace & the fashion of it perisheth : so also the rich man fadeth away in his ways" (James 1.11) = For all flesh is as grass & the glory of

✳ See No 72 Onion & No 53 Leek   ✳ Which may include those listed below ✳ Translated LEEKS Numb 11.5 (See No 53)

Note Grasses

Illustrative of Fodder Grasses PLEASE NOTE The Grasses Illustrated here are British Pasture Grasses. Some may occur in Palestine.

some four inches in diameter with four crumpled unequal petals ✗ numerous black stamens & stigmas forming a disc of ten or twelve rays. The have two concave sepals which are cast off as the flower opens. The leaves are pinnate, each lobe terminating in a boss the [continued at foot of next page]

✗ Two being smaller than the other two

Grass (continued)

man is as the flower of grass. The grass withereth & the flower thereof falleth away "(1 Peter 1.24)
HAY. The Hebrew word "Chatzir" (elsewhere translated "Grass") is translated "Hay" in
Proverbs 28.25 & Isaiah 15.6 ※ It does not signify Hay in the sense in which the term is
used in Britain today but grass mown with the sey that used green as fodder for stalled cattle.
Grass was never cut, dried, & stored for winter use in Biblical times ※. Dried Grass - Grass
which has dried naturally under the hot sun (natural hay) is signified by another Hebrew word
"Chashash" which occurs only twice in the Scripture & is on each occassion translated "CHAFF"
in the A.V ※ ("Dried grass" in the N.T.) Mown grass (Ps 72.6) & the after-grass following the
mowing (Amos 7.1) are also specifically mentioned in the Scripture.

No 44   GROVE

"ASHERAH" - GROVE Ex 34.13 ✡   TAMARISK (TAMARIX GALLICA) Illustrated
"ESHEL" - GROVE - Gen 31.33 ✿ TREE 1 Sam 22.6 ; 1 Sam 31.13 ※
Two Hebrew words are translated GROVE in the Authorised Version both erroneously.
(1) "ASHERAH" - This is supposed to be a wooden image of the godess Asherim. It is translated
"Asherim" in the R.V & "Asherah" in the N.T
(2) "ESHEL" - Occurring only three times, once translated "Grove" & twice "Tree" in the A.V.
Rendered "Tamarisk" in the R.V & N.T. Tamarisk is considered to the correct rendering as the
Modern Arabic name for the Tamarisk is "ASAL" Nine species of Tamarisk occur in Palestine
several of them in great abundance. The most widely distributed is Tamarix Pallasia.
Tamarix gallica occurs, as with us, on the sea shore. They are comparatively small trees, some
not much more than bushes, all bear very small leaves on long feathery branches very graceful &
delicate looking. The flowers are pink or white, small, but gathered in dense spikes.

MANNA

A sweet substance, which melts away & disappears as the sun gains power, is distilled in hot weather
from the Tamarisk. This exudation appears to be drawn forth upon occassion by the heat
of summer, at other times it is the result of the work of a species of Coccus. This is considered a
great delicacy by the Arabs who gather it before sun-rise, boil it, & strain it, & use it as honey is
used. After preserving for a period it forms a hard cake which melts upon exposure to the
sun. It only appears in small quantities & is given the name of "MANNA". The "Manna" of
medicine is a similar secretion obtained from incisions made in the bark of the Manna Ash,
Neither substance has any connection with the MANNA of Scripture. The only resemblence is that both
are sweet & both disappear beneath the heat of the sun, being found only early in the morning
The MANNA was not a vegetable product but a miraculous provision of God

No 45   HAZEL

"LUZ" - HAZEL Gen 30.37 (ALMOND R.V & N.T)   HAZEL (CORYUS AVELLANA) Illustrated
The Hebrew word "LUZ" occurs only once in the Scripture. It is translated "Hazel" in the A.V. &
"Almond" in the R.V & the N.T. As the modern Arabic name of the Almond is "Luz" it would seem
obvious that "Almond" is the correct translation. The Hazel (Coryus avellana) is found in
Galilee but is unknown elsewhere in Palestine. It occurs also on Lebanon. It is a small tree

※ HAY "Prov 22.25. "HERBAGE" Isa 15.6 N.T. ※ Nor is it the practice today in the East ※ - Isa 5.24 ; 23.11.
✴ Selected reference - mentioned also many times elsewhere in Scripture. Ex 34.13. "Groves" A.V. "Asherahs" N.T
with the holy images of the goddess ASHERAH. Possibly the same as ASHTORETH (ASTARTE)
✿ "Tamarisk Tree" R.V. "TAMARISK" N.T. ※ "Tamarisk Tree" R.V. "TAMARISK" N.T.

[continued from foot of Previous Page] The flower stalks are long & tender clothed with bristles springing from the
stalk at right angles. When broken they emit a milky, acrid, narcotic juice. This juice abounds throughout the whole plant
The plant is of annual duration.

Hazel (continued)

with broad leaves, prominently veined, & with irregularly serrated edges. The flowers precede the leaves & are arranged in catkins. The Staminate Catkins are usually found singly or in pairs. They are bright yellow, conspicuous, & pendant. The Pistilate Flowers are arranged in small, rounded, erect heads with imbricate bracts & pink stamens. The fruit is a nut almost globular in shape with a hard brown shell & a pleasantly flavoured sweet crisp white kernel enclosed in a leafy capsule so that only the apex of the nut is visible whilst the nut is green & immature but as the nut ripens the capsule withers & dries but still persists though in a wizened condition upon the mature nut. The Hazel occurs in woods & thickets in Britain & is very frequent. The nuts are greatly appreciated for desert & for use in confectionery.

No 46   HEATH
"ARAR" — JUNIPER Jer 17.6-X-48.6 | JUNIPER (JUNIPERUS SABINA) Illustrated
Mentioned only twice, & the Hebrew name is the same as the Arabic name used today (FRUIT) for a small Juniper which inhabits the driest & rockiest parts of the desert. In favourable situations it attains to the stature of a small tree but in the desert it is a small, stunted, often prostrate, shrub. The leaves are small, linear, & scale like, pressed closely to the stem. The shrub bears numerous purple berries which have the flavour of turpentine. Its stunted growth & generally unhappy appearance is used in the Scripture as a picture of the man who trusts in man — destitute & miserable. The R.V. gives "Tamarisk" in the margin but the plant is obviously Juniper. No species of Heath occurs in Palestine south of Lebanon & only one species occurs there.

No 47   HEMLOCK
"ROSH" — HEMLOCK Elsewhere "GALL"   CONIUM MACULATUM (Illustrated)
"LA'ANAH" — HEMLOCK Elsewhere "WORMWOOD"
Hemlock occurs as a weed of cultivated ground frequently in Palestine, being found in much the same situations as in Britain. It bears its white flowers in compound umbels, has a furrowed stem spotted with dark purple, almost black, stains & delicately cut compound pinnate leaves. It reaches a height, under favourable conditions, of some four feet. The Hemlock is a graceful looking plant but it has a strong unpleasant odour reminiscent of mice & is deadly poisonous.
Hemlock is mentioned twice in the A.V., once in Hosea 10.4 as a translation of "Rosh" elsewhere translated "GALL" ✱ & once in Amos 6.12 as a translation of "La'anah" elsewhere translated "WORMWOOD" ✱. The N.T. retains the rendering "HEMLOCK" in Hosea but gives "WORMWOOD" in Amos, in each instance without comment.

No 48   HERBS
"OROTH" — HERBS   CABBAGE (BRASSICA OLERACEA)
       2 Kings 4.39 : Isa 18.4 : 26.19 elsewhere "LIGHT"   Illustrated
"YARAK" — HERBS Prov 15.7   { Selected References · Mentioned also many times also many
"ESEB" — HERBS Gen 1.11 &2 {   times elsewhere in Scripture
A number of Hebrew words are translated "Herbs" in the A.V. (1) ESEB is used for herbs generally
✱ Jer 16.6 New Translation "Heath" in Text with note "Or a denuded (or forlorn) [man]", & so in Chap 48.6
✱ See No 41 for notes on gall   ✱ See No   for notes on the Wormwood

Herbs (continued)

in contrast to Grass (Gen 1.11 + 12). (2) YARÂK signifies herbs cultivated by man for food (Prov 15.7) (3) OROTH whose root meaning is "light" + is thus translated elsewhere is translated "Herbs" three times in the A.V. + is considered by some authorities to signify some specific food plant, such as the Cole wort or Cabbage *. In 2 Kings 4.39 "wild herbs are meant — wild plants which could be used as food. In Isaiah 18.4 + 26.19 it is considered that some specific cultivated plant is signified — possibly the Cabbage, not otherwise mentioned in Scripture. The Cabbage has been cultivated from an early date + was well known in Old Testament times. The Brussel Sprout, Cauliflower + Broccoli are derived from it. In its wild form it is indigenous to the coasts of Britain. The flowers have four petals + are bright yellow, turning to white as they decay. The fruit is a slender pod + the plant is (in its wild state) of biennial duration. As the root meaning of OROTH is "light" the R.V. gives "sunshine" in Isaiah 18.4 + "light" in Isaiah 26.19 instead of "Herbs" as in the A.V., but retains "Herbs" in 2 Kings 4.39. The N.T. retains "Herbs" in 2 Kings 4.39 + Isaiah 18.4 with the Note in Isaiah 18 "Or sunshine" but gives "morning" in Isaiah 26.19 with the Note "Lit 'the lights' others 'herbs'."

No 49

HUSKS

"Κερατια" – HUSKS Luke 15.16   The Fruit of the CAROB-TREE *
(CERATONIA SILIQUA)

Mentioned only once in Luke 15.16 as a food of   Illustrated
swine. The fruit of the Carob Tree. This is a very frequent tree in Palestine. It reaches a height of thirty feet + bears thick + heavy foliage. The leaves are divided into leaflets, usually six, opposite to each other on the stalk, they have uncut edges + without a terminal leaflet. They are evergreen + very dark + glossy. The flowers have no corolla + open in February. The fruit, borne in great abundance + maturing in May, is a shining purplish — pod, flat + narrow, from six to twelve inches long + about an inch broad. It contains a number of black seeds which are separated from each other by a fleshy pulp. This pod does not open. The fruit, which is very nourishing + which contains a great deal of sweet mucilage is used as a food for cattle horses + swine + is largely exported as a cattle food. The unripe pods are sometimes gathered + eaten as a fruit (The "Locust Beans" sold in shops in Britain being the dried pods of this tree). The ripe fruits are sometimes used as food by the very poor. They are given the name of "Locusts" + are popularly but erroneously believed to be the Locust which together with wild honey formed the food of John the Baptist

---

No 50

HYSSOP

"ÊZOB" – HYSSOP Ex 12.22:   CAPPER   (CAPPARIS SPINOSA) Illustrated
Lev 14.4: Numb 19.6:19.18: 1 Kings 4.33: Ps 51.7.
"Ύσσωπος" – HYSSOP John 19.29: Heb 9.19

Hyssop is frequently mentioned in the Scripture. It was used to sprinkle the door posts of the Israelites in Egypt with the blood of the Paschal Lamb (Ex 12.22) It was employed in the purification of the leper (Lev 14.14) + leprous houses (Lev 14.51) in the sin offering (Numb 19.6) + the sponge filled with vinegar at the Crucifixion of the Lord was filled with vinegar placed upon Hyssop (John 19.29) It was the lowliest of herbs (1 Kings 4.33)

* Others consider "Mallows." *- The R.V. gives "Husks" in the text + in the Margin "The pods of the Carob Tree" The N.T. gives "Husks" without comment

Hyssop (continued)

was found in Egypt, in the Sinai Desert, & in Palestine, & grew out of the walls &
cliffs. All this is quite clear from the Scripture but there is some doubt as to what
the Hyssop really was. It is generally accepted that it was the Capper (Capparis
spinosa) a creeping shrub common in the deserts & upon ruins, walls, & cliffs
throughout the East. Others consider that it was the plant known as Hyssop
today (Origanum maru) as, being used for sprinkling it would need to be a plant
with a hairy stem & leaves. The plant has thick, hairy, leaves & branches & is
common on walls & cliffs throughout Palestine. It bears purple flowers. Because
of it's lowly stature the Hyssop is the symbol of lowliness & humility in the
Scripture

CAPPER (CAPPARIS SPINOSA)

DESIRE Eccl 12.5 A.V   "Desire shall fail" Eccl 12.5 (A.V.)
CAPPER-BERRY Eccl 12.5 R.V. & N.T.   "The Capper - berry shall fail" Eccl 12.5 R.V.-✻-

                 "The Capper berry is without effect" Eccl 12.5 N.T. ✳

The Capper is a common plant in Palestine growing on walls, rocks, & ruins. It is frequent
in the Sinai desert & on the ruins & rocks of Egypt. It is a small spiny shrub
with weak trailing branches, oval, smooth, shiny, dark green leaves, large white
flowers & an oval fruit. The spines are small & re-curved, borne two at the base
of each leaf. The flowers have four petals, open wide, & have numerous pink anthers.
The fruit is a pod, oval, & about the size of a Walnut. The flower-buds are
pickled & used extensively as a condiment & are the CAPPERS of commerce.
The Capper is not mentioned in the A.V. but in the description of old age in Eccl
12.5 where the A.V. gives "desire shall fail" the R.V. gives "The Capper berry shall fail"
& the N.T. "The Capper-berry is without effect". The significance being that the
Capper eaten before a meal to stimulate the appetite cease to have it's effect upon
the aged

No 51   JUNIPER   (RETAMA RÆTAMA)   Illustrated
"ROTHEM" 1Kings 19. 4 + 5   RETAMA _____
"ROTEM" - JUNIPER - 1Kings 19. 4 + 5 ✳ Job 30.4 ✻ Ps 120.4 ✶

The Hebrew word "Rothem" is translated "Juniper" in the A.V. The plant intended was
a species of Broom — the Retama (Retama retama) known today to the Arabs as "RETAMA"
It is a shrub reaching a height of some ten feet which is found in Palestine only in the
Dead Sea basin & in the sandy ravines leading down into the Jordan Valley, but in
these localities is abundant. It is exceedingly plentiful in the Sinai Desert & is
essentially a desert shrub, never occurring on fertile ground. The Retama is deciduous &
the foliage is sparse at any time but the branches although slender & delicate in
appearance grow very densely & the shrub affords a grateful shade from the desert sun
& a shelter from the storms of the wilderness (1Kings 19.4 + 5) The flowers appear in
February before the leaves & are pinkish white. They crowd the tree like the flowers of the
Hawthorn do & are like the flowers of the White Broom of the garden — The tree is a
mass of delicate, pink & white & most conspicuous & very beautiful. The root-stock is
thick, in contrast to the slender stems & is made into a greatly valued charcoal (Ps 120.4)
The N.T gives "Broom bush" & the R.V. "Broom" in 1Kings 19.4 + 5 & in Job 30.4. In Ps 120.4

-✻- R.V. "Desire" in margin   ✳ N.T. Note ² Or it may be rendered "And desire hath failed"
✳ "Broom bush" N.T. "Broom" R.V. -✶- "Broom bush" N.T. "Juniper" Text R.V. "Broom" Margin
✶

Juniper (continued)

The N.T. again gives "Broom bush" whilst the R.V gives "Juniper" in the Text & "Broom" in the Margin. ✳ One of the resting places of the Israelites in the wilderness was Rithma — "the place of the Broom" (Numb 33.18)

No 52   LADANUM

LÔT - MYRRH Gen 37.25; 43.11 ✳ | Yielded by the GUM CISTUS Species Illustrated
"Behold a company of Ishmaelites came from Gilead with their \ CISTUS SALVIFOLIUS
camels bearing spicery ✳ & balm ✳ & myrrh ❀ going to carry it down to Egypt " NOTE
"Carry down the man a present, a little balm & a little honey ➝ ⌐Gen 37.25 ✳
spices ✿ & myrrh & nuts # & almonds " Gen 43.11 ✳
The Hebrew word "LÔT" occurs only twice in the Scripture (Gen 37.25 & Gen 43.11) & is
translated "Myrrh" in the A.V. It is translated "Ladanum" in the N.T. Ladanum is
considered to be the substance intended as Myrrh is not a product of Palestine but is imported
from Arabia & the "Myrrh" of Gen 37 & 43 was an export. ✳ Ladanum is the
fragrant resin which exudes from the leaves & branches of the Gum Cistus. It was
formerly greatly valued. Ladanum was gathered by brushing the plant (whilst the sun
was hot) with a loose brush consisting of long slender leather thongs. Several
species of Cistus yield Ladanum. They are all hill side plants favouring the same
situations which their relatives the Rock-roses inhabit in Britain. Cystus
Salvifolius bears yellowish white flowers & C. creticus & villosus bright pink flowers
All vary on occasion to white. The flowers of all species are large & conspicuous, densely
covering the plants which attain to a height of little more than two feet on the outside.
The leaves are simple, oblong, glossy & evergreen. These plants abound on Mount
Gum Ladanum whilst possessing a far sweeter fragrance has the properties ⌐Carmel
of Opium, though in a lesser degree, & it is from this fact that the name of
Ladanum was given to the essence of Opium. Ladanum was formerly greatly
valued for its medicinal properties but it is rarely used today

No 53   LEEK

"CHATZIR"   ALLIUM PORRUM (Illustrated)
"HHATZIR" — LEEKS Numb 11.5 Elsewhere "GRASS" (See No 43)
Mentioned only once in the Scripture log the with the Garlic & Onion amongst the
pleasant vegetables which the Israelites had enjoyed in Egypt & for which they longed
& lusted in the wilderness. The Leek was a favourite vegetable in Egypt where it was
held sacred. It bears a dense head of white flowers in June, has an Onion-like
scent, but does not produce bulbils. The bulb is more slender & the leaves broader
than those of the Onion. The leaves are linear, flattened & channelled & of a bright green hue.
The Leek is a greatly appreciated vegetable & is extensively cultivated in Egypt &
Palestine. The Hebrew word "CHATZIR" translated here Leek is of frequent occurrence
in the Scripture & is on every other occasion translated "Grass" & "Grass" is correct

✳ With in the Margin for "are their meat" "To warm them" — the suggestion being that the roots of
the Broom were used for fuel. ✳ MYRRH in these scriptures is Ladanum. Elsewhere the Hebrew word
"MOR" is translated MYRRH which is correct. X- Tragacanth ✳ Balsam ❀ Ladanum. Note "An aromatic
gum" N.T. ✿ "Myrrh" in Text "Ladanum" in Margin R.V ❀ Balsam ❂ Tragacanth § Ladanum
Pistacia Lutis N.T. ✦ "Myrrh" without comment in the R.V. ✸ For details concerning "Myrrh" see
No 65 ✿ Note Coloured Illustration CISTUS CRETICUS ✿ See No 42 Garlic ✳ See No 22 Onion

Leek (continued)

The Leek with it's bright green grass-like leaves might well be signified by the same word. Some authorities however considering that the usual meaning of the word is "Grass" claim that the plant intended here is the Fenugreek ~~Trigonella~~ (Trigonella foenum-graecum) a species of ~~Lucerne~~ commonly cultivated as a food plant in Egypt, the contention being that the ~~Hebrew~~ word "CHATZIR" signifies "Grass" in a general manner — all manner of ~~herbage~~ low growing edible herbage, true Grass & the edible & nutritious herbs which grow together with it (as Clover, Lucerne & Sain-foin). And the Fenugreek is the most likely plant intended, being in its wild state a plant of the meadows.

No 54   LENTIL

"ADASHIM"—LENTILS   ERVUM LENS (Illustrated)

Gen 25.34. 2 Sam 17.28 : 23.11 : Ezek 4.9.

Lentils are the small dark red lens-like seeds of a small Vetch-like plant — ERVUM LENS extensively cultivated in Palestine & the Orient. The plant bears much resemblance to some of the wild Vetches which are so frequent in England. It is a slender climbing plant bearing small white flowers & small rounded pods containing three or four seeds. The seeds are very ~~nutritious~~ & the Lentil has been appreciated & cultivated in the East from the earliest times. The amount of seed produced is apt to be scanty in comparison to the amount of room needed to develope the plant's but so much is the Lentil esteemed in the East that today it is the staple crop in some districts of Palestine. Several species of Lentil are cultivated but the Red Lentil is most valued. This is the species commonly used today in Britain for stews etc. Revalenta Arabica is the flour of Lentils & it is very nutritious. The seeds, stewed, are made into a red pottage as in the days of Esau (Gen 25.30) Lentils were amongst the provisions brought to David when he fled from Absalom (2 Sam 17.28) Shammah defended & preserved a field of Lentils from the Philistines (2 Sam 17.11) They were together with Wheat, Barley, Beans, Millet, & Spelt made into bread by Ezekiel (Ezek 4.9). The Lentil harvest is later than the Wheat harvest. The crop is cut & threshed like corn

No 55   LILY

"SHUSAN" 1 Kings 7.13 : 7.26 :   Species Illustrated WHITE LILY
-LILY   2 Chron 4.5 : Cant 2.1 & 2 & 16 : 4.5 : 5.13 : 6.2 & 3 : 55 (LILIUM
"KPLVOV"—LILY Matt 6.28 : Luke 12.27 Cant 7.2 : Hos 14.5. 55A TULIP

The Hebrew word "SHUSAN" translated Lily denotes some ~~~~ (TULIPA GESNERIANA) beautiful & conspicuous flower. There is much doubt however as to the particular flower intended. The modern Arabic word "SUSAN" is a generic term denoting any startlingly conspicuous indigenous flower & "SHUSAN" may have the same significance, but where mentioned in Kings & Chronicles some specific plant would seem to be intended. The Scarlet Martagon Lily (Lilium chalcedonicum) is indigenous to Palestine but is infrequent. Various Liliaceous plants abound there. The Tulip (Tulipa gesneriana) the Fritillary (Fritillaria persica) the Star-of-Bethlehem (Ornithogalum umbellatum) & the Autumnal Squill (Scilla autumnalis). Iris caucasicum occurs, also Gladiolus

Lily (continued)

Byzantinus & the Polyanthus Narcissus (Narcissus tazetta) Some authorities consider that the word "SHUSAN" is derived from a root signifying "to be white" & claim that the White Lily, the Maddonna Lily (Lilium   ) is the plant intended but this Lily though cultivated in Palestine is not known to grow wild there. Others consider that the ~~████████████~~ Lily of Scripture must be a red ~~████~~. ~~████~~ flower as it is ~~████~~ compared in the Song to the lips of the Beloved. The Tulip (Tulipa gesneriana) bears large, beautiful, brilliantly red, flowers. It is frequent throughout most of the country. It grows in valleys & on the plains amidst the thorny shrubs where the gazelles abound bearing out Song 2.1 & 2 & 4.5. It is cultivated in gardens (Song 6.2) It thrives on the rocky hillsides, springing up between the stones. It is of comparatively vigorous & rapid growth as would seem to be the significance of Hosea 14.5. It appears in the Spring. (As the flower of Roses in the spring of the year, as lilies by the river of waters. Ecclesiasticus 50.8) It is of a beautiful chalice-like form, eminently suitable for decorative work as it was employed in Solomon's temple (1 Kings 8.26 & 2 Chron 4.5). If a specific flower is intended the Tulip fits the Old Testament description of the Lily better than any. The Lily of the New Testament is more probably the Poppy Anemone (Anemone coronaria)

No 56   LILY-OF-THE-FIELD

"KPIVOV" - LILY Matt 6.28. Luke 12.27   SCARLET ANEMONE
(ANEMONE CORONARIA)
Illustrated

Many & liacious plants abound in Palestine of which the Tulip (Tulipa gesneriana) is the most striking & conforms most nearly to the Old Testament description of the Lily, but all these species although abundant & conspicuous all grow more or less individually — they do not grow in extensive colonies or carpet the ground over large areas. The Scarlet Anemone with it's large, bright red flowers covers extensive areas throughout Palestine in all regions, soils & situations. From February to April the plains & hillsides are a splash of with the abundance of the Anemone — The Scarlet Poppy covering the cornfields of Britain will give a picture of the effect. It is the most conspicuous of all the flowers of the wild & therefore the most likely to be the "Lily of the Field" used by the Lord Jesus as an illustration of the care of God. The flower concerned must have been very beautiful very brilliant or very conspicuous. The Scarlet Anemone is extensively cultivated as a garden plant under the name of Poppy Anemone. In it's wild state it bears crimson flowers but under cultivation they vary to pink white & purple as well as their original crimson. The flowers have no petals but the sepals (five to seven in number) are petaloid & brightly tinted. The foliage is bright green & richly cut as also are the bracts beneath the solitary flower. The root is tuberous.

No 57   MALLOWS

"MALLUACH" - MALLOWS Job 30.4 ✱   ORACHE (ATRIPLEX HALIMUS)
illustrated

Mentioned only as a food of the most abject & miserable of the poor: The root from which the Hebrew word is derived denotes "Saltiness", therefore both the R.V. & N.T. give "Saltwort". This however is unfortunate as it is misleading, the name Saltwort being given only to the Salsola Kali ✱ common on the sandy coasts of Britain, on the sea coast of Palestine &

✱ "Saltwort" R.V. & N.T.   ✱ For a description of the Saltwort (Salsola Kali) see under Soap No

Mallows (continued)

in the marshes of the Dead Sea Basin, which could not have been the plant intended as it cannot be said under any circumstances to be edible. It was most probably some species of Orache of which several species occur on the shores of the Mediteranean & the Dead Sea & in the salt marshes of the desert. There is one species Striplex halimus which forms dense thickets in such localities. It bears small thick leaves on dense thin twigs & terminal clusters of small purple flowers. It is a shrub reaching a height of from eight to ten feet. The leaves might be eaten as are those of its near relative the Garden Orache (A. hortensis) but they are sour to the palate & would make a most unsatisfying & miserable food.

No 58   MALOBATHRON

"BETHER" Suggested in the R.V. margin   CINNOMONIUM MALOBATHRON
Song 2.17 | as possibly the spice MALOBATHRON   (Illustrated)

Malobathron was a spice formerly much valued in the East. It was the fragrant leaf the the Cinnomonium malobathron steeped in wine or oil & used as a perfume or medicine. The tree is a native of India. It is not mentioned in the Scripture but in the Song of Solomon where is mentioned "the mountains of Bether" (2.17) the R.V. retaining "Bether" in the Text gives in the Margin "Perhaps the spice Malobathron". The N.T. also retains "Bether" in the Text with a note "Cloven or full of ravines". The suggestion being in the R.V. that "the mountains of Bether" denotes "the mountains of Malobathron" & in the N.T. "the mountains of Ravines" No information is available as to whether Malobathron was ever cultivated in Palestine but it is very doubtful.

No 59   MANDRAKE

"DUDÂÎM" – Gen 30.14 & 16: Cant 7.13 | MANDRAGORA OFFICINALIS
     (Illustrated)
The Mandrake is mentioned in two passages of Scripture.
In Genesis 30. 14 & 16 it is mentioned in connection with it's supposed ※ NOTE virtues in love incantations for which it has been widely famous from the earliest times & in the Song 7.13 the fragrance of the Mandrake is mentioned as one of the pleasures of Spring. The Mandrake is a plant of peculiar appearance. The dark green leaves, a foot long & some four inches wide, appear in very early spring, forming a dense rosette upon the ground. The flowers spring singly from their midst (the plant being stemless) some borne upon a short stalk & some stalkless, & open in favourable localities as early as December but but generally in January & February. They are cup shaped, five lobed, & of a bright purple colour. The succeeding fruit is a large spherical, yellow berry about the size of a large plum. It has a pleasant fragrance & is sweet & appatising to the palate & has narcotic properties but not in such a degree as to make it dangerous to eat. It matures with the Wheat harvest in April & May. The fruit

---

※ See Cassia No 17 & Cinnamon No 21 -※- Note.

Mandrake (continued)

is still valued in Palestine & the East today for the same superstitious reasons as in the days of Jacob. The large tap-root frequently forks & bears on occasion a rough resemblence to the human figure. The Mandrake is affiliated to the Potatoe & the Nightshade & is frequent throughout Palestine especially inhabiting neglected fields. Many strange superstitions attach to it. It was employed in love incantations. It resembled in shape a man & when dug from the ground it moaned & shrieked. As it's shriek was fatal to any who heard it the usual method of procuring it was to tie a dog to the base of the stout leaves. The creature in it's struggles tore it up but was instantly killed by it's shrieks. The fragrance of the Mandrake (save the fruit which, as already stated, is pleasantly scented) is not acceptable to Europeans but is not considered disagreable by the natives of the East. The Hebrew name "Dudaim" signifies "Love Plants" & it is perhaps for this reason that the R.V margin gives "Love Apples". This however is in correct as the name "Love Apple" belongs only to the Tomatoe which is an American plant. The N.T gives "Mandrake" without comment.

No 60   MELON

"ABATTICHIM" MELONS Numb 11.5   CUCURBITA CITRULLUS (Illustrated)

The Melon is mentioned once in the Scripture along with the Cucumber as being lusted after & longed for by the Israelites in the wilderness. The Cucumber, the Melon & the Pumpkin were extensively cultivated in Egypt from an early date. Their cool & refreshing juices make them invaluable in such hot climates & they would have been welcome indeed in the arid wilderness. Two closely allied fruits share the name of Melon & both have been cultivated from times immemorial. The Water Melon (Cucurbita citrullus) attains a gigantic size frequently exceeding thirty pounds in weight. The flesh is pink, interspersed with black seeds, icy cold, watery, & practicaly tasteless. Its abundant juices & its excessive coldness make it exceedingly valuable in the East especially in the long, hot, dry summers which characterise those regions. The juice is also used as a drink. The Common Melon (C. melo) is the species commonly sold in shops in Britain. It does not attain to the size of the Water Melon though never-theless it is a large fruit. The flesh is more solid, the juice less abundant but sweeter than that of the Water Melon. Both are widely cultivated in Egypt & Palestine today. There is a succession of fruits from May to November.

No 61   MILLET

"DOCHAN" - MILLET EzeK 4.9   Species Illustrated PANICUM MILIACEUM

Mentioned only once in Ezekiel 4.9 together with Wheat, Barley, Beans, Lentils & Fitches of which the prophet was commanded to make bread, obviously employing every substance which was used for that purpose. Several species of Millet are cultivated in the East, or perhaps rather, several species of small-seeded cereal are cultivated under the name of Millet. They supply a large amount of food in these regions. The most extensively cultivated species is Panicum miliaceum. The seeds are very small but are much eaten, often un-cooked by the poor. The plant is tall growing & is sometimes cultivated for fodder, being for this purpose cut whilst the stem is

Millet (continued)

juicy & green before the ripening of the seed. The straw is also employed for fodder being frequently fed to horses. The Arabic name of this species is _____ Dukan. The Indian Millet (Sorghum vulgare) is closely related to the last species & has likewise been cultivated in Palestine from an early date. The Arabic name of this Millet is Dhourrha. The seeds of this species are used in the same way as those of Panicum miliaceum but the stem is more woody & is of less value for fodder. The seeds of all species are used only for bird-seed in Britain.

PANNAG

"PANNAG" Ezek 27.17. An article of merchandise brought by the Israelites to Tyre. The word is the Hebrew left untranslated in the A.V. & N.T. but with a note in the latter "Perhaps a sort of confection". Rendered "Sweet cakes" in the N.T. "Balsam" in the Vulgate & "Millet" in the Syriac. Some suggest that it must be some sort of confection, others consider it to be the Panese but this is the Ginseng an Indian drug & does not fit the context. Others claim that "Pannag" is Millet.

No 62 — MINT

"Ηδνοσμον" – MINT   HORSE MINT (MENTHA LONGIFOLIA) ※
Matt 23.23 : Luke 11.4   Illustrated

Mint was used by the Jews as a condiment & is said to have been one of the Bitter Herbs used at the Passover ※ The Horse Mint (Mentha longifolia) is the species cultivated in Palestine. The leaf is broader & more hairy & the flavour is stronger than that of the Spear-mint (Mentha spikata) commonly used for the same purpose in Britain. The flowers are lilac & arranged in whorls. Mint is mentioned in Scripture only in Matt 23.23 & Luke 11.42 as one of the unimportant condiments which the Pharisees scrupulously tithed whilst neglecting the judgment & the love of God. For this they were rebuked by the Lord ✱ Several other species of Mint occur in a wild state in Palestine but Mentha longifolia is the species commonly cultivated.

No 63 — MULBERRY

"BECAÎM" – MULBERRY   ASPEN (POPULUS TREMULA)
1 Chron 14.14 & 15 : 2 Sam 5.23 & 24   Illustrated
Also occuring in Ps 84.6 as "BACA" signifying "WEEPING" ✦

MULBERRY occurs twice in the Scripture as the translation of the Hebrew word BECAÎM which also occurs in Ps 84.6 where it is rendered "BACA" – "Who passing through the valley of Baca make it a well" The A.V. gives in the Margin for this verse "Or. Who passing through the valley of mulberry trees make him a well ✦ The two other passages where this word occurs both relate one incident same incident

※ Formerly MENTHA SYLVESTRIS. ✦ See Note on BITTER HERBS No 12

✱ See also Notes on ANISE (No 4) & RUE (No) ✦ It is generally accepted that the significance of "BACA" is "WEEPING" & the N.T. gives a note "Or. Weeping" for this word which is retained in the text. The A.V. however gives no hint of "Weeping" but gives in the Margin "Or Mulberry trees". The implication being that the Valley of Baca" means "the Valley of Mulberry trees" & as already noted "BACA" in the original Hebrew
[continued at foot of next page]

Mulberry (continued)

"When David enquired of the Lord he said, Thou shall not go up; but fetch a compass behind them, & come upon them over against the mulberry trees And let it be when thou hearest of a going in the tops of the mulberry trees, that thou shalt bestir thyself for then is the Lord gone out before you to smite the Philistines" (2 Sam 5. 23 & 24) "Therefore David enquired again of God; & God said unto him, Go not up after them; turn away from them, & come upon them over against the Mulberry trees. And it shall be, when thou shalt hear a sound of going in the tops of the mulberry trees, that then shalt thou go out to battle; for God is gone forth before thee to smite the host of the Philistines" (1 Chron 14. 14 & 15) There is some doubt as to which tree is intended. The LXX gives "Pear Trees" which is not possible. The R.V. gives "Balsam Trees" in the margin, but the Balm - of - Gilead does not occur in the mountains. There is an Arabian gum - Tree which is known today by the name of "BACA" but this likewise does not occur in the mountain valley of Rephaim nor does the Mulberry given without comment in the A.V. & the N.T. It is generally considered that the tree in question is the Aspen (Populus tremula) — the Trembling Poplar. The leaves of this Poplar are practically always on the move. The leaf-stalk is long & slender & flattened & the leaves stir at the least breath of wind. "The sound of a going in the tops of the Mulberry Trees" would thus be the characteristic rustle of the leaves of the Aspen. This stirring was the signal for David to go into battle. The leaves of the Aspen are almost round & have serrated edges. — They are downy when young. The flowers open in March & April. The tree is tall-growing & the branches are of spreading habit. The bark is grey. The Aspen is common in woods in Britain & in the highlands of Palestine. The true Mulberry is mentioned in Scripture under the name of Sycamine (See Note on the Sycamine No 86)

No 64   MUSTARD

"Σιναπι" — MUSTARD   SINAPIS NIGRE   (Illustrated)

Matt 13. 31 & 32 : 17. 20 : Mark 4. 31 & 32 : Luke 13. 18 & 19 : 17. 6

Mustard is mentioned only in the New Testament & only in connection with three incidents. On each occasion the smallness of the seed is the significant point. In the the Parable of the Mustard Seed (Matt 13. 31) the smallness of the seed is contrasted with the subsequent largeness of the matured plant & used as an illustration of the small beginning of Christendom & the great proportions to which it eventually attains. Again the smallness of the Mustard seed is the significance of it's employment as the measure of faith in Matthew 17. 20 & likewise in Luke 17. 6. Mustard was used as a condiment in Palestine in the same manner as it is commonly used in Britain today & was obtained from the same plant — Brassica sinapioides. This plant (established, though not very frequently,

---

[continued from the foot of previous page] is "BECÂIM" which is translated "MULBERRY" in the other two passages where it occurs. Therefore the rendering "Mulberry trees" that is "Valley of Mulberry trees" is correct. Correct that is in denoting the valley as the valley of the trees mentioned in the previous passages — the same trees, though not Mulberries but more probably Aspens as explained above. Scofield omits the A.V. Marginal note "Mulberry

Mustard (continued)

in England as an original escape from cultivation) is indeginous in the Jordan Valley & on the maritime plains where it covers vast areas, in the Autumn with a sheet of gold as the Charlock (Sinapis sinapistrum) covers the cornfields of Britain. It grows very luxuriantly in the semi-tropical regions of the Jordan Valley reaching on occasion a height of eight feet, & throughout Palestine (where it is commonly cultivated in gardens for the sake of it's seeds from which the Mustard of commerce is produced) it's general height is four or five feet. In Britain it two or three feet. Some have suggested that the "Mustard Tree" (Salvadora persica) which bears pungent seeds which are used as Mustard by the Arabs was the "Mustard" intended in the parable as the Black Mustard does not "become a tree". But this tree is not found north of Engedi. It would not be familiar to those whom the Lord addressed (as would the Black Mustard), & it could not be described as the greatest amongst herbs, & the seeds are much larger than those of the Mustard. The Black Mustard meets all the requirements of the test. From a humble beginning (the smallness of the Mustard Seed was proverbial ✳) it attains to the greatest of herbs ▽, so as to become in effect a tree upon which the birds of the air can rest — The small birds of Palestine do so today, flocking after the seed to which they are very partial

No 65   MYRRH
BALSAMODENDRON MYRRHA

"MOR" – MYRRH Ex 30.23: Ps 45.8: Prov 7.17.   (Illustrated)
Cant 1.13: 3.6: 4.6: 14: 5.1: 5.13: Esth 2.12
"Σμυρνα" – MYRRH Matt 2.11: Mark 15.23: John 19.39
"LÔT" translated MYRRH in Gen 37.25 & 43.11 is LADANUM (See No 52)
A fragrant spice frequently mentioned in Scripture. It was an ingredient of the holy anointing oil (Ex 30.23) was used as a perfume (Ps 45.8: Prov 7.17) was used in the purification of women (Esther 2.2) as an anodyne (Mark 15.23) & for embalming (John 19.39). Myrrh was one of the gifts brought by the wise men to the Lord Jesus (Matt 2.11). It is a gum resin obtained from a small spiny tree found in Arabia & Eastern Africa & Eastern Africa. Incisions are made in the bark & a white viscid liquid oozes forth. This rapidly hardens on exposure to the air to a gum which is the Myrrh of commerce. The tree bears small bright green trifoliate leaves & small white flowers. The foliage is sparse & the spines long sharp & numerous. The bark & wood emit an aromatic odour. In Scriptural

---

✳ But the plant is always of annual duration however large a size it might reach
✳ Not literally the smallest seed there are many smaller but the Mustard seed was a symbol of smallness to the Jews "Small as a grain of Mustard seed" was a proverbial expression amongst them, & it was this common figure familiar & unmistakable to His hearers which the Lord Jesus employed.
▽ Matt 13.32. In this verse Mustard is stated to a herb "Λαχανον" (lit "garden herb") which becomes a tree "Δενδρον". Definitely a garden herb, tree like in growth
trees & gives instead a Note "Or weeping". Not a literal valley but any place of teats". The facts seem to be that the literal meaning is Valley of Mulberries — the Valley of the specific trees mentioned in 1 Chron 14.14 & 2 Sam 5.23. but the word has also a symbolical significance of Weeping

Myrrh (continued)

times the gum was obtained from Arabia & was used, in addition to the purpose already mentioned, as a stimulative medicine. Balsamodendron myrrha is of the same genus as the Balm of Gilead Tree (Balsamodendron Gileadense). Myrrh is sweetly fragrant yet of a very bitter flavour & typifies in Scripture the bitterness of death & the sweetness of the death of Christ

No 66   MYRTLE

"HADAS" MYRTLE   MYRTUS COMMUNIS (Illustrated)

Neh 8.15 : Isa 41.19 : 55.13 : Zech 1.8

"ETZ-ÀBOTH" – THICK TREES Lev 23.40 : Neh 8.15 : Ezek 20.28 ✡

Claimed by the Rabbinical authorities to be the MYRTLE

The Myrtle is a small tree indigenous to Southern Europe & Western Asia. It is frequent by the sides of streams on the hill sides of Palestine, & in the localities where the Sweet Laurel ✳ occurs both trees may be found growing together. The foliage of the Myrtle is semi-evergreen ✗, dark & glossy, ovate-lanceolate, & covered with transparent dots, resultant from the presence of a volatile strongly aromatic oil. The flowers are small white & sweetly fragrant. The fruit is an aromatic black berry. The dried flowers, fruit, & leaves are used as a perfume & further, from the flowers a fragrant water is distilled. Today the bark & root are used in Damascus for tanning leather to which they impart a distinctive perfume. Articles made of this leather are highly prized. The Myrtle has always been a valued tree where ever it is found. For this reason it is recorded as one of the blessings of the Millenial earth. (Isa 41.19 : 55.13) It was used by the returned remnant at the restoration of the Feast of the Tabernacles (Neh 8.15) & is still used today in synagogues at the celebration of this feast. It is maintained by the Rabbinical writers that the Hebrew "Etz-aboth" translated "Thick Trees" in Lev 23.40. Neh 8.15. & Ezek is the specific name of the Myrtle & that the Myrtle is especially intended. Therefore the boughs of thick trees used in the construction of the booths at the Feast of the Tabernacles were boughs of Myrtle. This reason the Jews employ the Myrtle (as already noted) in the celebration of the Feast of the Tabernacles. The N.T retains "Thick trees" in Neh 8.15 & Ezek 20.28 but gives "Leafy trees" in Lev 23.40

66

No 67   NETTLES

"KIMMOSH" – NETTLES Isa 34.13 : Hos 9.6 Species Illustrated   GREAT NETTLE

"KIMMESHONIM" – THORNS Prov 24.30 & 31 ✳   (URTICA DIOICA)

The Hebrew word "KIMMOSH" translated Nettles in Proverb. 24.31. Isaiah 34.13 & Hosea 9.6.

✳ Leafy trees Lev 23.40
Thick trees Neh 8.15 Ezek 20.28   ✳ Reaching a height of some twenty feet ✳ For Notes on The BAY-TREE see No 10
✗ The Laurel (   ) is a familiar example of a semi-evergreen. The foliage is glossy & has every appearance of an evergreen. In a mild winter the entire foliage will be maintained, in a normal winter few leaves will be shed, the tree maintaining along with branches of Citron & Willow most of its foliage even though frost & snow occur. The individual leaf will live for three or four years & ... in a severe winter all the foliage is shed & the tree has only bare branches but is unharmed

✳ "KIMMESHONIM" rendered thorns in the A.V is another form of "KIMMOSH" & would seem to obviously mean the same plant.

Nettles (continued)

Another form of the same word "KIMMESHONIM" is rendered "THORNS" in Proverbs 24.31. Nettles is indisputably the correct translation. Several species occur in Palestine infesting waste places & ruins. The most frequent species is the Roman Nettle (~~~~ Urtica pilulifera) a stout & vigorous plant & a persistant weed which reaches a height of five or six feet & has a most virulent sting. This plant is of annual duration & bears ovate coarsely-toothed leaves, small greenish-white flowers & a globous fruit arranged in stalked clusters. It is ~~~~ hairless except for the stings. The Roman Nettle occurs rarely & locally in Eastern England usually near the sea. It is much smaller here than in Palestine attaining but a height of some two feet & giving place in size to the Common Nettle (Urtica dioica) but it's sting is more painful than the sting of that species. The Common Nettle is almost as common as the Roman Nettle in Palestine frequenting like localities. It reaches much the same height but is of a slighter build & less virulent in the effect of it's sting. This is the species so common in Britain & is of perennial duration with a long creeping rootstock & cordate deeply serrated leaves square hairy stems & small green flowers arranged in long branching clusters. The plant is edible & can be cooked & eaten as a vegetable. It is said to have been used as one of the Bitter Herbs ✳ eaten with the Paschal Lamb.

Another word "CHARUL" is also translated "Nettles". The root meaning of this word is "that which burns" & the plant intended must therefore be one which stings as the Nettle. Some have thought that this is a general term & others that it ~~~~ denotes the Acanthus ✳

No 68   NUTS

"BOTNÌM" – NUTS Gen 43.11   PISTACHIA NUT (PISTACIA VERA)

Two words are translated "Nuts" in the A.V. Each word | ILLUSTRATED
occurring only once.

(1) BOTNÌM (Gen 43.11) Mentioned amongst the costly articles sent by Jacob as the present to the Governor of Egypt. Given "Pistachia Nuts" in the N.T. text & the R.V. margin. This is correct. The Pistacia Nut is the fruit of the Pistachia Tree a tree affiliated with to the Terebinth ✳ & Mastic ✳ & intermediate in height between the two. The nut consists of a hard shell enclosed in a dry outer skin with a green, sweet, oily kernel. The shape of the fruit is oval & the flavour reminiscent of the Walnut. An oil is compressed from the kernel. The shell is bright red or vivid green in colour. The Pistachio Tree is a native of rocky & mountainous places from Syria to Afghanistan. It was formerly found frequently on the mountain ranges of Palestine but is very rare there today. It has been cultivated throughout the East from an early date but it was not to be found in Egypt & so its fruit would be acceptable as a very rare & enjoyable luxury in that land. The foliage much ~~~~ that of the Terebinth but the leaflets are ~~~~. It's bright green & deciduous. The tree is dioecious ✳ & the fruit is born in clusters close to the main stem. The crop is very abundant but the nuts do not keep well so they are never imported into Britain. The name of the ~~~~ town of

---

✳ Because it contains a ~~~~ ~~~~ ~~~~ the ~~~~ Nettle or the Roman Nettle it is commonly class'd as the Water Nettle in Britain. ✳ See No 12 ~~~~ Notes on the Bitter Herbs ✳ See also THORN (IV) NETTLE (CHARUL) ACANTHUS. No 100. ✳ See FIL-TREE No   ✳ See No 8
~~~~ ~~~~ Notes on the ~~~~ ✳ ~~~~

Nuts (continued)

Betonium (Josh 13.26) is derived from "Botnim" signifies the abundance of the Pistachio Tree in Palestine at that date: The Arabic name of the Pistachio is "BATAM" today.

(2) EGOZ (Song 6.11) This is the Walnut (Juglans regia) which is indigenous in Persia & the highlands of Palestine & Syria. It has been appreciated & cultivated in Palestine from an early date. ✽

No 69   OAK

"EL" "ELAH" "ELON" "ILAN" "ALLAH" "ALLÔN" — OAK

Species Illustrated

"ALLONBACHUTH" — The Oak of Weeping" (Gen 35.8)

No 69 EVERGREEN OAK QUERCUS PSUEDO-COCCIFERA

"ALAMMELECH" — The King's Oak " (Josh 19.26)

No 69A VALONIA OAK QUERCUS ÆGILOPS

Six Hebrew words are translated "Oak" in the A.V.
They are El, Elah, Elon, Ilan, Allah, Allôn. Of these
"ELAH" is the Terebinth Tree (   ) ✽
The rest are interchangable, referring apparantly to any species of Oak, sometimes one word being used & sometimes another. The last two certainly denote exclusively the Oak & are invariably so translated in the A.V., R.V. & N.T.
Three species of Oak are indigenous in Palestine (1) The Evergreen Oak (Quercus Psuedo-coccifera) This is the most frequent species. It occurs in dense forests upon the hillsides if the term be not misleading when referring to trees which are little more than shrubs varying in height from eight to twelve feet. It abounds on Mount Carmel & Lebanon & under favourable conditions attains to an imposing size. The famous Oak at Mamre near Hebron called "Abraham's Oak" which according to tradition occupies the site of the Oak under which Abraham pitched his tent after his return from Egypt & where he was visited by the angels (Gen 13.18) is of this species. It formerly had a girth of twenty-three feet & a spread of some ninety feet. It has now however fallen into an advanced state of decay. This Evergreen Oak is frequent in Gilead & Bashan Its usual small size in Palestine is due to the indiscriminate ~~~~~ destruction of timber that carried out throughout the country over many years. The present conditions of of the forests of Palestine gives no indication of what they were like in Biblical Times. Roots of this species are found in regions where it is unknown today. Quercus psuedo-coccifera is essentially an upland tree & does not occur in the lowlands. It bears dark green, small, very prickly leaves, resembling the lower leaves of the Holly ✽ & produces a large crop of Acorns. The Arabic name is "SINDIÂN".

(2) The Valonia Oak (Q. ægilops) This species is deciduous with foliage resembling the Common Oak. It is very frequent in the north abounds on Carmel & Tabor & in Bashan being undoubtedly the Oak of Bashan (Isa 2.12 & 13: Zech 11.2) but it is infrequent in the South. It reaches a height of from twenty to thirty feet & is never shrub like as the Evergreen Oak so frequently is. The acorns are large with large rough cups. These cups contain a ~~large great amount~~ amount of tannin & are therefore greatly valued in the tanning industry. They are also used for dying under the name of Valonia. The acorns are used as food by the Arabs.

(3) The Gall Oak (Q. infectoria) Also deciduous, a small tree not exceeding twenty feet in height. It is less frequent than the previously mentioned species, occurs in the highlands in the North & is unknown south of Samaria. The Gall Oak gains its name from the

✽ See No 99 TEIL-TREE for Notes on the TEREBINTH   ✾ See No 114 for Notes on WALNUT
✗ Quercus psuedo-coccifera is in appearance more like the Holly than an Oak

Oak (continued)

galls with which it is infested. These galls are produced by a small fly (Cynips) which lays it's eggs in the bark of the new wood. They are used in the manufacture of ink.

"But it shall be a tenth, & it shall return, & shall be eaten: as a teil tree & as an oak, whose substance is in them, when they cast their leaves: so the holy seed shall be the ~~substance~~ substance there of". (Isa 6.13)

The Deciduous Oak & the Terebinth have this in common that both cast their ~~foliage~~ foliage in Winter & further the trunk of each species is rough barked, massive (in old trees) gnarled & twisted & the branches thick & rugged. So that in winter when both trees are leafless the resemblance is very striking. In Isaiah the deciduous nature of the two trees the fact that both cast their foliage in winter yet the trunk remains alive all through the season when the trees appear outwardly to be dead until in spring they burst into leaf again — into vigorous & manifest life is the characteristic common to the two species is ~~used~~ used as a symbol of the Jewish Remnant weak & feeble, reduced to a very few indeed & seeming ready almost to perish off the face of the earth, but preserved by the power & the grace of God through the long winter of the rejection until the summer of the restoration when "saith the Lord of Israel — I will gather the remnant of my flock out of all ~~the~~ countries whither I have driven them, & will bring them again to their folds; & they shall be fruitful & increase. And I will set up shepherds over them which shall feed them: & they shall fear no more, nor be dismayed, neither shall they be lacking saith the Lord. 'Behold the day cometh, saith the Lord, that I will raise unto David a righteous ~~Branch~~ Branch, & a King shall reign & prosper, & shall execute judgment in the earth. In his days Judah shall be saved & Israel shall dwell safely: & this is the name by which he shall be called, THE LORD OUR RIGHTEOUSNESS. Therefore the days which come, saith the Lord, that they shall no more say, The Lord liveth, which brought up the children of Israel out of Egypt; But, the Lord liveth, which brought up & which led the seed of Israel out of the north country, & from all countries whither I had driven them; & they shall dwell in their own land." (Jer 23.2 to 8)

In several passages in the Authorised Version "Oak has been rendered "Plain" ✳ The Plain of Tabor" (1 Sam 10.3) is realy "The Oak of Tabor", "The Plain of Moreh" (Gen 12.6) "The Oak of Moreh", "The Plain of Zaanaim" (Judges 4.11) "The Oak of Zaanaim". ✳ These passages are translated correctly with "Oak" in place of "Plain" in the New Translation. Idolatrous ceremonies were carried out under large & conspicuous Oaks (Hos 4.3) & important people were burried beneath Oaks. The Oak was a symbol of strength to the Hebrews. (Amos 2.9) Tradition claims that the tree of Nebuchadnezzar's dream (Dan 6) was an Oak.

No 78   OIL - TREE

"ETZ SHAMEN" - PINE - BRANCHES | OLEASTER (ELEGNUS ANGUSTIFOLIUS)
          Neh 8-15   "Olive Wood" N.T. ✳ (Illustrated)
    OLIVE - TREE 1 Kings 6.23 "Wild Olive Branches" N.T.
    OIL - TREE   Isa 41.19   "Oleaster" N.T.

The Hebrew name "Etz shamen" occurs three times in the Scripture & is translated differently in each ~~three~~ case in the A.V: R.V: & N.T. In 1 Kings translated "Olive Tree" Margin

✳ See also TEIL TREE No 99 For "Plain" | ✳ "Plain of Meonenim" Judg 9.37 A.V. "Magician", given in A.V. instead of Terebinth | ✳ With the text "Or word of the Oleaster (Wild Olive) Oak" N.T.

Oil Tree (Continued)

"Oily Tree "A.V", "Olive Wood" R.V, "Oil Tree "N.T.*. In Neh 8.15. "Pine Branches"
A.V. "Branches of Wild Olive" R.V. "Wild Olive Branches" N.T. In Isaiah 41.19 "Oil Tree"
A.V. "Oil Tree" margin "Oleaster" R.V. "Oleaster" N.T.   The Hebrew signifies OIL-TREE
and the tree intended cannot be the Olive as both are mentioned in connection in
Nehemiah 8.15.   The cherubim in the oracle in Solomon's Temple were made of the
wood of this tree (1 Kings 6.23), the branches were used together with those of the
Olive Myrtle & Palm in the construction of the booths at the re-institution of the
Feast of Tabernacles (Neh 8.15) & the tree is mentioned as one of the trees which will
clothe the wilderness in the Millenium (Isa 41.19). The tree is obviously the Oleaster
(Elægnus angustifolius) a small tree with, long, narrow, bluish leaves completely covered on the
back with silvery scales. * The flowers are small, green, highly fragrant & abounding in
honey, inconspicuous, & crowded at the junction of the leaves. The fruit is a small green berry
& has a very bitter taste. From this fruit an inferior oil is obtained.   The wood is fine, hard,
& closely grained.   The Oleaster abounds in Palestine.

<u>No 21</u>   # OLIVE
                                    OLEA EUROPÆA (Illustrated)

"ZAIT" - OLIVE Gen 8.11: Lev 2.1: Deut 6.11: 8.2 & 8.24.29: 28.40: 33.24: Judges 9.9:
Job 15.33: Ps 22.5: 52.8: Isa 17.6: Jer 11.6: Hos 14.6: Hab 3.17 & 18. ← ⌐ 1 Kings 6.31 & 33
"Ἐλαία" - OLIVE Matt 6.7: Luke 10.34: Rom 11.17: Jas 3.12: Rev 11.14 ⌐ Zech 4.3 & 11 & 14
"Ἀγριέλαος" — WILD OLIVE Rom 11.17 & 24.

The Olive is frequently mentioned in Scripture. The earliest reference is in Gen 8.11.
when the dove returns to the ark with an Olive-leaf – the symbol of peace & plenty throughout
all ages. It is one of the trees of the Parable of Jotham, the first parable in the Bible (Judg 9.9)
It was one of the blessings of the Land (Deut 8.2) & it failure a mark of Divine displeasure
(Deut 28.40) & it will be one of the blessings of the Millenial Earth (Isa 41.19) It is the symbol
of Divine favour, of beauty strength & luxuriance (Ps 52.8: Jer 11.16: Hos 14.6). Olive Oil was
used in the Golden Candlestick (Ex   ) & generally as a fuel for lamps (Matt   ), was
mixed with the Offerings (Lev 2   ) used in the anointing of priest (   ) of Kings
(   ) & of prophets (   ) & used as a dressing for wounds (Luke 10.14). *
The Olive is a small tree (rarely exceeding twenty feet) with blue-green oblong leaves
which are silvery white on the underside. The flowers are small, white, & crowded in
dense clusters. They are borne very abundantly & although so many are shed as
to whiten the ground beneath the trees * yet such an abundance is left that the succeeding
fruit weighs down the branches. This fruit is a green fleshy drupe from the pulpy
flesh of which Olive Oil is expressed. Olives are used as a desert & are eaten raw,
cooked or preserved. It is the oil however which makes the Olive so valuable. The
yield is great, thirteen or fourteen gallons of Olive Oil is frequently produced from one tree.
The Olive has been cultivated in Palestine from remote ages for the sake of its fruit.
Under Turkish rule a tax was levied annually on every Olive Tree, which had the
effect of restricting the planting of new trees, though the Olive was so prized that
even under this burden the tree was abundantly cultivated throughout the land.
Today with the tax removed it is more abundantly cultivated. The Olive frequently
* With the Note "Or wood of the Oleaster (Wild Olive)" * Making the undersides of the
leaves shine like silver. * Referred to in Job 15.33 *

Olive (continued)

attains to a great age when the trunk is rugged & often hollow & the branches are gnarled & twisted. ✻ The oldest exsisting Olive Trees in Palestine are the famous Olives in the Garden of Gethsemane which are claimed to have been flourishing in the days when the Lord Jesus was on earth. Olive wood is finely grained, of a rich amber colour with beautiful mottlings & veinings. It is highly prized today especially for cabinet work. & was as valued in ancient times. The doors & door-posts of Solomon's Temple were made of Olive wood (1 Kings 6.31:33). Oil in Scripture is the symbol of the Holy Spirit (see   ) which fact is the significance of the Olive Trees of Zech 4.3 & Rev.11.12. The Olive requires frequent attention or it ceases to yield fruit. It also requires grafting or it will produce only small & worthless fruits as does the Wild Olive (Rom 11.17 to 24).

No 72   ONION

"BETZALIM" — ONION   ALLIUM CEPA (Illustrated)
                 Numb 11.5.

Mentioned only in Numbers 11.5 along with the Garlic ✻ & Leek ✻ as one of the vegetables of Egypt after which the Israelites lusted. It has been cultivated in Egypt from the earliest times where it was an important article of food. The Egyptian Onion was mild & well flavoured & as large as the Spanish Onion of today. It was eaten cooked or raw by all classes save the priests to whom it was forbidden. It was offered in sacrifice to the gods (as depicted in ancient Egyptian sculptures & wall paintings) & was accorded divine honours. The Onion is extensively cultivated in Egypt today & is as valued as of old though its no longer sacred & no longer worshipped. It is of course widely cultivated in Britain & in all temperate countries. The Onion bears a dense head of white flowers without bulbils, the leaves are narrow, hollow & brittle. The bulb is large & spherical. The Onion is more appreciated than either the Garlic or Leek. It has important food values & is considered in the East to be a valuable preservative against thirst. Travellers in arid regions there for carry Onions with them & they would have been most acceptable to the Israelites in the wilderness

No 73   PALM

"TAMAR" — PALM   DATE-PALM (PHŒNIX DACTYLIFERA)
Ex 15.27: Deut 34.3: Lev 23.40: Judg 4.5. 1 Kings 6.29 to 35:   Illustrated (Fruit)
2 Chron 3.5: Neh 8.15: Ps 92.2: Ezek Chapter 40 & 41. Selected References
2 Esdra 2.45: Ecclus 24.14: 1 Mac 13.51:2 Mac 10.7:14.4. ✳
"ΦΟΙ'ΝΙξ" — PALM John 12.13 Rev 7.9 Selected References

PALM. The general name of the members of the Order PALMÆ an extensive order of tropical trees & shrubs but in Scripture signifying one tree only — The Date Palm (Phœnix dactylifera)

✻ The bark is bitter & astringent ✻ See No 42 Garlic ✻ See No 5 Leek
✳ There be they that have put off their mortal clothing, & put on the immortal & have confessed the name of god: now are they crowned & receive palms" 2 Esdra 2.45.
"Tree is tall like a palm tree in Engaddi" Ecclus 24.14. "Entered into it --- with thanksgiving & branches of palm trees" 1 Mac 13.51. "Therefore they bare branches, & fair boughs & branches also, & sung psalms unto him that had given them good success in cleansing his place
"He --- came to King Demetrius in the hundred & one & fiftieth, presenting   2 Mac 10.7
unto him a crown of gold, & a palm" 2 Mac 14.4.

Palm (continued)

The Date Palm ranges from India to the Atlantic coast of Africa. It is the principle tree of Egypt & Arabia, & the characteristic tree of the African & Arabian deserts. It was very abundant in Palestine in former times & was noted as the typical tree of the country — The Roman coin struck to commemorate the capture of Jerusalem by Titus depicted Judaea as a woman sitting weeping under a Palm Tree. It is still very plentiful there today ✡ but in the upland regions it could never have been frequent & the Palm Tree of Deborah (Judges 4.5) near Bethel was probably a noted land-mark being the only Palm in the region. Phoenicia was named after the Palm — the name signifying "The Land of Palms". Phenice in Crete (   ) was the city of Palms". Jericho (Deut 34.3) "The city of Palm-trees". Baal-tamar (Judg 22.33) "the sanctuary of the Palm". The Date Palm is a very graceful tree with a long ✳ slender trunk reaching a height of from thirty to eighty feet ✳ & crowned with the feathery leaves which are often twelve feet long. The leaves are often called branches in the Scripture (Lev 23.40: Neh 8.15. John 12.15) the Palm leaf is the symbol of victory & triumph (2 Esdra 2.44 : 1 Macc 13.51: 2 Macc 10.7 : 14.4) & this is the significance of the Palms in Rev 7.9. The graceful form of the Palm & its symbolic significance of victory made it a favourite architectural ornament. It was employed to decorate walls, doors & pillars in Solomons Temple (1 Kings. 6.29 to 36 : 2 Chron 3.5), will decorate Ezekiel's Temple (Ezek 41 & 42) & was used in Herod's Temple. For this reason also it was a favourite woman's name "Tamar". Three women are mentioned in Scripture with the name of Tamar — Judah's Daughter-in-law (Gen 38.6), David's Daughter (2. Sam. 13.1) & Absalom's Daughter (2. Sam 14.27) The Date is one of the most important items of food in the Near East yet frequently as the palm tree is mentioned in the Scripture the Date is never mentioned. ✳ The Dates are borne in enormous bunches springing from the base of the leaf. The tree is diæcous & the fruit bearing trees are more frequent than the staminate. Under cultivation this fact is exaggerated. The tree although bearing a good crop when growing wild requires attention under cultivation or the fruit will not mature ✳ This might be because in a wild it survives only in the most favourable situations. The Date Palm is a very valuable tree in the regions where it flourishes. It's fruit is a most important article of food, its leaves are manufactured into mats & baskets, a drink is made from the juice of the fruit, & sugar is manufactured from the syrup, the fruit-stalks are fed to horses & the ground stones to camels, whilst the crown of the staminate tree is sometimes used as a vegetable. The Palms are the chief Endogenous trees. The trunk is composed of a solid mass of fibre, hard on the outside & soft & pithy in the middle. It does not (as in the case of the majority of trees) increase in bulk from year to year but only in height.

✡ The Date Palm has disappeared from many localities in Palestine where it was abundant in Biblical times. It is no longer found at Jericho nor at Engeddi or on the Mount of Olives but it still a frequent tree in various parts of the country & some

✳ Occassionaly reaching a height of a hundred feet. Palms still flourish inside the walls of Jerusalem.

✳ It has been claimed that "clusters of grapes" (Cant 7.7) should be "clusters of dates" But the A.V. R.V. & N.T. all give "grapes" without comment. Indirectly Dates are mentioned on one occassion — Bethany means "the house of Dates"

✳ It requires watering & care is needed to ensure fertilization.

Palm (continued)

producing an annual ~~coronet~~ of leaves which persist for some seven or eight years & then wither. The bases of the old leaves persist as a sheath on the stem. When the Palm is growing wild the dead leaves often persist for years, sheathing the stem & hiding its graceful shape. The flowers are enclosed in a spathe which bursts when they ~~become~~ mature. A large number of flowers are borne in a branched tuft. ~~All~~ Palms are diœcious. ✱

No 74   PINE

"TIDHAR" - PINE Isa 41·19: ~~44·14~~ ⌐ ELM (ULMUS CAMPESTRIS) (Illustrated)
The word "TIDHAR" occurs only twice in Scripture both times in Isaiah ﬁrst as the name of a tree mentioned in conjunction with the Fir & the Box as clothing the wilderness during the Millenium & second as one of the trees from which idols were made. It is translated "Pine" in the A·V· R·V & N·T· but with "Plane" in the margin in the R·V· & with the Note "Or perhaps "plane tree" or "evergreen oak"" in Isa 4·19, & the Note "Or mountain ash" in Isa 44·14 in the N·T· There is some doubt as to which tree was actually intended. Several species of Pine occur in the mountainous regions of Palestine. The Plane is frequent by the side of streams & the Evergreen Oak on hill sides. It cannot be the Rowan (the so-called Mountain Ash) as that tree is unknown in Palestine but the Manna Ash (Fraxinus ornus) which bears a superficial resemblance to it is not infrequent & might be intended in the N·T· Note ✱. Some suggest the Elm (Ulmus campestris) which is indigenous to Lebanon. The Elm attains to a large size. It bears inconspicuous purple flowers which open before the leaves appear. The fruit is winged, the leaves are of an oblong shape, coarsely toothed at the margin & prominently veined. It is the most frequent road-side tree in most of the rural areas of England. "PINE - BRANCHES" in Neh 8·15 is a mis translation & should be "Branches of the Oleaster" ✱

No 75   POMEGRANATE

"RIMMÔN" - POMEGRANATE   PUNICA GRANATE (Illustrated)
Ex 28·33 & 34; 39·24 & 26: Numb 8·8: 13·23: Deut 8·8: 1Sam 14·2: ⌐ 75. Flowers & ~~Fruit~~
1Kings 7·18: 2 Kings, 25·17: 2 Chron 3·16: Cant 4·3 & 13: 6·7·10: 7·12: 8·2.
The Pomegranate is a small tree, eight to fifteen feet in height ✗ which is indigenous in Southern France, Northern Africa & Western Asia & is extensively cultivated in all semi-tropical regions for the sake of its fruit. It bears small glossy evergreen leaves which are lanceolate with uncut edges & a bright green hue. The flowers are blood red with (if present) a cluster of bright yellow stamens in the centre. They are large & conspicuous with from five to eight petals. The flowers sometimes bear the pistil & stamens together, sometimes only stamens & sometimes only the pistil. The three sorts of flower occur together on the same tree & as the barren flowers predominate the amount of fruit produced is much less than the quantity of blossom would seem to ~~promise~~: The

It has been said "You cannot bark a Palm Tree, you cannot kill it (as for example you could kill the Oak) by removing the bark, it cannot be destroyed by outside influence". The truth of this lies in the fact that the Palm being Endogenous grows from the inside & does not form bark

✱ See also Notes on the Ash No 8 for more details concerning the "Mountain ✱ See "Oil Tree" No 70
✗ The Pomegranate under which Saul tarried ~~was~~ (1 Sam 14·2) must have been a well grown Specimen

Pomegranate (continued)

succeeding fruit is spherical, crowned with the remains of the calyx, bright red in colour, with a hard rind enclosing numerous seeds which are attached to a white membrane which is exceedingly bitter to the palate & surrounded by a delicious red pulp. It is the seeds which have gained for the fruit it's name of Pomegranate which is from the Latin signifying "grained apple" & refers to the orderly manner in which the seeds are arranged. The enclosing pulp is cool, deliciously flavoured & very refreshing in the hot climates in which the tree flourishes, causing the fruit to be greatly appreciated. The juice was made into a pleasant & refreshing drink (Cant 8.2) The rind & the bark have powerful astringent properties & are used in the East in medicine & for tanning. The Pomegranate has been appreciated in Egypt & Palestine from the earliest time & is still extensively cultivated there today. Its wide cultivation in Palestine in earlier days is seen in the frequency with which it's Hebrew name of "Rimmon" occurs in place names in the Scripture—Rimmon (Josh 15.32: 1 Chron 4.39: Zech 14.10) Gath—Rimmon (Josh 21.25: 1 Chron 6.39) & Rimmon in Zebulon (1 Chron 7.22) The Pomegranate figured in the ornamentation of the high-priest's robe — pomegranates in blue, purple & scarlet alternated with golden bells on the hem. The Pomegranate owing to it's numerous seeds was the emblem of fruitfulness & this is it's significance upon the high-priest's robe — Pomegranate = Fruitfulness, Bells = Testimony — a fruitful walk acceptable to God (Ex 28.33 & 34: 39.24 to 26) Pomegranates were also carved on the capitols of the pillars of the porch of Solomon's Temple (1 Kings 7.18) The Pomegranate is indigenous in Palestine & is not unfrequent in a wild state but the fruit of the Wild Pomegranate is very bitter & astringent & of no service as food. The rind & bark have powerful astringent properties & are used in the East in medicine & for tanning. ✳ The budding of the Pomegranate is mentioned in the Song of Solomon & an orchard of Pomegranates in 4.13 whilst in 4.3 the temple of the beloved is compared to the Pomegranate ✳ The Syrian deity Rimmon is considered by some to be a personification of the Pomegranate, embolising the fructifying principle of nature. Worshiped in conjunction with Hadad the Syrian Sun God at an annual ceremony in the autumn he typified the Sun God who ripened the fruit & then died with the dying summer & the perishing fruit & was mourned for with great lamentation — The Mourning of Hadadrimmon (Zech 12.11)

No 76   POPLAR

"LIBNEH" — POPLAR Gen 30.37: Hos 4.13 | WHITE POPLAR (POPULUS ALBA)

Species Illustrated
No 76 WHITE POPLAR
No 76A BLACK POPLAR
POPULUS NIGRA

The Hebrew word "Libneh" meaning white & derived from the same root as Lebanon = "The White Mountain" occurs only twice in Scripture (Gen 30.37 & Hos 4.13) The R.V. suggests "Storax" in the margin in Gen 30.37 & gives "Poplar" without comment in Hos 4.13. The N.T. gives "White Poplar" in Genesis & "Poplar" in Hosea. The Storax (Styrax officinalis) ✳ is frequent in most parts of Palestine. It bears white flowers & pale green leaves which are white with down beneath, so that it would well accord with "Libneh" but it would not fit the Scripture in Hosea as it is little more than a bushy shrub, not (as the passage requires) a large tree

✳ The rind of the wild Pomegranate is employed in Morocco in the preparation of the finest Morocco leather to which it imparts a bright red colour.
✳ In reference to the red colour of the fruit. ✳ See No 94 STACTE for notes on the Storax Tree

Poplar (continued)

under which sacrifices could be offered. The White Poplar would seem to be the tree intended in Hosea. It is a noble tree with acutely lobed light green leaves which are covered with a wet of white down on the upper surface & white & wooly with a thick down on the under. It is abundant in the upland regions of Palestine by the side of rivers & streams. The Euphrates Poplar (P. euphratica) is abundant on the banks of the Jordan & by the side of ~~brooks~~ in the low-lands of Palestine. It receives it's name from it's abundance by the Euphrates & it is frequent by the Tigris — the regions where the land of Haran was situated & where Jacob peeled the rods of Poplar. The Euphrates Poplar ~~could~~ therefore be the Poplar of Genesis 30·37. Two other species of Poplar occur in Palestine. The Black Poplar (P. nigra) by some considered to be the Poplar of Genesis ✳ & the Aspen (P. tremula) the "Mulberry" of Scripture ✳. Populus dilatata occurs in Syria

---

No 77   PULSE

"ZEROIM" — PULSE Dan 1·12:16   Species Illustrated GARDEN PEA
"PULSE" 2 Sam 12·28.   (PISUM SATIVUM)

The word "Zeroim" occurs only the first chapter of Daniel & is translated "Pulse" without comment in the A.V: R.V & N.T. The word however in the original Hebrew means "Seeds" & is not confined, as is the word "Pulse" to Peas, lentils & other Leguminous seeds. It signifies in Daniel a plain vegetable ~~food~~. The word "Pulse" occurring in 2 Sam 12·28 is supplied by the translators & is not in the original. Here it signifies parched Peas which were a favourite article of food in the East. Peas of various kinds have been cultivated in Palestine from the earliest times. ✣

No 78   PURSLANE

"PURSLANE" Job 6·6. R.V. Margin   PORTULACA OLERACEA (Illustrated)
in place of "the white of an egg"

"Can that which is unsavoury be eaten without salt? or is there any taste in the white of a egg?" Job 6·6. R.V. Margin "Is there any taste in the juice of Purslane". Purslane is an ~~annual~~ fleshy prostrate herb with small simple entire succulent leaves which has been cultivated in the warmer regions from times immemorial as a pot herb. It is sometimes grown in Britain but cannot be called popular here. It occurs as an escape from cultivation at Richmond in Surrey. In the
✳ This a large tree with large oval leaves which have an lid y an acutely pointed apex. They are of a dark green hue with trace of white about them. It seems difficult to associate this tree with the Poplar of Scripture when we consider that the word "Libneh" means "White" & in other that the White Poplar is frequent in the highlands of Palestine & undoubtedly fulfills all the requirements of the text. The Black Poplar is not infrequent in Palestine & favours like situations to those of the White Poplar. It is a large tree with grey bark & spreading branches. The catkins open in April & May.
✳ See No 63 "Mulberry" for Note on the Aspen. ✣ See No 11 Beans & No 54 Lentil

Purslane (continued)

East it is much more appreciated. Purslane is not mentioned in Scripture but in Job 6.6 for "the white of an egg" the R.V. suggests in the margin "the juice of Purslane". The herb is practically tasteless & would be as fitting an illustration of insipidity as "the white of an egg". The A.V. & N.T. give "white of an egg" without comment. The plant bears inconspicuous flowers which only open in sunny weather. It is indigenous to Palestine where it is frequent in moist places throughout the country.

No 79   ROSE

"CHABATZELETH" – ROSE Cant 2.1 Species Illustrated   POLYANTHUS
                    Isa 35.1   NARCISSUS
"I am the rose of Sharon & the lily of the vallies" Cant 2.1 ✳   (NARCISSUS TAZETTA)
"The wilderness & the solitary place shall be glad for them; & the desert & the desert shall rejoice & blossom as the rose" Isa 35.1. ✳

The Hebrew word "CHABATZELETH" occurs only twice in the Scripture. It is translated "Rose" without comment in the A.V. "Rose" with in the margin "Autumn Crocus" in the R.V. & "Narcissus" without comment in the Song of Solomon 2.1, & "Rose" with the note "Or Narcissus" in Isaiah 35.1. in the N.T. The root denotes a bulbous plant. Many bulbous plants occur in Palestine. The Scarlet Martagon Lily (Lilium chalcedonicum) the Tulip (Tulipa gesneriana), the Fritillary (Fritillaria persica) the Star of Bethlehem (Ornithogalum umbellatum) the Autumnal Squill (Scilla autumnalis), the Autumn Crocus (Crocus autumnalis) the Polyanthus Narcissus (Narcissus tazetta) & Gladiolus Byzantinus. The New Translation rendering of "Narcissus" is most probably correct. The Narcissus indigenous to Palestine is the Polyanthus Narcissus (N. Tazetta) the species so frequently grown in hot-houses in Britain, opening its flowers in February & March. It abounds on the Plain of Sharon & is exclusively cultivated throughout Palestine. It bears numerous pale yellow, richly scented flowers in an umbel at the summit of a stout stalk. The Autumn Crocus (C. nudiflorus) suggested in the Revised Version produces purple flowers in September & October without a sign of a leaf, the foliage appearing in March & withering away by June. It is the most frequent of the Crocuses occurring in Britain & the only one with any real claim to be considered indigenous. It occurs in colonies in meadows in the Midlands but it is not common. This Crocus is frequent throughout Palestine. The Narcissus has the advantage however in that it is as beautiful as the Crocus & in addition is sweetly fragrant – the Crocus being scentless. True Roses occur only in the mountains in Palestine & have no place in Scripture.

No 80   ROSE-OF-SHARON

"I am the Rose of Sharon & the lily of the valleys" Species Illustrated AUTUMN CROCUS
      Autumn Crocus" R.V. Margin.   Cant 2.1   (CROCUS NUDIFLORUS)
"I am a Narcissus of Sharon, A lily of the valleys" 2.1
The Rose of Sharon was a beautiful & notable flower which abounded on the Plain of Sharon. It could not have been a true Rose as no species of wild Rose occurs

---

✳ "Autumn Crocus" Margin R.V. "Narcissus" Text N.T   ✳ "Autumn Crocus" Margin R.V.
"Rose" Text Note "Narcissus" N.T.

Rose - of - Sharon (continued)

in Palestine save in the mountains. The New Translation gives "Narcissus" the Revised Version suggests "Autumn Crocus". Both the Polyanthus Narcissus & the Autumn Crocus are frequent on the Plain of Sharon. The Narcissus (as already noted) is most likely to be the Rose of Scripture. (The Rose of Sharon & the Rose of Isaiah are the same plant). The plant under common cultivation as the Rose of Sharon & therefore almost invariably associated with the name is the large flowered St John's Wort (Hypericum calycinum). It is a small evergreen shrub not exceeding a foot in height & bearing large yellow solitary terminal flowers of which the five petals are crumpled & the stamens very numerous. The stems are square & hairless, the leaves oblong blunt & leathery, light green beneath & dark green above with the main vein picked out in light green. It flowers from June to September. Hypericum Calycinum bears the largest flower of any species of St John's Wort & is a very handsome plant but it cannot be the Rose of Sharon.

No 81   **ROSE (Ecclesiasticus)**

"ROSE" Eclus 24.14 : 39.13 : 50.8   **OLEANDER (NERIUM OLEANDER)**
                                                                                    Illustrated

"I was exalted like a palm tree in Engaddi & as a rose plant in Jericho" Eclus 24.14.

"Harken unto me ye holy children & bud forth as a rose growing by the brook of the field" Eclus 30.13.

"He was as the flower of Roses in the spring of the year" Eclus 50. 8 :

The Rose is mentioned three times in the Apocrypha, on each occasion in Ecclesiasticus. First in Ecclesiasticus 24.14. Wisdom who is speaking, says, "I was exalted like a Cedar in Libanus & as a Cypress tree upon the mountains of Hermon. I was exalted like a Palm tree in Engaddi & as a Rose plant in Jericho as a fair Olive tree in a pleasant field & grew up as a Plane tree by the water. Second in 39.13 "Harken unto me ye holy children & bud forth as a Rose growing by the brook of the field. And give ye a sweet savour as Frankincense, flourish as a lily, send a smell, & sing a song of praise, bless the Lord in all His works." Third in 50.8 speaking of Simon the high priest, the son of Onias "He — — — as the flower of Roses in the spring of the year, as lilies by the rivers of waters, — as the branches of the Frankincense in the spring of the year in the time of summer — — As a fair Olive tree budding forth fruit, & as a Cypress tree which groweth up to the clouds." From these passages it will be seen that the Rose of the Apocrypha was a water-side plant of suitable beauty, luxuriance & vigour abounding at Jericho. The plant which meets all these requirements is the Oleander (Nerium oleander) the rhododendron of the Greeks. The oleander clothes the banks of the Jordan almost down to the Dead Sea (though it does not occur in the Dead Sea Basin) It is very frequent at Jericho* by the sides of the streams of Gilead & Sharon, by the waters of Merom & on the shores of Gennesaret. It luxuriates by the brooks of the valleys of Lebanon & plains of Phoenicia & the waters of Syria & Moab. The oleander really assumes the form of a tree.

* Not to be confounded with the "Rose of Jericho" of horticulture (   ) which is native of the Peak. Why this plant has been given this name is a mystery.
    Not to be confounded with the fabulous "Rose of Jericho" (Anastatica hierochuntica) a small inconspicuous Crucifer which grows in the sand of the desert around the Dead Sea & whose translation = Resurrection-flower Hierochuntica = Jericho). continued overleaf

Rose (continued)

shrub but occassionally reaches the proportions of a forest tree. It bears
dark green, narrow lanceolate evergreen leaves (reminiscent of the narrow-
leaved willow) & large, pink, very beautiful flowers which open in June. *
It is frequently grown in hot-houses in Britain. The wood of the Oleander is
virulently poisonous & has caused deaths when brought into contact with the food
* It is sometimes powdered & used to kill rats. The Oleander is claimed by some
to be the Willow of Scripture ✳ ❋. It was the Rhododendron of the Greeks - The Rose
Tree, but it must not be confounded with the Rhododendron of today - Rhododendron
Ponticum, a relative of the Heath. J. Keeble in his "Christian Year" gives the
following lines (Third Sunday in Advent. The Travellers)

> — "Where Gennesaret's wave
> Delights the flowers to lave
> That o'er her western slope breath airs of balm
>
> All through the summer night
> Those blossoms red & bright
> Spread their soft breasts unheeding to the breeze "

To these lines he gives a Note thus "Rhododendrons, with which the western
bank of the lake is said to be clothed down to the water's edge" The 'plant'
concerned is the Oleander

No82   **RUE**

"Πηγανον" - RUE Luke 11. 42.   **RUTA GRAVEOLENS (Illustrated)**

Mentioned only in Luke 11-42 along with Mint as amongst the garden herbs which
the Pharisees were so careful to tithe whilst neglecting the great & important
matters of the Law thus bringing themselves under the rebuke of the Lord. The
garden Rue (Ruta graveolens) has been cultivated in Palestine from the earliest
times; being greatly valued for it's medical properties. This is the same species
commonly cultivated in Britain today, the bitter juice procured from the boiled leaves
& stems being held in some repute as a corrective for stomach complaints. The
whole plant has a strong foetid odour due to the presence of a volatile oil. It was
formerly held in great repute as a disinfectant & was scattered in courts of justice to protect

---

*

---

in the revolts of Egypt. It is also called the Resurrection Plant. It receives it's name
from the fact that it will lie for months amidst the hot arid sand like a dead withered
mass of tangled branches yet upon being plunged into water it will open its flowers, & further
will do so if it has been gathered for months

Rue (continued)

the officials from Typhus Fever (at that date known as Gaol Fever) which swept the prisons in those days & often spread from the prisoners to the judges & other officials at the court. A relic of this practice of strewing the courts is retained today in the ceremony observed [formerly general & habitual on certain particular occasions] of scattering rue over the floor of the courts. The rue is a small herb reaching a height of two or three feet. Its leaves are divided into blunt lobes & the flowers are yellowish-brown with four distinct petals. Two species of Rue grow wild in Palestine Ruta bracteosa & R. chalepensis R. bracteosa is the more frequent. Both are handsome species, much more showy than Ruta graveolens.

RUSH

Six Hebrew words are translated BULRUSH, FLAG, PAPER-REED, REED & RUSH the words with their translations are as follows: (1) GOME — BULRUSH (Twice) RUSHES RUSH. (2) ACHU — FLAG, MEADOW. (3) AGMON — RUSH (Twice) HOOK, CAULDRON, BULRUSH, REED. (4) AROTH — PAPER-REEDS. (5) SÛPH — FLAGS (Twice) WEEDS (6) KANEH — REED (frequently. Occurs in many Old Testament passages as the generic name of any species of reed). It will be seen that BULRUSH occurs twice as the translation of GOME & once as the translation of AGMON. That RUSH (RUSHES) occurs twice as the translation of GOME & twice as the translation of AGMON. That FLAG occurs once as the translation of ACHU & FLAGS twice as the translation of SÛPH. That REED occurs once as the translation of GOME & generally as the translation of KANEH & once as the translation of AGMON. Further it will be seen also that GOME twice translated BULRUSH is also twice translated RUSH (RUSHES). That AGMON twice translated RUSH is also translated BULRUSH & REED It will be noted from this that the names BULRUSH RUSH &c are not confined by the translators to the rendering of one Hebrew word but are used indiscriminately. A Hebrew word being translated BULRUSH in one passage is translated RUSH in another, whilst another Hebrew word is likewise translated RUSH in one passage BULRUSH in another & REED in a third. The Revised Version & the New Translation renderings are less confusing, as will be seen from the following list — (1) GOME — REEDS, PAPYRUS, RUSHES (Note PAPYRUS). N.T.: BULRUSH (MARGIN PAPYRUS) (Twice) PAPYRUS. R.V (2) ACHU — REED-GRASS (Twice) R.V. & N.T. (3) AGMON — RUSH, BULRUSH, SPIKE, CAULDRON. N.T. (4) AROTH — MEADOW R.V & N.T. (5) SUPH — SEDGE (Twice) WEEDS (6) KANEH — REED R.V & N.T as in A.V. There is however still some overlapping, so the best arrangement seems to be to group all together as "RUSH" & describe the appropriate species under the six Hebrew names as follows —

No 83   RUSH (1) BULRUSH
"GOME" — BULRUSH Ex 2.3 : Isa 18.1&2 :   PAPYRUS (CYPERUS PAPYRUS)
        RUSHES Isa 35.7 : RUSH Job 8.11 / "BULRUSH" Margin "Papyrus" Ex 2.3
Job 8.11 "PAPYRUS" Isa 18.1&2 : 35.7 R.V. "SEDGE" Ex 2.3 "PAPYRUS" Isa 18.1&2 : Job 8.11
Translated "Bulrush" "Rushes" & "Rush" (see above). The [RUSHES "Note" Papyrus" Isa 35.1
rendering "Papyrus" in the R.V & N.T is correct. The Papyrus (Cyperus papyrus)
was formerly very abundant by the side of the Nile forming dense thickets, though
today it is extinct in Egypt though it is still found in Nubia in the marshes of

Rush (continued)

the White Nile. It is found in two localities in Palestine growing in
abundance in a marsh at the northern end of the Plain of Gennesaret &
covering many acres of the shallow Waters of Merom. It is not found elsewhere in
Asia but in Sicily. The Papyrus has a triangular stem reaching a
height of eight to ten feet & terminating in a bushy top of slender leaves among st
which the seeds are produced. The root is bulky fleshy & spreading. The flowers
appear in September. The ark in which the infant Moses was placed was made
of Papyrus (Ex 2·3) & it was used for making light vessels as mentioned in Isa 35.7.
but it is famous in that it supplied the first paper known to history. This
paper was obtained by removing the outer covering of the stems & cutting the
soft white pith lengthwise into long thin sheets which were laid alongside one
another in a flat surface. Similar sheets were then laid across at right angles
(gum having been first applied to hold them together) This done the resultant
large sheet was subject to severe pressure & thoroughly dried, after which it
was ready for use. This paper was used from the early days of Egypt to the
seventh century A.D. when it was superseded by parchment. ✗

No 84   R U S H (2)   F L A G
"ACHU" - FLAG Job 8.11   Species Illustrated FLOWERING RUSH
          MEADOW Gen 41.2.18.   REED-GRASS R.V. & N.T.   (BUTOMUS
                                                                UMBELLATA)
"Can the flag grow without water? Job 8·11
"There came up out of the river seven well favoured Kine & fat fleshed & they
fed in a meadow" Gen 41.2. A.V. "Doth the reed-grass grow without water? Job·8·11
"There came up out of the river seven Kine, fine looking & fat fleshed, & they fed
in the reed-grass" Gen. 41.2. N.T.
"Achu" Translated "Flag" Job 8·11 & "Meadow" Gen. 41.2. It refers to the luxuriant
vegetation on the banks of the rivers. As it is mentioned in Job 8·11 along
with the Papyrus ("Doth the Papyrus shoot up without mire T. Doth the
reed-grass grow without water" N·1) it would seem that some specific
plant was intended & not just river-side vegetation in general. From the
passages in Genesis it must have been a plant eaten by cattle. The R·V & N·T give
"Reed Grass" & the Edible Rush (Cyperus esculentus) a very nutritious Reed luxuriates
on the banks of the Nile & by the sides of rivers of Palestine. The Flowering Rush
(Butomus umbellata) ✶ also abounds in the same localities & is likewise very
nutritious (being eagerly sought out by cattle when they have the opportunity) It
would perish if the water failed. Either species would therefore fulfil the
requirements of the Scriptures.

─────

✗ The Papyrus belongs to the Order CYPERACEÆ
✶ The Flowering Rush is a tall growing aquatic plant with a creeping
rhizome & sword-shaped radical leaves which each a length of two & three feet.
It throws up stout stems to a height of some three feet which are crowned with
a simple umbel of handsome pink flowers which are an inch across, & (unlike
the majority of plants of the Order Alismaceæ where the perianth leaves are in two clearly
defined whorls the three inner leaves coloured & the three outer green) have six petaloid
perianth leaves. It flowers in May & June, is of annual duration & bears in...

No 85   RUSH (3) REED

"AGMON" – REED Isa 9.14 : 19.15   ARUNDO DONAX (Illustrated)
BULRUSH Isa 58.9   HOOK Job 41.2   CAULDRON Job 41.20

"RUSH" Isa 9.14 : 19.15. "BULRUSH" Isa 58.9 "SPIKE" Job 41.2 "CAULDRON" Job 41.20

"Agmon" Translated "Rush" in Isaiah 9.14 + 19.15 in a proverbial expression [N.T.
"Head & tail, branch & rush" — top & bottom, absolutely. The contrast of the Palm
-branch & the Rush signifying the esteem of the great & the small. This
is however only comparative for from the passage in Isaiah 58.7 where Agmon
is translated "Bulrush" "to bow the head like the Bulrush" must denote some plant
which bowed it's head to the wind & which therefore possessed a high yielding
stem & a tufted head. The Reed of Palestine (Arundo donax) reaches a
height of twelve feet. It has a long slender elastic stem & bears a dense
plumed panicle of flowers. It's plumed head bends low to the wind & from the
elasticity of the stem immediately rises again. This Reed is the "Reed
shaken in the wind" of Matthew 11.7 * It is a magnificent plant & could
only denote smallness comparatively by contrast with the greater size of the
Palm Tree. The Reed grows very luxuriantly by the Dead Sea especially on
the western shore where nourished by the fresh springs it attains an enormous
size it forming a dense cane brake including willow It occurs in large patches
along the banks of the Jordan & is the common Rush of Egypt. Agmon is
translated "Cauldron" in Job 41.2 & "Hook" in Job 41.2 where it is thought to
⑤ refer to a reed put through the gills of fish to carry them

No 86   RUSH (4) PAPER REEDS

"AROTH" – PAPER-REEDS Isa 19.7   Species Illustrated YELLOW–IRIS ✳
MEADOWS R·V·+ N·T.   FLEUR–DE–LYS
(IRIS PSEUDO-ACORUS)

"Aroth" occurs only in Isaiah 19.7 where it   Illustrative of the green herbage of the
is translated "Paper-reeds" in the A.V.   river side ✳
This would be the Papyrus if correct but as the "Bulrush" of Isaiah is that plant PAPER-
in this Scripture is in error. The R·V & N·T. both give "Meadows". [REEDS
This is correct, the word refers to the green herbage of the marshes & river-sides
which would wither & die if the water to dry up.

Iris Pseudo-acorus is frequently found fringing the banks of the rivers & streams
of Palestine. It occurs frequently in like situations in Britain, opening it's yellow
flowers in June ✳

No 87   RUSH (5) FLAGS

"SUPH" – FLAGS Ex 2.3+5 : Isa 19.6   Species Illustrated 87(a) COMMON RUSH

WEEDS Jonah 2.5 :   "SEDGE" Ex 2.3+5 : Isa 19.6   87 b WHITE-WATER-LILY

"WEEDS" Jonah 2.5 N.T.   87 c YELLOW WATER-LILY

"Suph" Translated "Flags" in Ex 2.3 where the mother of Moses   87 D L.F & g.

✳ See No 88 Rush 3. Reed   87 e SEA-WEEDS

✳ The Yellow Iris (Iris Pseudo-acorus) bears handsome yellow from June   87 D PORPHYRA VULGARIS

to August. It has sword shaped leaves, a round stem & a creeping   87 e

rhizome. It is usually found growing in the shallow water at the edge of   87 F

slow-moving rivers, ponds & lakes it occasionally occurs on the bank   87 G

above water and it always in a wild state necessarily though sometimes

cultivated, it can be grown in an ordinary garden bed away from any

a slow-moving river. It is not common in England, though frequent in some localities

Rush (continued)

placed the ark amongst the Flags by the side of the Nile. Also translated "Flags" in Isaiah 19.6 where it is prophesied that the river of Egypt would dry up & the Reeds & Flags wither. Translated "Weeds" in Jonah 2.5. The N.T. gives "Sedge" in Ex 2.3 & 5 & Isa 19.6 & gives "Weeds" in Jonah 2.5. "Weeds" is the correct translation, the word signifying water weeds in general — aquatic vegetation either of the rivers or the sea. In Jonah it denotes Sea Weeds. The Red sea because of the abundance of Sea Weeds in it's waters was from an early date nominated "the Sea of Suph" by which it is still known by the Arabs today.

The following species are figured & described as typical aquatic plants of Palestine they are not mentioned by name in Scripture.

COMMON RUSH (JUNCUS CONGLOMERATUS) ✱ The Common Rush is as common a marshland plant in Palestine as in Britain ✱ It has a long slender cylindric stem which tapers to a point, & bears on it's upper portion in July a densely crowded globose panicle of brown flowers. The capsule is pointed. It has a rhizom. The Common Rush occurs only on majstoy ground, where it is abundant.

WHITE WATER-LILY (NYMPHÆ ALBA) ✱ Occurring in abundance in the lakes & pools of the marshes of the Upper Jordan. It bears large white fragrant flowers with many golden stamens, many large fleshy petals which have no honey glands, & four large sepals which are green on the outer surface & white on the inner. These flowers are sometimes five or six inches across. They are very beautiful. They float upon the surface of the water (which enhances their beauty) during the day but at twilight they close & sink beneath the surface, rising & expanding again the following morning. The leaves float on the surface & are rounded, thick, & leathery, & from five to ten inches across. The White Water-lily occurs in Britain in slowly moving rivers & clear lakes & ponds. It flowers from June to August. The fruit ripens under water.

YELLOW WATER-LILY (NUPHAR LUTEUM) Also found in abundance in lakes & ponds amidst the marshes of the Upper Jordan. It has both floating & submerged leaves. The floating leaves being heart-shaped, large, thick & leathery, & the submerged being membranous & of a lighter hue. The flowers have five conspicuous petaloid sepals yellow on both surfaces but brighest on the upper & many small inconspicuous petals which are rendered more inconspicuous by being almost hidden by the multitude of yellow anthers. The petals produce honey at their base. The stigma is rayed & conspicuous. The fruit matures above water & is flagon shaped ✿ From the odour of the flowers & from the shape of the fruit the Yellow Water Lily is locally called "Brandy Bottle" in some parts of Britain. It flowers from June to August. The flowers (which are raised on stout stalks about two inches above the water) are far less pleasing than those of the White Water-Lily & the Yellow Water Lily is altogether more untidy & in-elegant than that plant. It occurs in Britain in like localities to those chosen by the

✱ Illustrative of semi-aquatic & marshland vegetation.
✱ Illustrative of lake & river vegetation ✿ Pulpy, with the seeds embedded in the pulp
✱ Claimed to smell like brandy

<u>Rush</u> (continued)

White Water-Lily & is the commonest & most widely distributed of the two.
SEA-WEEDS   See <u>Note</u> Below

<u>No 88</u>   R U <u>S H</u> (6) R E E D

                              Species Illustrated SUGAR-CANE
<u>KÁNEH</u>" — REED. Occurring in many Old Testament passages ⌐ (SACCHARUM
       as the generic name of any species of Reed   ⌐ OFFICINARUM)
Used to denote Stalk of Wheat Gen 41.5 & 22   Branches of Candlestick
Name of a measure of length equal to six cubits Ezek 40.2.   Ex 25.31
     The bone of the upper arm — the Humerus.

"Καλαμος" — REED Matt 11.7 : 3 John 13 : Rev 11.1 ✳

"KANEH" signifying "REED" or "CANE", the English word "CANE" is derived from the same root. It occurs in many Old Testament passages as the Generic name of any species of Reed — not as the name of any particular species. It is used to denote a stalk of wheat (Gen 41.5 & 22) the branches of the golden candlestick (Ex 25.31) ✳, the bone of the upper arm — the Humerus, & is farther the name (translated "Reed" in the A.V. & R.V.) of a measure of length equal to six cubits (Ezek 40.2). The equivalent of "Kaneh" in Greek is "Καλαμος". It is applied in the New Testament to the growing Reed (Matt 11.7) ✳, to a measuring rod (Rev 11.1) & to a pen made of reed (3 John 13)
     Measuring rods were made of cane. The stiff upper portions of the stem of the Sugar Cane were ideal for this purpose. The measuring rod of the New Testament was very likely made from the Sugar Cane but that of the Old Testament would probably be the Common Reed as the Sugar Cane was unknown to the Jews in Old Testament times. For this reason it is considered that the Sweet Cane of Isaiah 43.24 ✳ cannot be the Sugar Cane. The Sugar Cane (Saccharum officinarum) was introduced for cultivation into Palestine in the times of the Crusades & has from that time been cultivated in the Lower Jordan Valley. It was however imported into Palestine from the east at an early date cut into pieces & ready for use. The Sugar Cane is the source of the world's best sugar

<u>No 89</u>   R Y E
                      SPELT   (Illustrated)

✳ Deleted References. Mentioned also many time elsewhere in the Scripture
  ✳ The "Reed shaken in the wind" is the Common Reed of Palestine (See No 85 Rush 3 Reed)
<u>Note</u> SEA-WEEDS

Rye (Continued)

"CUSSEMETH" – RIE Ex 9.32 : Isa 28.25. (Margin "Spelt")

FITCHES EзeK ~~~~.4.19. (Margin "Spelt")

"SPELT" Ex 9.32 : "RYE" Isa 28.25 "RYE" EзeK 4.19 N.T.

CUSSEMETH – Translated "Rie" in Exodus 9.32 & Rie with "Spelt" in the margin in Isaiah 28.25 in the A.V. Rendered ~~Rye~~ without comment in Exodus 9.32 & "Rye" without comment in Isaiah 28.25 in Spelt → the N.T. Given "Spelt" in the R.V. "Spelt" is the correct translation. Spelt is an inferior kind of Wheat which has the chaff & grain adhering. The sheath is rougher than that of Wheat & the awn is long. The flour is inferior in value to wheaten flour & is usualy mixed with it. Spelt has been cultivated in Egypt from the earliest times. The modern Arabic name for Spelt is "Chirsanat". "Cussemeth" is translated "Fitches" in Ezekiel 4.9, this is an error, "Spelt" in the R.V. & N.T. is correct.

No 90   SAFFRON

"KARKÒM" – SAFFRON Cant 4.14.   SAFFRON CROCUS (CROCUS SATIVUS)

(Illustrated)

Mentioned only once in the Scripture as a fragrant plant of the garden. The Saffron Crocus bears large purple flowers with a large prominent orange-coloured stygma. It abounds in Palestine both in a wild & cultivated state where it is much appreciated for it's beauty & fragrance. The Saffron of commerce consists of the style & stamens which ~~possess a~~ penetrating aromatic odour & flavour. It was formerly used far more extensively than today in cookery, as a spice & seasoning. It was greatly esteemed for this purpose & though not so generally appreciated today it is yet highly valued by many. In the East it's esteem has never decreased in any measure & there it has also a medical reputation. Saffron is used as a dye & as a flavouring & colouring agent in confectionary, imparting a distinctive spicy flavour & a rich yellow colour though the Saffron itself is a deep orange tending toward red. Saffron is prepared by pressing the styggmas & stamens into cakes which are dried in the sun ✳ or the style & stamens are dried in the sun & then pounded ✲ The Arabic name of the Saffron is "Kurkum" today & the name Saffron itself is derived from the Arabic "Zafran" signifying "Yellow"

No 91   SHITTAH TREE

ACACIA (ACACIA SEYAL)

(Illustrated)

SHITTAH TREE – Isa 41.19   ACACIA R.V & N.T.

SHITTIM WOOD – Ex 25.5 : 10 : 13 : 23 : 28 : 26.15 : 26 : 32 : 37 : 27.1 : 6 : Deut 10.3 ACACIA R.V & N.T

SHITTAH TREE & SHITTIM WOOD

The Hebrew names untranslated in the A.V. rendered "Acacia" in the R.V. & N.T.
The tree is mentioned only once in Scripture in reference to the Millenial earth when the desert will be fruitful (Isa 41.19) The wood is mentioned many times, being used in the construction & fittings of the Tabernacle. The tree is the Acacia (A. seyal) the only timber tree of any size occurring in the Arabian desert. It grows in the driest & hottest situations, is scattered frequently throughout the Sinaitic Peninsula, & is abundant in the arid ravines on the Western shores of the Dead Sea. Acacia seyal is a small tree (fifteen to twenty feet) with angulas, twisted, branches, delicate feathery leaves ✲, long sharp thorns, & curved twisted & tapering pods. The tree is very beautiful

---

✳ Rye is a northern grain & is rarely if ever grown in Egypt or Palestine · ✳ The Saffron Cakes of the East
✲ The Saffron Powder of the East

in spring when covered with its fragrant yellow flowers, & elegant at any season & very conspicuous in the barren desert. The wood is hard & very durable, close grained, & orange red in colour withy the heart wood of a darker hue. Shittim Wood typifies Christ in His humanity — "a root out a dry ground" & incorruptable. "A root out of a dry ground" for the Acacia flourishes only in the arid & waterless desert. Incorruptable for Acacia wood is exceedingly durable. Gum Arabic is obtained from the Acacia, It exudes from the branches spontaniously in sticky patches but is obtained in greater quantities by making incisions in the bark.

Twice in Scripture are places named after the Shittah Tree. In Numbers 34.48+49 we are told the Israelites "encamped in the plains of Moab by the Jordan of Jericho. And they encamped by the Jordan from Beth-jeshimoth unto Abel Shittim in the plains of Moab" (N.T.) Abel Shittim means "the plain of acacias" (N.T. Note) or some claim "the marsh of acacias" In Joel 3.18 "And it shall come to pass in that day, that the mountains shall drop new wine, & the hills shall flow with new wine — —& a fountain shall come forth from the Lord, & shall water the valley of Shittim". The valley of Shittim signifying "the valley of acacias" (N.T. Note is Joel 3.18). Acacia bark is astringent & is used in tanning leather. The tree must not be confounded with that commonly cultivated under the name of Acacia in Britain which is the Robinia or False-Locust Tree (Robinia pseudo-acacia) a native of America. This tree although of the same Botanical Order (Leguminoseæ) as the Acacia is far removed from that species both generically & in appearance. The Acacia bears flowers which have neither calyx nor corolla, their numerous yellow stamens causing them to look like little golden balls whilst the foliage is bi-pinnate with very narrow leaflets feathery & delicate looking. The Robinia bears flowers which are of the typical papilionaceous form, reminiscent in form size & arrangement of white Laburnum flowers, whilst the foliage is rather heavy, pinnate, with some four to six broad, almost ovate, leaflets reminiscent (though deciduous) of the foliage of the Carob-tree ✱. The trees have therefore nothing in common save the name, & why the name should have been bestowed upon the Robinia is a mystery, but the fact that the Robinia is popularly & erroneously called "Acacia" in Britain should be well noted if mistakes are to be avoided

No 92   SOAP

"BORITH" – SOAP Jer 2.22: Mal 3.2.

Soap was manufactured in Old Testament times by burning certain alkaline plants & thus obtaining Potash which was mixed with Olive Oil. The most important potash-yielding plants in Palestine are the Salsola Kali which is abundant in the salt marshes of the Dead Sea Basin & equally abundant in the salt-marshes on the coasts of Britain, & Salicornia fruticosa frequent on the eastern shores of the Mediterranean but not occurring in Britain ✱. Salsola Kali is the Saltwort, a small plant bearing minute red flowers & scale-like, yet succulent, awl-shaped, spine-tipped leaves. The stems are hairy, glaucous, square, ridged, & fleshy, but the main stem becomes woody & very hard. This plant which is of annual duration, is called "El Kali" by the Arabs & from this name the word Alkali is derived. Salicornia fruticosa is a species of Glasswort, a leafless much branched, many jointed, smooth, glossy, reddish green plant which bears its minute green flowers at the joints & is fleshy throughout its entire growth, never becoming in any degree hard or woody. The soap described above was

✱ It is probably for this reason that the tree has received its alternative name of "False Locust" Tree, an alternative name for the Carob tree being "Locust Tree" ✱ Both these plants belong to the same Botanical Order — Chenopodiaceae. "Salsola – from the Latin SAL – "salt" the plants being rich in soda". "Salicornia – from the Latin SAL – "salt", CORNU-"horn" from the abundance of soda (continued on leaf)

Soap (continued)

used for the same purposes as is soap today. It is the cleansing properties of soap which are stressed in Scripture. Israel who had deserted the Lord who had brought her out of Egypt, who had gone in the way of the heathen, forsaken the fountain of living waters to hew out broken cisterns which could hold no water, she whom God had planted as a noble vine but who had degenerated into a worthless wild vine, though she wash herself with nitre & use much soap could not make herself clean in the sight of God, He who knew all her iniquities (Jer 2.22) But when the Lord shall come suddenly to His temple -- Who may abide the day of his coming? & who shall stand when he appeareth? for he is like a refiner's fire, & like fuller's soap: And he shall sit as a refiner & purifier of silver: & he shall purify the sons of Levi, & purge them as gold & silver, that they may offer unto the Lord an offering in righteousness. Then shall the offering of Judah & Jerusalem be pleasant unto the Lord, as in the days of old, & as in former years (Mal 3.1 to 4). The N.T. does not mention soap but instead gives "Potash" in Jeremiah & "Lye" in Malachi ✸
Important for No 94 SPICERY see Note at foot of Next Page

No 93   SPIKENARD

"NERD" — SPIKENARD cant 1.12: 4.13 & 14 | NARD (NARDOSTACHYS JATAMANSI)
"Ναρδος πιστικη" - SPIKENARD Mark 14.3: John 12.3.   (Illustrated)
SPIKENARD. A perfume made from the fragrant root of the Nardostachys jatamansia, an Indian plant of the Order Valerianaceæ which is found only in the heights of the Himalayas. The perfume therefore was very rare & costly in Palestine, the alabaster vase of pure (that is "genuine") Nard (Mark 14.3 to 5) being so valuable that was worth three hundred Roman Pence equal to £10/12/0 in English money. Two Hebrew words are covered by the name Spikenard in Mark 14.3 & John 12.3. The A.V. gives "Spikenard" in the text & in the Margin "Pure Nard" or "Liquid Nard" & The R.V. gives "Spikenard" in the text & in the Margin "Greek. Pistic Nard, Pistic being perhaps a local name. Others take it to mean genuine Nard, others "liquid". The N.T. gives "pure Nard" in the text without comment. Most authorities consider that the significance is "Pure (that is Genuine") Nard". The Hebrew word "Nerd" translated "Spikenard" in the three passages in the Song of Solomon where it occurs (being found no where else in the Old Testament) in the A.V.; R.V. & N.T. is so translated in all versions & is undoubtedly correct. Nard was employed by the ancients in both a solid & liquid state, liquid Nard being used by the Romans for anointing the hair.
No 94 see Above

No 95   STACTE

"NATAP" — A DROP (of sweet spice)   Yielded by the STORAX-TREE (STYRAX
     A DROP (of water) Job 36.27 Ex 30.24 "STACTE" A.V.R.V.&N.T.   OFFICINALE)
                        (Illustrated)
Translated "STACTE" in Exodus 30.24 in the A.V. R.V. & N.T. ✸
"And Jehovah said to Moses, Take fragrant drugs — stacte, & onycha, & galbanum — fragrant drugs & pure frankincense; in like proportions shall it be" Ex 30.34 N.T.
The Hebrew word "NATAP" which has the meaning of "A DROP" occurs twice in the Old

✸ LYE. Water made alkaline with wood ashes, etc, for washing "Dictionary
✳ The stems of this plant are hairy & the root-stock thick & very fragrant. The root-stock is [Nerd]
✸ Denarii. Denarion (Latin "Denarius") A silver coin worth about 8½
† Stacte "NATAP" is in the Hebrew "a drop" = a drop of sweet spice in Ex 30.24 a drop of water in "Stacte" Ex 30.24. A.V.R.V.& N.T. drops of water Job 36.23 A.V.R.& N.T.   Job 36.23
(continued from one-leaf) in the plant, & it horn-like (in appearance, in texture fleshy) branches" Johns

Stacte (continued)

Testament. In the Hebrew Bible (that is the Bible used by the Jews & literally translated in English) it is rendered "a drop" on each occassion. This rendering is retained in Job 36·27 in the A·V: R·V & N·T but the passage in Exodus 30·34 rendered "A drop of sweet spice" in the Hebrew Bible is rendered "Stacte" in all these versions.✻ The R·V· margin suggests that STACTE IS OPOBALSAMUM but it is generally considered that the substance is STORAX the gum-resin of the Storax Tree (Styrax officinale). This gum was greatly valued in the East in former times & is today held in esteem by the Arabs, & used by them medicinally to sooth coughs & give ease in throat complaints. The Storax of commerce is a different substance & is obtained from liquid-amber orientale a tree indigenous to Asia Minor. The Storax Tree is more properly described as a shrub. It is commonly found in thickets on the lower hills of ~~Palestine~~, in Galilee it is the predominant shrub, & it occurs on the lower slopes of Lebanon. It is of a some-what tender constitution & is not found in the heights, perishing in exposed situations. The Storax is a very beautiful & conspicuous shrub bearing single simple ovate leaves which are light green above & covered with white down on the under-side. The large white fragrant flowers, which open in March, are six petaled & arranged in small spikes of four or five. In the flowering season the tree is covered with a snowy mass & is most beautiful & conspicuous, whilst the fragrance spreads far & wide. The bark is of a pale hue. The whiteness of the Storax Tree has caused some to consider it to be the Poplar of the Scripture but it's small stature makes this impossible. ✱

✻ Without comment save in the R·V· which gives "Or OPOBALSUM in the Margin
✱ See No 94 for notes on the Poplar

Note No 94   SPICERY

"NECHOTH" — SPICERY   ASTRAGALUS (ASTRAGALUS TRAGACANTHA
          Gen 37·25.   (Illustrated)
          SPICES Gen 43·11.   TRAGACINTH R·V·Margin N·T· Text
"NAKAH" — SPICES   2·Kings 20·13 : Isa 39·2.
✻ Behold, a caravan of Ismaelites came from Gilead ~~their~~ camels bore tragacinth, & balsam, & ladanum - going to carry it down to Egypt." Gen 37·25 N·T.
✻ Carry down the man a gift: a little balsam & a little honey, tragacinth & ladanum, pistacia-nuts & almonds" Gen 43·11. N·T.

The Spicery carried by the Ismaelites into Egypt for sale & the Spices sent by ~~Joseph~~ as a present to the governor of Egypt are believed to have been Gum Tragacinth. This gum is a natural exudation found upon the twigs, thorns, & leaves of several species of Astragalus especially Astragalus Tragacantha. It is drawn out by the hot sun & is gathered in the same way as ladanum. The genus is a very large one consists of herbs & shrubs very numerous in Asia. Fifty species of Astragalus are indigenous in Palestine. They range from the heights of Hermon to the shores of the Dead Sea. The gum bearing species are stunted, hoary, thorny shrubs inhabiting the deserts. The flowers are papilionous & usually yellow though in a few species they are white & in Astragalus Tragacantha alone purple. Astragalus Tragacantha that is the most important of the gum producing species bears pinnate leaves (the mid-riff of which is terminated with a spine) & long thorns. Only when growing under the most favourable conditions does it lose its usual stunted form. The spicery of Genesis was together with the other substances mentioned in conjunction with it ✱ a product of Palestine (continued over-leaf)
✱ See Notes on ladanum No 52

No 96   SYCAMINE

"Συκάμινος" — SYCAMINE Luke 17.6   BLACK MULBERRY (MORUS NIGRE)
MULBERRY 1 Mac 6.34   (Illustrated)

"And the Lord said, If ye had faith as a grain of mustard seed, ye might say unto this sycamine tree, Be thou plucked up by the root, & be thou planted in the sea; & it ~~should~~ obey you." Luke 17.6

"And to the end that they might provoke the elephant's to fight, they showed them the blood of grapes & mulberries" 1 Mac 6.34

SYCAMINE. Mentioned only once in the Scripture when the Lord Jesus, teaching His disciples the power of faith, said "If ye have faith as a grain of mustard seed, ye might say unto this sycamine tree, Be thou plucked up by the root, & be thou planted in the sea; & it should obey you". The Sycamine is the Black Mulberry (Morus nigre) still called "Sycaminos" in Greece & must not be confounded with the Sycamore which is a species of Fig* This tree has been cultivated in Palestine from an early date & would be a very frequent & familiar object in the days when the Lord was upon earth & therefore to hand to serve as an illustration to His exhortation. It has been valued from antiquity for it's timber & it's fruit. This fruit (which is as valued in the East today as it was in earlier times) is something like a Blackberry in appearance but in reality each drupe is the product of a seperate blossom. The flowers are small, green, inconspicuous, & crowded closely together. It is stated in 1 Maccabees 6.34 that the juice of Mulberries was used to excite the elephants of Antiochus who mistook it for blood. Formerly cultivated in Palestine for the sake of its fruit & its timber it has today an added attraction in the value of it's leaves as food for the silk-worm. Since the introduction of the silk-worm into the Holy Land the rearing of it has become an important industry in various parts of the country & the cultivation of the Mulberry has greatly increased. It abounds in Lebanon* & upon the hill sides near Jerusalem reaching a maximum height of some forty feet. The Mulberry of the Old Testament is the Aspen *.

No 97   SYCOMORE

*SHIKMIN" — SYCOMORE   FICUS SYCOMORUS (Illustrated)(Fruit)
*SHIKMOTH" — SYCOMORE 1 Kings 10.27; 1 Chron 27.28; 2 Chron 1.15; 9.27 Isa 9.10;
*Συκομορεα" — SYCOMORE Luke 19.4.   Jer 24.2; Amos 7.14.

The Sycomore is a species of Fig & is not related to the Sycamore of Britain which is the Great Maple (Acer pseudo-plantanus) & is not mentioned in the Scripture. The resemblance (which is very slight) is in the shape of the leaves yet it was for this reason that the Great Maple was in mediaeval times confounded with the Sycomore & so recieved it's common name. Sycomore fruit is a Fig in miniature, it is green, & although edible is unsatisfying to the palate having but a mild insipid flavour, & this at it's best when prepared for consumption, which is done by cutting a hole in the top of the still growing fruit when it has almost reached maturity. This results in an acrid juice (which would otherwise make the fruit entirely ineatable) being discharged, leaving only the

---

* Though both are of the same Botanical Order "Urticaceae" * In a cultivated state, It is also found away from cultivation & may be polygamous.
* See Notes on the Mulberry No 63

(continued from overleaf). & as the spice bearing trees are natives of India & the Tropics & do not ascent in Palestine Tragacanth seems to obviously be the substance intended. The N.T. gives Tragacanth in the text without comment & the R.V. spicery in the list & *Gum Tragacanth in the Margin. Some consider that the spices of 2 Kings 20.13 & Isa 39.2 were also Gum

Sycomore (continued)

the faint sweetness already mentioned ⁂ The Sycomore is a large tree with wide-spreading branches springing out from the trunk from a very low level & making the tree one of the easiest to climb (Luke 19.4) The foliage is evergreen, downy on the under-surface, & aromatic. The fruit is formed by numerous minute flowers within a hollow receptacle ⁂ produced all the year round but is most abundant in early summer. It is borne in small bunches which sprout from all parts of the trunk & branches. The Sycomore is the commonest timber tree in Egypt & its wood is employed extensively in the manufacture of furniture, doors, boxes & mummy cases. Although soft & porous its durability is proved by the survival of mummy-cases after lying in the tombs for thousands of years. The Sycomore is very tender & cannot bear frost (Ps 78.47) It occurs in Palestine only in the Jordan Valley (which is sub-tropical) & on the Maritime Plains (where frost is very infrequent & mild)

No 98 TARES

"Ζιζάνια" – TARES BEARDED DARNEL (LOLIUM
Matt 13.24 & 30:36 DARNEL N.T. TEMULENTUM)

TARES. The Bearded Darnel (Lolium temulentum) a species of Rye-grass (Illustrated) & the only Grass which produces poisonous seeds. It occurs rarely as a weed in cornfields in Britain & frequently in the cornfields of Palestine & other Mediterranean countries. Whenever possible it is scrupulously eradicated. It is a dangerous plant in that the seed when ground with the corn & made into bread produces poisonous symptoms frequently ending in death. It is also poisonous to animals. The Arabic name is "Zawān" signifying "Vomiting" & is very fitting for the symptoms of Darnel poisoning are sickness, convulsions & diarrhoea. In its earlier stages it is not easy to distinguish in the cornfields as it has a broader leaf than most grasses & closely resembles Wheat until the appearance of the ear after which, of course, it is at once detected. It is only mentioned once in the Scripture in the Parable of the Wheat & the Tares ⁂. The Tares of Botany ✡ are entirely different plants, they are not grass-like but resemble Vetches, being papilionous climbing plants. Their only point of resemblance with the Tares of the Bible is that they are cornfield weeds, but they do not resemble Wheat which is the essential characteristic of the Tares of the Parable.

No 99 TEIL-TREE

TEREBINTH (PISTACIA TEREBINTH
– US)
"ELAH" – TEIL-TREE Isa 6.13 ■ ❀ ₰ (Illustrated)
ELM Hos 4.13 ₰ ❀
OAK Gen 35.4 ₰ ⚲ Judg 6.11 ₰ ⚲ 9.6 ■ ₰ 2 Sam 18 ₰ ⚲ 1 Kings 13.14 ₰ ⚲
1 Chrom 10.12 ₰ ⚲ Ezek 6.13 ■ ⚲ ₰

"The valley of Elah" 1 Sam 17.2 & 19:1 Sam 21.9 A.V. "The valley of Terebinths" R.V. Margin
Teil is an obsolete English name for the Lime Tree (Tilia vulgaris) & means] N.T. Text
⁂ Yet it was much eaten by the poor · ※ See Notes on the Fig (No 33) for further details on the construction of this form of fruit. ⚲ The R.V. gives "Teil" in the Text & "Darnel" the Margin. The N.T. gives "Darnel" in the Text & note "A useless weed resembling Wheat" ✡ The Hairy Tare (Vicia hirsuta), the Smooth Tare (V. gamella) & the Slender Tare (V. gracilis) ❀ "Terebinth" R.V. ₰ "Turbinth" N.T. ⚲ "Oak" with "Terebinth" in Margin R.V.
→ Tragacinth but the A.V. R.V. & N.T. all give "Spices" without comment.

Teil-Tree (Continued)

only once in the A.V. in Isaiah 6.13 as the translation of the Hebrew word ELAH. This is erroneous as the time does not occur in Palestine. The same word is translated (again erroneously) "Elm" in Hosea 4.13 & elsewhere "Oak" save, in two passages in the First of Samuel where it occurs in conjunction with the word "Valley" & is left untranslated, so giving the erroneous impression of a place name. The R.V. gives "Terebinth" in Isaiah 6.13 & Hosea 4.13 & elsewhere "Oak with "Terebinth" in the Margin. The N.T. gives "Terebinth" invariably, & without comment. The tree intended is the Terebinth (Pistachia terebinthus) a small tree frequent in Palestine on hill sides & in rocky places. From a distance it resembles the Oak in appearance but is smaller, & in winter when it has shed its foliage the resemblance is very marked for the trunk of the Terebinth is gnarled & the branches are massive & twisted in the manner so characteristic of that tree. The Terebinth is closely related to the Mastic (Pistachia lentiscus) & the leaves are pinnate as in that species but larger & of a sombre dark-green hue. The flowers are borne in clusters & are small, green & inconspicuous. The succeeding fruit is a red berry about the size of a Holly berry. This is a very common tree in Southern & Eastern Palestine but is less frequent toward the north. It is frequent in the Grecian Archipelago & carries the alternative name of the Chio Turpentine Tree, Chio Turpentine being the aromatic resin of this tree, which is obtained by tapping the trunk. It has never been known for turpentine to be obtained from this tree in Palestine, its value in this respect being apparently unknown there. Tradition claims that Judas hanged himself on a Terebinth.

THORNS

Nine Hebrew words are translated variously BRAMBLE, BRIARS, THORNS & THISTLE in the in Authorised Version as follows — (1) ATAD — BRAMBLE Judges 9.14 : THORNS Ps 58.9 (2) CHOACH — BRAMBLES Isa 34.13 THICKETS 1Sam 13.6 THISTLE 2 Kings 14.19 THISTLES Job 31.40 THORNS 2 Chron 33.13 : Prov 26.9 : Cant 2.2 : Hosea 9.6 (4) CHEDEK — THORNS Prov 15.19 : BRIER Mic 7.4 (5) KOTZ — THORNS Gen 31.18 & frequently as the Old Testament word for Thorns without reference to any specific plant. (6) SHAMIR — BRIARS Isa 7.23 & 27 (7) NAATZOTZ — THORNS Isa 7.19 : 55.13 (8) BARKANIM — BRIERS Judges 8.7 & 16 (9) SILLON — BRIERS Ezek 2.6 PRICKLING BRIER 28.24. It will be seen that the names are given indiscriminately, for THORNS occurs once as the translation of ATAD, four times as the translation of CHOACH, generally as the translation of KOTZ & once as the translation of NAATZOZ. BRAMBLES (BRAMBLES) occurs once as the translation of ATAD & once as the translation of CHOACH. THISTLE (THISTLES) occurs twice as the translation of CHOACH & twice as the translation of DARDAR, BRIERS occurs once as the translation of CHEDEK, once as the translation of BAKKANIM & twice (with Prickling Brier) as the translation of SILLON. Thus ATAD occurring twice is translated once Bramble & once Thorns, CHOACH once rendered Bramble is twice translated Thistles & four times Thorns, CHEDAK occurring twice is rendered Thorns once & Brier once. The New Translation gives identical renderings save in the following instances —

Thorns (continued)

ATAD Judges 9.14 rendered Thorn-bush. CHOACH 2 Kings 14.9 rendered Thorn-bush 2 Chron 33.11 rendered Fetters. SILLON Ezek 28.24 rendered Wounding Sting

Some of the Hebrew name obviously refer to specific species but several are general terms applied to thorn-bearing plants without any thought of any particular species.

Palestine abounds in thorns & thistles, its weeds & wild shrubs almost invariably bear an abundance of spines & prickles. Combined heat & dryness always encourage the production of thorns & the climate of the country is very favourable for the development of spinous plants, such species form a considerable portion of the Flora.

Thorns & Thistles are the fruit of the curse (Gen 3.18) & their abundance in Palestine is a promised sign of the dis-favour of God for the disobedience of His people "Upon the land of my people shall come up thorns & briers"

Owing to this indiscriminate rendering of the Hebrew & the fact that several of these words are in the original only general terms it has seemed most satisfactory to group all together under "THORNS" & to describe the appropriate species under the nine Hebrew names & where the term is not specific to describe some notable thorn weed of Palestine whose characteristics most nearly approach the essential conditions, as follows —

No 100   THORNS (1) BRAMBLE   ILLUSTRATED

"ATAD" — BRAMBLE Judges 9.14,   BOX—THORN (LYCIUM EUROPÆUM)
THORNS Ps 58.9.   "THORN-BUSH" Judges 9.14: THORNS Ps 58.9 N.T.

Translated "BRAMBLE" in the parable of Jotham, Judges 9.14, & "THORNS" in Psalm 58.9 in the A.V. "THORN-BUSH" & "THORNS" respectively in the N.T. Translated "RHAMNUS" in the Septuagint & the Vulgate. The Rhamnus is the Box-thorn (Lycium europæum) a thorny shrub or, under favourable circumstances, a small slender tree, which is used in Palestine for the construction of hedges as the Hawthorn is employed in England. It has slender light green branches, narrow strap-shaped pale blue-green leaves, slender needle like thorns & pale purple trumpet shaped flowers which turn buff after fertilisation. The fruit is an oblong red berry. The Box thorn is of frequent cultivation in Britain & is not infrequent in a wild state in limestone districts as a naturalized exotic. It is a member of the Order Solanaceæ

The shade of the Box thorn is at the best very slight by reason of its slender branches & narrow leaves & then, as often, it is a mere shrub its protection is less than ever whilst its wood, when cut, soon becomes very dry & (lacking bulk) burns away very quickly. From these particulars Rhamnus therefore seems to be undoubtedly the correct translation & the Box-thorn the plant intended.

No 101   THORNS (2) BRAMBLES   species illustrated

"CHOACH" BRAMBLES Isa 34.13.   SPOTTED THISTLE (SCOLYMUS MACULATUS)
THICKETS 1 Sam 13.6
THISTLE 2 Kings 14.9 "THORN-BUSH" N.T.; THISTLES Job 31.40
THORNS ... 1.8: Prov ... : Cant 2.2 Hos 9.6
2 Chron 33.11 "Fetters" N.T.: Prov 26.9: Cant 2.2: Hos 9.6 THORNS N.T.

Mentioned eight times in the Old Testament. Translated "BRAMBLES" once (Isa 34.13) "THICKETS" once (1 Sam 13.6) "THISTLE" once (2 Kings 14.9) "THISTLES" once (Job 31.40)

Thorns (continued)

& "THORNS" four times (2.Chron 33.18 : Prov 26.9 : Cant 2.2 : Hos 9.6) in the R.V.
"BRAMBLES" once (Isa 34.13) "THICKETS" once (1 Sam 13.6) "THORN-BUSH"
once (2 Kings 14.9) "THISTLES" once (Job 31.40) "THORNS" three times (2 Chron
33.18 : Cant 2.2 : Hos 9.6) "FETTERS" once (Prov 26.9) in the N.T.

From the references it would appear to be a vigourous weed infesting both
waste places & cultivated ground. It was of sufficient height to hide a man when
crouching behind it (1 Sam 13.6) but was not stout enough or woody enough
to resist the trampling of the wild beasts "The thistle that was in Lebanon sent
to the cedar that was in Lebanon, saying, Give thy daughter to my son to wife, &
there passed by a wild beast that was in Lebanon, & trod down the thistle."
(2 Kings 14.9) It grew amongst ruins & deserted buildings in the mountains
in the valley meadows & in cultivated ground. Several species of Knapweed
& thistle occur very frequently in waste places & infest cultivated ground,
especially cornfields. Any of these might be the plant intended. The most
widespread & vigorous Thistles in Palestine are Scolymus maculatus ✱ a tall
plant which greatly resembles the Carline Thistle (Carlina vulgaris) of Britain
but is much more vigorous. It bears bright Orange flowers & very numerous
spines on the leaves, stem & involucre. This is very troublesome, covering the
cornfields in dense patches & choking the corn, & it is very difficult to
suppress. Carthamus oxycantha bears yellow flowers & has numerous sharp
& poisonous spines which inflict a painful wound. Notabasis syriaca is
a tall weed bearing pink flowers & strongly armed with numerous sharp spines.
These species also are very difficult to erradicate.

No 102   THORNS (3) THISTLES

"DARDAR" — THISTLES Gen 3.18.
     THISTLE Hos 10.8.

"Τρίβολος" THISTLES Matt 7.16
     BRIERS   Heb 6.8

Species Illustrated KNAPWEED
        (CENTAUREA
          VERBUTUM)
     STAR-THISTLE
     (CENTAUREA CALCITRAPA

The Hebrew word "DARDAR" occurs in Genesis 3.18
& in Hosea 10.8 where it is translated "THISTLE" & "THISTLES" in the A.V: R.V:
& N.T. In the Seventy it is translated "ΤΡΙΒΟΛΟΣ". ΤΡΙΒΟΛΟΣ occurs in
Matthew 7.16 & Hebrews 6.8 where it is translated "THISTLES" & "BRIERS"
in the A.V: R.V. & N.T. It is the Tribulus of the classical authors, a species of
Centauria of a spiny habit ✱. The majority of Centaurias are innocent of spines
but a few species (the Star Thistles) have the scales of the involucrum elongated
into formidable spines. Two such species are of frequent occurrence in Palestine,
infesting cornfields. Centaurea calcitrapa, the Common Star Thistle which occurs in
Southern England where it is never vigorous enough or frequent enough to be a plague
& is named Common only because it is more common than the Yellow Star Thistle (Centauria
solstitialis) & is in actual fact rare. Throughout Southern Europe & Western Asia it is

✱ The Spotted Thistle, so called because the leaves are usually spotted with white
✱ The Tribulus is frequently mentioned by the classical writers in conjunction with the
Thistle. This species cannot therefore be a Thistle but it is a thorny plant allied to
the Thistle & found frequently with it. It is generally accepted that it is a Centauria

<u>Thorns</u> (continued)

is however indeed common — far to common, a very abundant cornfield weed very difficult to eradicate. It is a stout spreading stiff looking much branched plant. It has pinnatifid leaves & sessile, lateral flower heads & purple flowers. This species is un-armed except for the involucrum, each bract of which is elongated into a long stiff spine. It flowers from July to August & is of annual duration *

Centaurea raeutieum infests cornfields & covers large areas of waste ground especially in Galilee. It has very formidable spines an inch & a half in length upon the involucrum. The stem & the leaves are entirely un-armed. It bears purple flowers in late summer.

<u>No 103</u>   T H O R N S (4)   T H O R N S

"CHEDEK" — THORNS Prov 15.19.   Species Illustrated SOLONUM
          BRIER Mic 7. 4.   (SOLONUM SANCTUM)

The Hebrew word "CHEDEK" occurs in Proverb 15.19 & Mic 7.4. where it is translated in the first Scripture "Thorn," & in the second "Brier." "The way of the slothful man is as a hedge of thorns." "The best of them is as a brier: the most upright is sharper than a thorn hedge." The context clearly shows that no herbaceous or low growing plant is intended but some vigorous thorny shrub or tree capable of being used in hedge making. There is a species of Solonum (S. sanctum formerly S. Sodomoeum) familiarly but erroneously called "The Apple of Sodom *" which is very frequent in the warmest parts of Palestine, especially the Jordan Valley. It infests waste places in the vicinity of towns & cultivated land, luxuriating in hedgerows & thickets. This Solonum is of shrubby habit, attaining to a height of some four feet. It bears much branched, very prickly stems, & large leaves which are wooly beneath & thorny on the midriff. The flower is large & white resembling a large Potato flower & the fruit has the appearance of a large Potato Apple. It is spherical, yellow when ripening, & brilliant red when fully mature. The fruit is borne abundantly & contains a large number of seeds. When growing in hedgerows its many prickles, & dense growth proves a valuable addition to the hedgerow trees. & as the Arabic name of the Thorny Solanum is CHADAK it seems very probable that this plant is the species intended by the Hebrew CHEDEK.

<u>No 104</u>   T H O R N S (5)   T H O R N S

"KOTZ" — THORNS Gen 3.18   Species Illustrated SPINY REST-HARROW
"ἄκανθα" — THORNS Matt 7.16; 13.7-2; 27.29 Heb 6.8.   (ONONIS SPINOSA)

The Hebrew word "KOTZ" occurs very frequently in the Scripture & is usually translated

* The instrument of war, known as the "Todstuy" or the "Caltrops" was either modelled upon the spines of this plant or the resemblance was noted & the plant received its name from this fact. The "Caltrop" was a metal ball from which were spikes projected in all directions. & was so constructed that however it lay at least one spike projected upwards. Its purpose was to impede cavalry by laming the horses. Many examples exist & are preserved in museums.
* See No

▽ The Rest-Harrow is a. ed not as an illustration of the plant intended by the word "KOTZ" but illustration of a thorny cornfield weed. It is a low growing shrub with a tough slim
(continued over leaf)

Thorns (continued)

"THORNS" as in Gen 3.18 "Thorns also & thistles shall it bring forth for thee" It is a general term for any prickly or thorny plant, sometimes used for a bush, at other times for a cornfield weed. No specific plant is signified. This seems clear for the LXX renders "KOTZ" "ἄκανθα" the word which is invariably translated "THORNS" in the New Testament, as Matt 7.16 "Do men gather grapes of thorns?" Matt 13.7 "And some fell amongst thorns & the thorns sprung up & choked them" & Hebrews 6.8 "But that which beareth thorns is rejected." This is also the word which is used to describe the crown of thorns placed in mockery upon the head of the Lord Jesus. *

No 105   THORNS (6) BRIERS   ILLUSTRATED

"SHAMIR" – BRIARS. Isa 7.23–22   CHRIST'S – THORN
                                        (PALIURUS ACULEATUS)

Occurs in Isaiah where it is rendered Briers. It is usually mentioned in conjunction with SHAIT (an indefinite term which cannot be identified with any specific plant) which is translated THORNS. The Christ's Thorn (Paliurus aculeatus) a straggling shrub with thorns at the base of the leaf & frequently used for hedges is called SAMUR by the Arabs today. This is the tree which is traditionally claimed to have supplied the material for the crown of thorns. The straggling flexible branches would conceivably be quite easily plaited & used for such a purpose but as already noted * the wood used to describe the crown of thorns is a general term & does not denote any particular species. The plant employed in the construction of the crown of thorns cannot therefore be identified from Scripture. The Christ's Thorn bears clusters of small white flowers & a remarkable winged fruit. It is frequent throughout Palestine & is abundant around Jerusalem. The Arabs also give the name SAMUR to the Buckthorn (Rhamnus alaoides) which is closely affiliated to the Christ's Thorn & is as frequent on the high ground. It is however of a very different appearance to the Christ's Thorn being a stiff erect shrub (reminiscent in habit of the Black-thorn) It bears small greenish-yellow flowers, small leaves & short spines. The name SAMUR is used only for these two shrubs & either might well be the SHAMIR of Isaiah, the Christ's Thorn being the most generally distributed of the two is most likely.

No 106   THORNS (7) THORNS   Species Illustrated
                                              JUJUBE-TREE

"NAATZOTZ" – THORNS. Isa 7.19; 55.13.   (ZIZYPHUS SPINA CHRISTI)
The Hebrew word "NAATZOTZ" occurs in Isaiah as the name of a tree & translated "THORN". "And they shall come, & shall rest all of them in the desolate valleys, & in

* The Rest Harrow could not have been used for the crown of thorns. ‡ See No 104

RESTHARROW (continued from the foot of the previous page)
& needle-like spines occurring with frequency as a troublesome weed in pastures & upon arable land. It is difficult to eradicate & with its dense growth can prove a serious hindrance to growing crops & grass. It is a common cornfield weed in Palestine. The Spiny Rest-Harrow is also a common plant in England in waste places & on rough pasture land. The flowers are pink pea-flowers & are found all the summer.

Thorns (continued)

the holes of the rocks, & upon all thorns, & upon all bushes " Isa 7.3. " Instead of the thorn shall come up the fir tree " Isa 55.13. The largest thorn-tree in Palestine is the Jujube Tree (Zizyphus spina-christi). It occurs in all the warmer regions of the country, is found about Jerusalem & Jericho, & luxuriates in the Jordan Valley, forming impassable thickets in many places. The Jujube Tree & the Christ's Thorn are closely related both being members of the Order Rhamneae. The Jujube Tree has however neither the trailing habit nor the weak branches of the Christ's Thorn but is a large, upright, stoutly though crookedly branched tree bearing long, strong, piercing, recurved & very formidable thorns. The fruit also is vastly different, being a bright yellow berry about the size of a large cherry with enjoyable acid flesh & a hard stone in the centre. The fruit is borne in clusters & is produced profusely from December to June. It is from this fruit which is called Jujube that the tree has received it's name. The foliage is oval & bright green whilst the flowers are small, white, & born in clusters - Like the Christ's Thorn the Jujube Tree is claimed to be the source of the material which formed the crown of thorns & like that tree it could have well been used for the purpose, its branches being tough & flexible & the thorns far stouter & more numerous than is the case with that species.

No 107   THORNS (8) BRIERS   Species Illustrated

"BARKANIM" - BRIERS Judges 8.7 & 16   BRAMBLE
(RUBUS FRUTICOSUS)

Occurs only in Judges 8.7 & 16 where it is translated "BRIERS" (I was the threat of Gideon to the men of Succoth who refused him food when he pursuing the Midianites = When the Lord hath delivered Zebah & Zalmunna into mine hand, then will I tear your flesh with thorns of the wilderness & with briers " Judges 8.7. And afterwards he fulfilled his threat "He took the elders of the city, & thorns of the wilderness & briers & with them he taught the men of Succoth". Judges 8.16. The thorns of the wilderness would seem to be the Acacia (Acacia syal). Briers would appear to be some thorny plant which could be used as a flail. The most likely plant is the Common Bramble (Rubus fruticosus) which is as frequent in Palestine as in England & luxuriates about the fords of Succoth. Its trailing, slender, prickly branches would be ideal for the purpose & ready to hand. The Bramble is a very variable plant but it is always a trailing shrub with prickly stems. The foliage consists of from three to five leaflets. The flowers are white with numerous yellow stamens, like little white roses, & the succeeding fruit consists of a number of loculi connected together. It is at first green, next red, & finely black when ripe, edible & of a very pleasant flavour. The flowers appear in June & continue opening until the ripening of the fruit in September.

No 108   THORNS (3) BRIERS   Species Illustrated

"SILLON" - BRIERS Ezek 2.6.   BUTCHER'S BROOM
PRICKING BRIER Ezek 28.24   (RUSCUS ACULEATUS)

The Hebrew word "SILLON" occurs twice in Ezekiel where it is translated "Brier" Ezek 2.6 & "A Pricking Brier" Ezek 28.24. There is an Arabic word "SULLAON" which is applied to the sharp points at the apex of Palm leaves & also to the Butcher's Broom (Ruscus aculeatus) the branches of which are leaf-like & terminate in a sharp point. The Arabic "SULLAON" is probably identical with the Hebrew "SILLON" & if this be so the Brier of Ezekiel would seem to be the Butcher's Broom. This remarkable shrub occurs rather infrequently in woods in Southern England but it is very frequent in many parts of

Thorns (continued)

Palestine. It belongs to the Order Liliaceae* It reaches a height of three or four feet & is a stiff looking plant with erect stems & flattened branches which have the appearance of stiff dark green spiny-tipped leaves. The true leaves are minute & scale-like. The flowers are minute, green & grow singly from the centre of the leaf-like branches. They open from February to May. The succeeding fruit is a round scarlet berry as large as a Cherry & does not ripen until the Autumn.

No 109   THORNS (10) NETTLES   Species Illustrated

"CHARUL" - NETTLE Job 30.7 ·   ACANTHUS
                    Prov 24.31· Zeph 2.9.   (ACANTHUS SPINOSUS)

Two words are translated "Nettle" in the Scripture

1 KUMMOSH   This refers to the true Nettle. Two species of which are frequent in Palestine*

2 CHARUL   This word is derived from a root "meaning that which burns," & must essentially denote some plant which stings as the Nettle. The plant intended could not have been the Nettle however as it is mentioned along with it in Proverbs 24.31 (Nettle being there translated "Thorn") The plant was a weed of quick growth infesting arable land (Prov 24.31) & waste places (Zeph 2.9) It reached a considerable height as men could creep beneath it (Job 30.7) & it had a burning sting.

The Acanthus (A. spinosus) fits the description. It is a prickly plant with a burning sting. It infests cornfields & is frequent in waste places & amidst ruins. It is a handsome plant with conspicuous purple flowers. The stems (which upon withering become woody) are gathered for use as fuel by the Bedouins. This explains several Scriptures which speak of thorns being used for this purpose (Ps 58.9 : Ecc 8.6: Is 33.12) Such fuel crackles & flares & consumes very quickly

---

There is one thorny plant very frequent in Palestine today which is not mentioned in the Scripture. It is a recent introduction – The Prickly Pear† a native of America which has over-run all the warmer parts of Europe & is very troublesome in Palestine. It is used to form hedges, but it is also a persistent weed difficult to eradicate.

No 110 (Ξύλον Θύϊνον) THYINE WOOD

     – THYINE WOOD. Rev 18·12   THYINE TREE
Mentioned only once in the Scripture amongst the   (THUYA ARTICULATA)
precious commodities of the Babylon of the Book of   (ILLUSTRATED)
Revelation. It was held in the greatest esteem by the Greeks & Romans & used for the most expensive furniture fetching fabulous prices. It is very heavy, close grained, fragrant & reddish-brown in colour, sometimes being variegated by knots when its value is greatly enhanced. It is still highly prized in Algeria for inlay work. Thyine Wood is the wood of a small Cypress (Thuya articulata indigenous to the Atlas Mountains). This is a very small tree of very slow growth. It is almost leafless, the leaves being reduced to very small scales at the top of each joint of the jointed branches. The resin which exudes from the Thyine Tree is known as "Gum sandarach & is used in the manufacture of parchment. The tree was called "CITRUS" & its wood CITRON WOOD by the Romans.

---

* It is the only shrubby Monocotyledon found in England ※ See also 67. † Opuntia

No III   <u>VINE</u>

"GEPHEN" - VINE. Gen 9.20 : 40.9 + 10 :   GRAPE VINE (VINIS VINIFERA)
49.11 : Numb 8.23 : 20.5 : Deut 8.7 & 8 : Ps 78.47 :   Illustrated
80.9 & 13 : 105.33 : Cant 2.15 : Isa 16.8 & 11 : Amos 9.13 : Mic 4.4 : Zech 3.10.

"αμπελος" - VINE   John 3.10   "SÔREK" - CHOICE VINE Gen 49.11 : Isa 5.2 : Jer 2.21

"YAYIN" - WINE   Gen 14.18 : Ps 75.8 : Prov 23.30 : Isa 48.32 + 33 : Ezek 27.18 :
Hos 14.7 : Isa 25.6 : OΣVOS - WINE Matt 9.17.

DEBASH - SYRUP   Gen 43.11 : Ezek 27.17   Translated "Honey" but in these
Scriptures it is considered that the syrup of grapes is intended .   "Honey" N.T.

GRAPE JUICE   Gen 49.10 : Numb 6.2 :

RAISENS — 1 Sam 25.18 : 30.12 : 2 Sam 16.1 : 1 Chron 12.40.

FLAGON OF WINE   2 Sam 6.19 : 1 Chron 16.3 : Cant 2.5 : Hos 3.1. (Flagon of
Wine in these Scriptures, should be CAKE of Raisens). Translated RAISEN CAKES N.T.

VINEYARD - Ex 22.5 : Jos 24.13 : Lev 19.10 : Cant 1.14 : Isa 5.2 : Matt 21.33 :
Mark 12.1 : John 15.2.

WINE-PRESS - Gen 49.11 : Judg 7.25 : Isa 5.2 : 63.2 & 3 : Jer 25.30 Joel 3.13
     Zech 14.10 : Matt 15.13.

The Vine is frequently mentioned in Scripture . It is first mentioned in Genesis when Noah planted a vineyard after the Flood (Gen 9.20) It has been cultivated from the earliest times & was grown in Egypt (Gen 40.9) & in Canaan in the days of Abraham (Gen 14.18) & in Assyria from antiquity. The Promised Land was a land of vines (Deut 8.8). The Vineyards were always fenced (Isa 5.2) This was essential as grazing animals are fond of Vine-leaves. The Tower (Isa 5.2) was also essential as the Vineyards were outside the towns & villages, often in lonely situations, & the residence of some person was imperative to keep watch against marauders during the whole time that the grapes are ripening. The vintage was a time of rejoicing, thus the desolation of Moab is stressed by the lack of revelry at this season "In the vineyards shall be no singing neither shall there be shouting : the treaders shall tread out no wine in their presses. I have made their vintage to cease" (Isa 16.10) The vintage commences in September & in the colder regions continues until the end of October, whilst the Wheat sowing season starts in November. Therefore the fruitfulness of the Millenial earth is foretold in Amos depicted in the length of the Vintage — "Behold the days come saith the Lord, that the ploughman shall overtake the reaper & the treader of grapes him that soweth seed" (Amos 9.13.) The grapes were crushed on the spot, the wine press being situated in the vineyard (Isa 5.2. Matt 15.33) The press consisted of two tanks, one higher than the other, In the upper the grapes were crushed (by treading with the feet (Jer 25.30 : Gen 49.11) & the must ran into the lower. The treading was always done by several men & in this fact lies the significance of Isa 63.2 & 3 . The Vine if it is to develope an abundant crop requires constant & drastic pruning. The whole of the wood is often cut back to the main stem. Only by this means can an abundant crop be produced. It has many enemies which destroy it's fruit, outstanding are the Wild Boar (Ps 80.13) & the Jackal (the Fox of Song 2.15) Both Red & White grapes were cultivated in Palestine, the red being the most valued for wine making. Several sorts of wine are mentioned in Scripture. The Hebrew word for ordinary wine is YAYIN. The sweet wine of Acts 2.13 is

Vine (continued)

the finest wine made from the juice compressed from the grapes by the weight of the bunches only & collected before the treading commenced. Wine on the lees (Isa 25.6) was wine that had been kept on the lees (dregs) in order to increase it's body. The mixed wine of Prov 23.30 & the wine of full mixture of Ps 25.8 was wine mixed with spices to increase it's potency. This sour wine is translated Vinegar in Ruth 2.14. & is by some considered to be the Vinegar offered to the Lord Jesus Christ on the cross (Matt 27.48) The fresh juice of grapes was also used as a drink (Gen 40.11) & this when boiled down to a third of it's bulk becomes a thick & treacly syrup of a light brownish yellow colour & a very sweet flavour. The Hebrew name DEBASH is translated Honey in the A.V. It was this substance which Jacob included in his present to the governor of Egypt (Gen 43.11) & which was an article of commerce between the Israelites & the men of Tyre (Ezek 27.17) not as would appear bee's honey. The choicest berries of the white grapes selected specially for the purpose are laid in the sun & dried when they become Raisens. The Raisen was as much esteemed in Biblical times as today (2 sam 6.19; 1 Chron 16.3; Cant 2.5; Hos 3.1 where "flagons of wine" should read "cakes of raisens" & is translated "Raisen cakes" in the N.T. The Nazarene was forbidden to drink wine or grape juice, grapes or raisens. To dwell every man under his own vine & fig tree is the expression of peace & prosperity 1.Kings 4.25; Mic 4.4; Zech 3.10)

BÖSER - WILD GRAPES Isa 5.2: 18.5.   FOX GRAPE
    UNRIPE GRAPES Job 15.33. RIPENING GRAPE. N.T. Hs.18.5.

The Wild Vine is Fox grape indigenous to Palestine & other countries bordering on the Mediterranean. It is frequent in waste places trailing over bushes & by the highways covering the hedges. The fruit is small rounded & black. It is very acid & astringent & is not fit to eat. Neither is it of any value for wine though it is sometimes used for vinegar. Some authorities consider that BÖSER translated "wild grapes" Isa 5.2 & 4: 18.5. & translated "unripe grapes" Job 15.33 signifies the fruit of the Wild Grape as opposed to the grape of the cultivated Vine. This word in the singular is translated COCKLE in Job 31.40. A.V. & R.V. & TARES N.T.

"GEPHEN SEDOM" - VINE OF SODOM (Deut 32.32)   Species Illustrated
Only mentioned once in the Scripture (Deut 32.32 &   CALOTROPSIS GIGANTEA
believed to be identical with the Apple of Sodom = Dead sea fruit, that tempt the eye But turn to ashes on the lips. " - The Dead Sea Fruit whose fruit was pleasant to the eye but turned to ashes in the mouth. Some consider the plant to be the Coloquinth * which is abundant in the desert around the Dead Sea, is vine-like & bears attractive orange fruit which contain a bitter & poisonous pulp which when the fruit ripens dries up to powder. This fits both the description of the Vine of Sodom & the Apple of Sodom Some suggest Solanum Sodomum a thorny plant bearing large red apple-like fruits which are poisonous & acid. This plant however is frequent throughout Palestine & is not peculiar to the Dead Sea Basin. Others claim the Calotropis Tree a member of the order Asclepiadaceae a tropical & semi-tropical order. This tree is frequent in Nubia & Southern Egypt but

*See No 39 Wild gourd   *See No 109 Thorn. (4)

Vine of Sodom (Continued)

in Palestine it is found only in the Dead Sea Basin, the extreem northern limit of it's range. It is a small tree of a height some twelve feet with light, thick, spongy, cork-like bark & large glossy oval leaves which when broken emit an acrid milky juice reminiscent of the Spurge on like occasions. The flowers are large & white, & the fruit, borne in bunches of three or four is large, oblong, bright yellow & soft to the touch. The outer covering contains a slender pod which encloses numerous flat seeds, each fitted with a tuft of beautiful long white silky hairs. This is another fruit beautiful to the eye but containing no food.

No 114   WALNUT

"EGOZ" - NUTS   Cant 6.11   JUGLANS REGIA   Illustrated

Two words are translated "Nuts" in the Scriptures & each word is mentioned only once.

1/ BETNIM (Gen 43.11) is the Pistachio Nut, the fruit of the Pistachio Tree. Much cultivated & appreciated in the East & indigenous to Palestine ✱

2/ EGOZ (Cant 6.11) is the Walnut (Juglans regia) a native of the uplands of Palestine, Syria & Persia. Cultivated in the cooler regions of these lands from the earliest times & from thence introduced into the rest of Western Asia & Europe. The foliage is heavy & dense & the branches ends spreading, casting a graceful shade which is very attractive in the hot summers of the East. The heat of the sun draws a sweet fragrance from the leaves, & the tree is of a graceful appearance. For these reasons (apart from the value of the fruit) it has always been an extensively cultivated garden tree in the East & well worthy of a place in the gardens of Solomon. The leaves (which are pinnate like those of the Ash but with larger & broader leaflets) appear in Palestine in the middle of March & the flowers open with the leaves. The fruit ripens in August. It is in Northern Palestine where the Walnut is extensively cultivated for the sake of it's fruit & the oil extracted from the immature nuts. In this region it takes the place of the Olive but in the hottest regions of Palestine it is not found. The Walnut is cultivated extensively throughout Europe for the sake of it's fruit & it's valuable timber.

No 115   WILLOW   Species Illustrated

"ARÂBIM" - WILLOW   Lev 23.40: Jb,& 40.22   **No 115**   SALLOW

Ps 137.1&2 Is 21.5. 7:44.3&4.   SALIX CINEREA

"TZAPHTZAPHAH"   Ezek 17.5.   **No 115A**   ALMOND-LEAVED WILLOW

Two Hebrew words are translated "Willow"   SALIX TRIANDRA

in the Scriptures.   **No 115B**   OSIER

1/ ARÂBIM. ✱ It is described as a water-side tree   SALIX VIMINALIS

of the valleys (Job 40.22: Is 21.5. 7: 44.3 & 4: Ps 137.1 & 2) & was used in the construction of the booths at the Feast of Tabernacles (Lev 23.40)

2/ TZAPHTZAPHAH & Mentioned only in Ezek 17.5. referring to a water-side tree. Eight species of Willow occur in Palestine. All are found only by the sides of rivers & streams, are frequent in locality but of a somewhat scattered distribution & are (in that country) of an inconspicuous & unattractive appearance save in the very early spring when the staminate trees are wreathed with their golden catkins. The Almond leaved Willow (Salix triandra) The Sallow (S. cinerea) The Common Osier

---

✱ See No 68. NUTS for notes on the Pistachio Nut.   & Arabic GHARAB   & Arabic SAFSAF. The name used today by the Arabs is almost the same.

Willow (continued)

(S. viminalis & the Black Willow (S. nigricans) are the most frequent species. The Common Sallow (Salix cinerea) is a large shrub or small tree with glaucous obovate-lanceolate leaves which are hairy beneath, downy twigs & buds & pale yellow anthers which appear in early spring. It is frequent in damp places. This is a frequent shrub of such situations in England, flowering in March & April.

The Almond-leaved Willow (Salix triandra) is a tree which reaches a height of some thirty feet with smooth oblong-lanceolate, serrated leaves which are two to four inches long, pale on the under surface & possessing large stipules. The anthers are golden & mature in April & May. This is a common riverside tree in Palestine & also in England.

The Osier (S. viminalis) is a shrub or small tree with linear-lanceolate leaves from five to ten inches long, with wavy margins. The catkins first appear in April before the leaves but may occassionally be found in June when the tree is in full leaf. The branches are long, slender & flexible, downy when young, polished when mature. This is the Willow extensively cultivated for it's branches, used in basket making etc. (The Almond-leaved Willow is also used for this purpose)

The Weeping Willow (S. Babylonica) has been introduced & is frequently found by wells & ponds in the coastal regions. This species is said to be native of China & Japan & not to occur in a wild state in Babylonia. Some authorities claim that the Oleander (Nerium oleander) the "Rose" of the Apocrypha ✱ is the Willow of Scripture. This is a small indigenous tree frequent by the side of lakes, rivers & streams throughout the country save in the Dead Sea Basin. It has narrow uncut leaves, which are dark green & large & beautiful red flowers in June. The whole tree is poisonous.

No 116   WILLOW OF BABYLON   ILLUSTRATED WEEPING WILLOW (SALIX BABYLONICA)

"ARABIM" – WILLOW Psalm 137.142.
"By the rivers of Babylon there we sat down, yea we wept when we remembered Zion. We hanged our harps upon the willows in the midst thereof". The association of the Willow with sadness is thought by some to have originated from this Scripture when the Israelites in their Babylonian exile in the sadness of their hearts, hung up their harps on the Willows by the side of the rivers. The people of God exiled in a far away alien country "How shall we sing the Lord's song in a strange land?" It was for a long time thought that this Willow was the Weeping Willow – the Willow of Babylon (Salix Babylonica) so familiar in gardens & parks, but it is now claimed that this is out of the question as Salix Babylonica is confined in it's wild state to the Far East & would not have been introduced in to Babylon at that early period. There is no doubt however that some species of Willow is intended. Several species occur by riversides throughout Mesopotamia. The Weeping Willow is one of the most graceful of trees. A characteristic of the species is that owing to it's pendent habit the catkins point to the base of the stem instead of it's apex as in all other species of Willow

---

✱ See No 81 ROSE (Ecclesiasticus) for notes on the Oleander

WORMWOOD   Illustrated

LA'ANAH — WORMWOOD. Deut 20.18: ~~~~ ARTEMESIA ABSINTHIUM
  Prov 5 4: Jer 9.15: 23.15: Lam 3.15:19: Amos 5.7: Translated Wormwood Amos 5.7

"ΑΨΙΝΘΟΣ" — WORMWOOD Rev 8.11.

Wormwood is mentioned several times in Scripture but always illustratively as signifying bitterness or misery. Five species of Wormwood bitterness or misery. Five species of Wormwood are indigenous to Palestine — Artemesia Judaica. A cinerea A. nilotica, A. fruticosa & A. deltiliana. They abound on the sea coast & in the deserts. They are characteristically marked by a strong odour & a very bitter taste. All species are of a very graceful appearance with much divided leaves & clusters of small yellow flowers. The Common Wormwood (Artemesia absinthium) has long been cultivated for medicinal purposes. It was greatly valued in early times & was of common cultivation in Palestine. It has silky, hoary (almost silvery) much divided leaves & bright yellow flowers which open from August to September. Only the outer florets produce seed. The whole plant is strongly aromatic. It occurs in a wild state in waste places in England but is of local distribution.

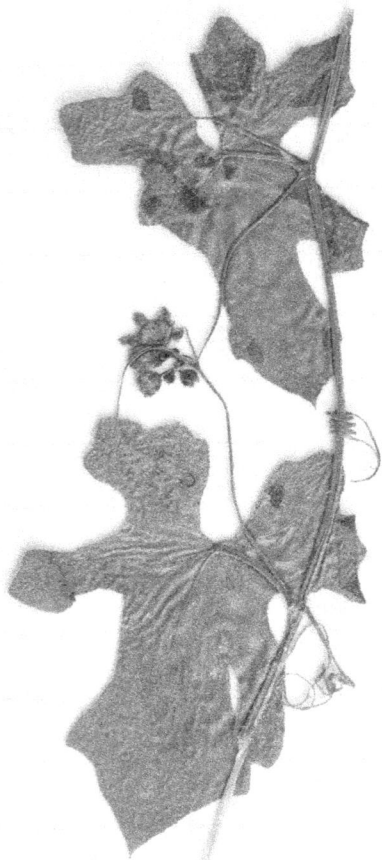

www.ingramcontent.com/pod-product-compliance
Lightning Source LLC
Chambersburg PA
CBHW081656270326
41933CB00017B/3185